# Studying the
# Old Testament

*Henry McKeating*

**EPWORTH PRESS**

7162 0339 1

First published 1979
by Epworth Press
Room 195, 1 Central Buildings
Westminster London SW1

Fourth impression 1990

Printed in Great Britain at
The Camelot Press plc
Southampton

# Contents

# Abbreviation

GBS   David Stacey *Groundwork of Biblical Studies* (Epworth Press 1979)

**Note for Methodist Local Preachers on trial studying for the Connexional Examination in the Old Testament**

*Studying the Old Testament* is a companion volume to *Groundwork of Biblical Studies* and the student, whether taking a correspondence course or not, should pay careful attention to the Study Scheme printed at the end of this book. The Scheme indicates the passages of the Bible required to be read.

Examination questions may be set on the whole of *Studying the Old Testament* save only the paragraphs on the apocryphal literature in smaller print (Section 5). These paragraphs, however, should be read in order to understand the development of the biblical ideas. The chapters from *Groundwork of Biblical Studies* referred to in the Study Scheme (Sections 3–10) should be carefully read as they provide essential background knowledge.

# Author's Introduction

THIS book is intended for use by those studying to become Local Preachers in the Methodist Church, but the author hopes that it will be read with profit by others. It attempts to introduce its readers to the *message* of the Old Testament. It therefore does not say any more about matters of history or of literary introduction than is necessary to put that message in its setting. Questions of history and of literary introduction (dates and authorship of Old Testament books and the manner of their composition) are fully dealt with elsewhere (notably in the companion volume *Groundwork of Biblical Studies* by David Stacey).

We would stress that it is an *introduction* to the message of the Old Testament. It does not aim at being comprehensive. It selects the most important religious figures and the most important themes and the hope is that the reader will be encouraged to explore matters further for himself. Thus, for instance, it does not deal with the less important prophetic figures such as Joel, Zephaniah, Malachi, or even Trito-Isaiah. It omits any treatment of the work of the Chronicler. Students approaching the Old Testament are often daunted by the sheer bulk of its material. It does, after all, cover nearly two thousand years of history and of religious development. To make the Old Testament manageable for such students an introductory book needs to be selective. In the process of selection material is left out which is of undoubted value.

There are many possible ways of dividing up the Old Testament for study purposes. All of them have advantages and disadvantages. This book divides it into broad categories of literature. It looks first at Pentateuchal Traditions, excluding Deuteronomy, then at Deuteronomy and the Deuteronomic History (which means the books of Joshua, Judges, Samuel and Kings), then at the earlier prophetic traditions, the later prophets, the Wisdom Traditions, the Psalms and the Apocalyptic Writings. This means that in some sections material from quite different dates has to be dealt with. A chart is included which it is hoped will help the student to relate the main events of Old Testament history to the religious and literary developments going on at any given period.

In each section an attempt is made to pick out the principal themes and images employed in the class of literature being examined. Some of the themes appear in one form or another in every section. Each category of literature, for example, has its own contribution to make to our knowledge of the person of God, or to our understanding of man. Other themes and particular images may appear in one body of literature but not in another. This is a book primarily for Christian preachers, and it tries to indicate not only how the themes and images of the Old Testament point forward to the Christian revelation but how they can speak to us today. Many books have been written about the Old Testament which try to discover what its words meant to the people who spoke or wrote them first, and to the people who first heard them. It is proper for the academic student of the Old Testament to rest content with such questions. The preacher too ought to start with the same questions, about what the Old Testament *meant* in its own time, but he cannot stop there. The preacher must go on to ask what the Old Testament *means* for our time.

Studying the Old Testament has its problems. This book is written in the conviction that the problems are worth battling with because through the words of the Old Testament God is still speaking.

# Time Chart

| Major kings and principal historical events | Major religious figures (prophets, etc.) and developments of literature |
|---|---|
| Before 1500 BC    Patriarchs | Individual stories handed down by word of mouth |
| Thirteenth century    Exodus<br>About 1250–1200    Settlement | Moses ⎫ Traditions of exodus and<br>Joshua ⎭ settlement preserved orally |
| 1200–c. 1020    Judges<br>About 1020    Saul | |
| About 1000–961    David | Samuel    About this time the Yahwist<br>Nathan    (J) collects many of the<br>earlier traditions |
| 961–922    Solomon | The 'Succession Narrative' giving account of the reign of David, written |
| 922   Division of the kingdom | Ahijah |

| Judah | N. Israel | Judah | N. Israel |
|---|---|---|---|
| 922–915<br>Rehoboam | 922–901<br>Jeroboam | | E traditions possibly collected at about this period |
| | 876–869 Omri<br>869–850 Ahab | | Elijah and Elisha Legends about these prophets composed orally |
| | 842–815 Jehu | | |

EIGHTH CENTURY

| | | |
|---|---|---|
| 783–742 Uzziah | 786–746<br>Jeroboam II | Isaiah of Jerusalem<br>(742 to about 685)  Amos (about 746)<br>Hosea (about |
| 735–715 Ahaz | 722 Fall of<br>N. Kingdom | Micah    740–725) |

| | |
|---|---|
| 715–687   Hezekiah | Northen traditions probably brought south by refugees after the fall of N. Israel |
| 687–642   Manasseh | The Law Book probably composed during this period |
| 640–609   Josiah | Jeremiah (called in 626) |
| | The Law Book found (621) |
| 597   First Fall of Jerusalem | Ezekiel deported to Babylon, where he receives his call to prophesy |
| 586   Second Fall of Jerusalem<br>582   Murder of Gedaliah | Jews flee to Egypt, taking Jeremiah |

| Major kings and principal historical events | Major religious figures (prophets, etc.) and developments of literature |
|---|---|
| | During exile the Law Book is expanded into Deuteronomy. The Deuteronomic History is written—incorporating earlier traditions. The words of the pre-exilic prophets are also collected at this time |
| 539  Cyrus takes Babylon | Deutero-Isaiah |
| 538  Jews allowed to return | |
| 520–515 the temple rebuilt | Haggai and Zechariah |
| | The Priestly Writing probably produced at this period |
| 457  Ezra arrives in Jerusalem (traditional date) | |
| 444  Nehemiah arrives in Jerusalem | Books of Proverbs and Job produced around this period |
| 397  Ezra arrives in Jerusalem (alternative date) | |
| 336–33  Alexander the Great conquers the Middle East | Ecclesiastes probably written at about this time |
| | Ecclesiasticus (Jesus ben Sira) writes his book (about 180) |
| 167  Outbreak of Maccabaean revolt | Book of Daniel published |
| | Wisdom of Solomon written, perhaps about 100 BC |
| 63  The Romans take over Palestine | |

# Section 1

# The Pentateuchal Traditions

IF we leave aside the book of Deuteronomy, there are basically three different strands of tradition in the Pentateuch. There is the Yahwistic or 'J' tradition, which is generally regarded as the oldest and is usually said to have been drawn together around the time of Solomon. There is the Elohistic or 'E' tradition, which runs parallel to J, and evidently covered much of the same ground. But whereas enough of J survives to give us an idea of what the complete work must have been like, E survives only in fragments. It seems to have been used simply to supplement or fill out J's picture. Perhaps, indeed, E never did exist as a single, coherent body of traditions, with its own shape. Perhaps it was merely a scattered collection of materials. In any case, there are many places where the J and E traditions are not easy to disentangle and we have to be content with saying that a particular story comes from 'JE'. For all these reasons, we shall not attempt in this book to give any independent account of E's themes and theology, but will deal with the J and E traditions together.

The third pentateuchal strand is the Priestly or 'P' strand. It was put together during the post-exilic period. We shall have more to say about it shortly when we consider it in detail. (See GBS, Chapter 21, g–e).

## The J and E traditions

We have already spoken about the date of J. This is important, for it means that the background to the thinking of the Yahwistic author has to be sought in or around the reign of

Solomon. This is the historical period into which we find his ideas to fit. His preoccupations are the sort that we might expect of a man living in the heady days of the early monarchy, when Israel had just achieved nationhood, her prestige and power stood high, and her culture was flowering as perhaps it never did again. (The closest parallel to this period in the history of our own country is the Elizabethan age.)

You will find older books which characterize J as a 'naive storyteller'. They will speak of his unsophisticated, artless style and his rather childlike (not to say primitive) way of talking about God. The E traditions used to be thought of as perhaps slightly less naive than J, but still rather primitive in their thinking. Most scholars now regard such views as misjudgements. They see the 'artlessness' of these early traditions as concealing profound theological thinking.

### The content of the JE material
(See GBS, Chapter 21, h, i)

J begins with an account of creation (starting at Gn. 2.4b); not the one that speaks of God creating the world in seven days, but the story of the garden of Eden. He goes on to tell of the fall of Adam and Eve; Cain and Abel; and gives us a version of the story of the flood. (P also had an account of the flood, and the two have been carefully amalgamated in our Bible, so that they take a little untangling. The J account is the one that speaks of the flood lasting forty days and forty nights, and says that Noah took one pair of every species of animals.) J goes on to give us the story of the tower of Babel, and then moves to the Patriarchs, Abraham, Isaac and Jacob. (E has nothing corresponding to the primeval history and only begins its account with the patriarchs.) The long cycle of tales about Joseph is partly from J, partly from E. J had an account of the deliverance from Egypt and the wanderings in the wilderness (these too have later been combined with E and P materials). There is also a JE account of the revelation on Sinai.

J and E may originally have completed their work with an account of the conquest, and some scholars claim to be able to trace J and E material in the book of Joshua, but this does not concern us for the moment.

J appears to have contained no legal material with the possible exception of the ten commandments. The great collection of laws in Exodus *21–23*, which we call the Book of the Covenant, is sometimes ascribed to E, sometimes treated as a quite separate body of material. The large body of laws relating to worship and sacrifice, etc., to be found in Numbers and Leviticus, belong to P.

The outline given above of the content of the JE traditions exhibits a pattern, and this pattern gives us some important clues about the thinking behind these early traditions. J begins with paradise, the ideal state for which God intended man; in which man, in his innocence, has daily, unaffected dealings with God; seeing him, speaking to him. Then man sins. The eating of the fruit is only, in itself, a little disobedience, but it is the beginning of disobedience and spreads to greater things. In Gn. *3* it is only eating forbidden fruit; by Gn. *4* it is murder, and murder of brother by brother. Human sin does not remain a matter for human beings only. It involves the whole earth, for the ground is cursed because of it. By Gn. *6*.1–6 it has acquired a cosmic dimension, for it now involves heavenly beings. We thus have the ramifications of sin spreading out like tentacles gripping the universe.

The flood represents God's attempt to make a fresh start. Noah is the new ancestor of all mankind. But the disgraceful episode of Noah's drunkenness (Gn. *9*.20 ff.) shows that even Noah's righteousness is of a qualified kind, he has his little weaknesses. Sin has not really been got rid of, it lurks there still. Noah's drunkenness is the first of the sins of civilization. It is followed quickly by the much more momentous sin of the Babel builders, who in their headstrong pride use their new-found technology to challenge God himself, and build a tower with its top in the heavens. In spite of the measures God has taken, therefore, sin prevails more and more. As a consequence, mankind is divided and scattered.

With Gn. *12* begins the next phase of God's dealings with man. From the scattered peoples he chooses one man and his offspring. From the offspring of the one man Abraham he chooses Isaac. From the offspring of Isaac he chooses Jacob, and from the offspring of Jacob he builds the one nation out of all the nations through whom the rest are to be saved and the world set right. He makes a beginning of the process of setting right by rescuing this people from slavery, and giving them the law, and giving them a land.

The foregoing is simply an outline of J and E's thinking and it may reflect primarily J's. We shall now look at some aspects, of this thinking in more detail. What the outline does not reflect is the subtlety of much of the thought. In these traditions character is drawn with great refinement, and above all, with great consciousness of ambivalences and ambiguities. J's stories in particular are not peopled by 'goodies' and 'baddies', but by real people, who never fit quite neatly into the slots the reader has mentally prepared for them. We have men like Cain, who is accursed, and yet divinely protected; or Jacob, who is a liar and a swindler, and yet chosen and blest.

## The nature of God and his relationship with man (1)

As we saw above, man's relationship with God in paradise is seen as an entirely easy and natural one. Man shows no fear of God; is not overcome by the sight of the divine majesty. Man's reticence in God's presence, and his reluctance to face him, begin when man is conscious of sin.

Sin, therefore, is a disaster. It mars that original relationship between man and God. And yet for J there is an ambiguity even about sin. Through sin man has lost much, and yet he has also gained a little. He sinned through an unrestrained quest for knowledge, yet the gaining of knowledge is not in itself evil. The quest for knowledge led to sin, and yet the sin itself did lead to further knowledge, knowledge of the self, and knowledge of the other; for it says that, after the fall: 'And Adam knew Eve his wife, and she conceived . . .' (Gn. 4.1). Now the primary reference of these words is to sexual intercourse, 'carnal knowledge', to use the antiquated phrase, and yet it is not mere accident that the Hebrew chooses the word 'to know' as a euphemism for sexual intercourse. The sexual experience is a genuine and intimate *encounter* with another person. And this encounter is not merely reproductive, but productive of understanding and love. To revert from a Hebrew euphemism to an English one, in that encounter man and woman do genuinely '*make* love': infinite possibilities of human love are involved with and emerge from the sexual encounter. At the fall man loses immortality, but he gains all this. The need now to reproduce himself leads to possibilities of knowledge and understanding; to the institution of family life; and immediately to the joys and sorrows of parenthood. This is by no means all to be regretted.

Man's loss of paradise also leads directly to the possibility of civilization. Adam in the garden knows nothing of civilization. He is, in a word, a savage—a noble savage, doubtless; a happy savage, certainly, but a savage none the less. Fallen Adam learns to labour. His descendants build cities, they invent arts and sciences. This, too, is not all loss.

In J's account of human prehistory God responds to human sin and failure not by undoing it, but by helping man to live with its results, and by showing him how something can be *won* from failure. And what is won is not necessarily a poor substitute for what was lost, but often has in it the seeds of something better still. This is illustrated by the incident in Gn. 3.7–11, 21, where Adam and Eve become conscious of their nakedness. They have lost innocence. But God does not leave them to cope with their embarrassment by their own inadequate devices, by ridiculous fig leaves. He himself takes the initiative by making, and showing them how to make, more adequate garments. They have lost innocence, and it is lost for ever. God does not restore it to them. They have to learn to live with the consequences of their actions. But he himself introduces them to the civilized man's substitute for innocence, which is respectability. And though J himself does not make this clear, from the rest of scripture we see that this is the beginning of a long road to something better still, better even than innocence, and that is purity. At the end of the history of salvation God offers his people not garments of skins, but robes made white in the blood of the lamb.

J is acutely aware of the ambiguities of civilized life itself. The story of Noah's drunkenness, already referred to (Gn. 9.20 ff.) demonstrates this. Vine-growing and wine-making are characteristic of the settled life. Those, like the Rechabites, who rejected settled life, expressed this rejection by shunning wine (see, for example, Jer. 35). Wine, throughout scripture, is seen as one of God's great blessings, 'making glad the heart of man' (Ps. 104.15). It is that with which the messianic feast is to be celebrated, and can therefore in the

NT symbolize the kingdom of God (Mk. *14*.25 and parallels) and the new dispensation of Christ (Jn. *2*.1–11). Yet in Gn. *9* J is pointing to its ambivalence. It brings blessing, and yet it can destroy reason and dignity. It leads here to one of the most reprehensible of offences, the dishonouring of a parent. What J is telling us is that the blessings of settled life are two-edged blessings.

J expresses a parallel thought by the use he makes of the image of the city. The city is an image which appears again and again in the pages of the Bible. Like the image of the vine, it is interpreted very positively by later writers. J introduces it first in a quite neutral way. Cain (not, admittedly, an auspicious character) first became a city builder (Gn. *4*.17). Other civilized arts and sciences likewise antedate the flood. Jubal invented musical instruments, and Tubal-Cain the craft of metal-work.

But after the flood, as men's command of technology increased, their ambitions grew, and they set out to build a city, and a tower with its top in the heavens, the tower of Babylon. This is civilization gone wrong. Men are using their God-given intelligence and technical skill not in the service of God's purposes, but to challenge God, to assert their own independence of him. From here onwards Babylon becomes in scripture the name of the dark side of civilization, the symbol of pride, impressive but sinful. Once having left paradise and savagery behind man must become a citizen. But he has a choice of cities, Babylon, or the city of God.

The story of salvation begins in this same chapter, chapter 11, with Abraham, who starts out by *leaving his city,* and becomes a wanderer, so that after many generations his descendants might find a better one.

## Covenant and promise

For J and E, the patriarchs are men in transition. They receive little for themselves, except promises. Yet such is their faith and faithfulness that promises are enough for them. God makes a *covenant* with Abraham. The key chapter is Gn. *15*. (The alternative account of covenant-making in Gn. *17* belongs to P.) The important points to note about this covenant with Abraham are that, first, there are no conditions attached. God does not lay down any prior conditions which Abraham or his descendants must meet, or any rules which they are required to keep. The covenant is offered purely from God's grace. Secondly, the covenant, having been freely offered, is freely responded to. The offer of grace meets the response of *faith*, for Abraham believed the Lord (Gn. *15*.6). Thirdly, the substance of the covenant is *promise*. God promises Abraham multitudinous offspring, and a land.

We have mentioned the Yahwist's grasp of the two-sideness of human character. This serves to bring out the doctrine of grace. The patriarchs are not, for the most part, exemplary characters. They hold the position they do, not because they are of surpassing virtue, but because God has chosen them, and for no other reason. Abraham is the exception here. In the JE traditions Abraham's response to God appears to be a perfect response. He accepts the promises. He believes without further evidence or proof. (The mention of Abraham's incredulity in Gn. *17*.17 is by P and not JE.)

Abraham's faith contrasts sharply with the response of those around him. Sarah, who is likewise chosen by God, is incredulous (Gn. *18*.12) yet she becomes the mother of the holy people. Lot, Abraham's nephew, is the Bible's best example of the fifty-one per cent believer, the man who has *just* enough faith to be saved. With enough virtue to mark him out among the inhabitants of Sodom and Gomorrah, he nevertheless exhibits extreme reluctance to flee from the wrath to come (Gn. *19*.15–23). He is ready enough to *believe* the angelic messengers. He does not question their message, but he still lacks the initiative to do more than the absolute minimum about it.

Lot's wife, famous for looking back and being turned into a pillar of salt, is even less whole-hearted. She insisted on looking back to see what happened to the wicked cities. Von Rad, in his commentary on Genesis, has an acute comment on her case. When God acts in this world, says Von Rad, there are only two possibilities for men; to be saved, like Lot, or to be judged and destroyed, like the people of Sodom. Lot's wife wants a third option. She just wants to watch, to be a spectator. But when God acts in the world, there are no mere spectators.

Abraham's faith is presented by J as perfect. The outstanding episode which demonstrates this is his willingness to sacrifice Isaac, the son of promise. All the contradictions and
paradoxes of faith are summed up here. The promise rests on
Isaac. Only through him can it be fulfilled. Yet when God
seems to command that he be sacrificed, Abraham is ready to
comply. In hope, he is prepared to sacrifice even the ground
of hope. Abraham has the faith that is prepared to put faith
itself at risk.

For the Yahwist himself, Abraham's faith is the central
point of the story, and generally, this is what Christian interpreters have stressed. Interestingly, Jewish interpretation has
often taken as its starting point the words (which are signific-
antly repeated) 'And they went on, both of them
together . . .' (Gn. 22.6, 8) and has emphasized the unanimity
of father and son, and the son's willingness to be sacrificed.

It is also probable that for the Yahwist the *place* of Isaac's
sacrifice is significant. He tells us with great deliberation (Gn.
22.4) 'And Abraham lifted up his eyes and saw *the place*'.
What was this 'place'? It is called by JE 'Moriah', and it is
referred to in 22.14 as 'the mountain of the Lord'. Now in all
the Old Testament only two places are ever designated as 'the
mountain of the Lord', one is Sinai, the other Mount Zion.
Later tradition, which we find already in the Chronicler (2
Chr. 3.1) identifies the place of Isaac's sacrifice as Mount
Zion, the place that was afterwards the site of the temple, the
place where, and where alone, valid sacrifices might be
offered. Jewish interpreters have said that this is because all
sacrifice that ever took place at Jerusalem derived its efficacy
from that archetypal sacrifice; the one willing sacrifice of the
only begotten son. There is no evidence that J and E themselves take this view, but the use of the phrase 'the mountain
of the Lord' does suggest the identification of Moriah and
Zion. Be that as it may, if we are to consider the 'topography
of salvation' as we find it in the OT, Moriah must certainly be
included as one of the places of encounter with the divine.

Gn. 22 contrasts strikingly with Gn. 18.22–33. Both of
them exemplify Abraham's faith. Gn. 22 exemplifies *unques-
tioning* faith, which obeys God, however irrational and
unlikely the command. Gn. 18 exemplifies *reasoning faith*, the
faith which does question. The difference is that in Gn. 22 it is

Abraham and Abraham's own that are at risk. In Gn. *18* those at risk are others. The context is again the threatened destruction of Sodom and Gomorrah. Questioning Abraham in Gn. *18* is a forerunner of the later questioning Job. He questions God's justice, and insists on being answered. The underlying assumption of Abraham's argument is that God cannot be less just than human beings. His challenge is summed up in the words of *18*.25, 'Shall not the judge of all the earth do right?' It would not satisfy human justice, he urges, to destroy the righteous and wicked together. Yet is this not what God is proposing to do?

What is established by this argument is something akin to the 'doctrine of the remnant' for which Isaiah later became so famous. God is challenged to save the many for the sake of the faithful few. He ends by saving the few, to preserve the seed of a new and more faithful community. Abraham conducts a sort of 'Dutch auction', beating God down and down. Will he not save the city for the sake of fifty righteous? If only forty-five are found there, would he condemn it for lack of five? Down and down he drives his bargain, until he gets God to allow that even ten righteous would be enough to save the city.

Why does he stop at ten? Jewish tradition said that it was because he knew that in the days of the flood eight righteous persons (Noah, his wife, his three sons and his sons' wives) were not enough to save the world, and so there was obviously no point in going much below ten. Every Christian reader, however, must will Abraham to go on. 'And if there is only *one* righteous? Will you not save a city—will you not save the world, for one, righteous man?' But the JE traditions do not press matters so far. For *that* completion of the argument we have to wait (Rom. 5.18–19).

Comparing this account in Gn. *18* with the account in Gn. *22* we discern that the conception of faith exhibited in JE is not a simple one. Faith does not always or necessarily translate itself into blind obedience and acceptance. There is a time to question, and a time to obey without questioning.

If the wholeheartedness of Abraham's response to God contrasts with the response of those around him it contrasts no less strongly with that of his heirs and successors. Jacob is a very ambiguous character indeed. JE not only tells of Jacob's deviousness quite unblushingly, but even seems to exult in it.

Jacob is the man of blessing—but even the blessing was obtained by a confidence trick. It is noteworthy that the prophet Hosea, some time later, presents a very negative picture of Jacob. He sums up his criticisms of his people Israel by saying that they are like Israel their ancestor (Hos. *12*), who was crooked from the very womb, and resisted God to the point of physical combat. And yet God spoke with him.

Jacob, as these early traditions present him, is not a nice man, or at all a good man, but he is a man, nevertheless, whom God could use, and to whom God could speak. Above all, Jacob learns by experience. It is one of the strengths of these traditions that their characters are not flat stereotypes. As the longer stories are built up the characters develop and grow.

Jacob appears first as a thoroughly reprehensible character. He deceives his blind father, taking advantage of his blindness. He cheats his brother out of his inheritance. And then, not surprisingly, he has to leave home. And he meets God.

There is a curious unsatisfactoriness about Jacob's encounter with God at Bethel in Gn. *28.* Certainly, God renews to Jacob the sort of promises he had earlier made to Abraham (*28.13–15*). Yet Jacob's response to the promises seems hardly adequate. There in the night he seems suitably impressed, overcome with awe (*28.16–17*), but in the morning the old Jacob reasserts himself. He tries to drive a bargain with God. God in the night had offered his promise freely, without conditions, as he had to Abraham. It is Jacob who introduces conditions. *If* God will indeed look after him, and if Jacob sees concrete results from this association, why, then Jacob will reward God by offering him ten per cent of the profits (*28.22*).

If this reaction strikes us as lacking in proper appreciation of the situation then it is probably fair to guess that the story teller thought exactly the same of it.

This initial experience at Bethel is remarkable for its lack of any obvious effect on Jacob's life. He flees to Syria, takes up residence with Laban, and lies and cheats until he has well outstayed his welcome, and there is nowhere to go but home.

Arriving back in his old territory, he hears that Esau is coming to meet him, with a small army of retainers. Now Jacob is forced to face his past, and to face himself, and to face the person he has become. 'And Jacob was left alone; and a man wrestled with him until the breaking of the day' (*32.24*). The man never gives his name, and we are left to guess his identity. We guess that for Jacob, facing himself and facing his past meant facing God.

Jacob's career thus revolves round these two meetings, as around two foci. The first meeting was apparently abortive, the second less so. The patriarchs, in the J work, are entirely human. Even God's chosen do not necessarily respond immediately to the heavenly vision. Some of them have to learn the hard way, and come back by a long road before they hear with profit what God is saying to them.

But perhaps the JE traditions' greatest creation is the figure of Joseph. The stories themselves are not only of infinite subtlety, they enshrine some of the profoundest theological ideas in the Bible. And the character of Joseph himself is probably the nearest the Bible ever comes (before Christ) to trying to define the ideal of humanity.

It is not that Joseph is perfect, for the ideal man is not the man who needs to learn nothing, but the one who knows *how* to learn. For Joseph begins as something of an upstart 'daddy's boy', flaunting his dreams of greatness and his splendid coat of parental favouritism. All one's sympathies are with the brothers, violent as their reaction was.

Yet when Joseph has actually *achieved* greatness, and as in the dreams, so in real life, his brothers do bow down to him, he makes no exulting. He never says, 'I told you so'. He does not even hold their wickedness against them, but sees everything as having been ordained by God for good. By oppression and judgement he was taken away, 'but God meant it for good; to bring it about, as it is this day, to save many people alive' (Gn. *50.20*).

But this not holding their wickedness against them does not mean that Joseph *excuses* the brethren. He does not say that it was all done by God, therefore they are not morally responsible. Their wickedness *was* real wickedness. Joseph is quite blunt about it, he prefaces the text just quoted: '*You intended evil against me,* but God meant it for good . . .' Neither is the salvation wrought through Joseph due to the blind workings of destiny either. There was nothing *automatic* about the way Joseph's career turned out. God does not bring about his ends through Joseph willy nilly. Good comes out of malevolence only because, in the midst of that malevolence, one man keeps faith. Joseph succeeds because he accepts his sufferings as a God-given task. He accepts humiliation, taking the form of a slave, and ultimately being numbered with transgressors: and he learns obedience through the things that he suffers. Only for this reason has God highly exalted him, dividing him a portion with the great.

In Joseph, then, we see the archetype (or *an* archetype) of the suffering servant of God. But what is distinctive about the JE picture is that the traditions show how God's purposes prosper when men *respond* to experience; when they *learn* from experience; when they mature and grow. They also show that it is part of Joseph's maturity that he not only learns and grows himself, but enables others to learn and grow too. The complicated devices by which Joseph engineers the accusation of theft against Benjamin are all to give Judah the opportunity to make the declaration which he does indeed make in *44*.33 f., and offer himself in Benjamin's stead. Judah, who had once connived at a brother's destruction, is here acknowledging that he is, after all, his brother's keeper. The excellence of Joseph's reconciling work is that he enables Judah, for himself, to come to this atoning act, and to find (unlike another Judas, of another Twelve) a place of repentance.

There is yet another striking feature of the Joseph story, as J presents it. There is nothing narrow or nationalistic about J's idea of salvation. Salvation is given, as J sees it, *through* God's chosen. It is not given only *to* God's chosen. '. . . to bring it about, as it is this day, to save *many people*.' Most of those whom Joseph saved by his presence in Egypt, saved from famine and death, were Egyptians.

## The places of encounter with God

It is a feature of the J stories of the patriarchs that the patriarchs encounter God in many different places. God speaks to Abraham first in Haran (Gn. *12*.1). The great encounter in which God announces his covenant with Abraham (Gn. *15*) occurs at a place which is unnamed. His argument over the cities of the plain happens at Mamre. Jacob meets God first in what was apparently at the time open country, though having been a place of encounter it is named 'God's house' (Bethel). He later struggles with God again at the Jabbok ford. And that place is in consequence called 'God's face' (Penuel). For JE God is not at first attached to particular *places*. He is the God of particular *people*. He may reveal himself wherever his people happen to be.

Yet, although there is nothing special about the places at which God chooses to reveal himself, once he *has* revealed himself there they *become* special, more often than not. They are marked out. Their names may be changed. Their locations are remembered. They become definite staging posts in the experience of the people of God, which can be pointed to. They are identifiable milestones along the Way by which the people have been led. The encounters of Israel's ancestors with her God are not, for the most part, episodes that happen in some dream world, some vaguely indicated land of fairy tale or make believe. The Israelite can stand on a piece of real ground, a spot that has a name and a location on a map, and say, 'Here, in this place, God spoke.' It is not merely in myths and stories that God communicates with men, but in the real world.

So for the JE authors, God can encounter men wherever they are. And yet, on two occasions at least, we are told how men are summoned to *particular* places to meet God. The first we have already mentioned. The patriarchs build altars and offer sacrifices wherever they happen to be. Why could not Abraham sacrifice Isaac just where he happened to be? But he is summoned to go on what is apparently quite a long journey in order to make that offering at one particular place, Moriah. What the significance of that place was in the minds of the shapers of the tradition we have already explored. Only in Zion can the only begotten son be offered up.

The second place to which God's people are specifically summoned comes later, beyond the patriarchal narratives. This is Sinai, where God reveals himself to Israel and makes his other covenant. Now in the paradise story, as we observed, one of the striking things about man's relationship with God (as J portrays it) is that the dimension of awe is lacking. There is no feeling of God's holiness or separateness. This awe, this element of fear in relations between God and man, comes in abruptly and dramatically with the fall. It is only after he has disobeyed God and become fallen man, separated man, that Adam has to say: 'I heard you coming, and I was afraid . . . and hid myself' (Gn. *3*.10). Such is Abraham's closeness to God that sometimes we might almost imagine that paradisal conditions had been restored. Several times we are told: 'And God said to Abraham . . .', as if God's conversation with Abraham was a daily occurence (e.g. *12*.1, *13*.14, *22*.1). And in these passages no mention is made of dream or vision, or sense of overpowering holiness. In Gn. *18*.22–23, though Abraham is very *respectful* to God, as one might be to an earthly superior, it *is* essentially respect, not awe, which he shows. Yet on at least one solemn occasion, the important one of the covenant-making in Gn. *15*, the feeling is quite different, and God's word is revealed to Abraham 'in dread and great darkness' (*15*.12).

Jacob's two greatest experiences of God both have this dimension of awe in strong measure. After his meeting at Bethel Jacob is overcome and says: 'This is nothing other than the house of God; this is the gate of heaven' (Gn. *28*.16–17). And few descriptions in the Bible are as mysterious and awesome as the account of Jacob's struggle with the 'man' at the ford at Penuel.

The awe and mystery are related from the start to that other specific place of encounter with the divine, Sinai (or Horeb) the 'mount of God'.

We are first introduced to Sinai in Exodus *3*, when Moses encounters God there. Ex. *3* is a JE tradition, and perhaps the E elements predominate. In the E material the holy mountain is called not Sinai but Horeb, and this is the name which prevails in Ex. *3*. There has been much discussion about where Moses' ideas about the God Yahweh came from . Some have suggested, very plausibly, that Yahweh was originally the tribal God of the Kenites, with whom Moses was residing, and into which tribe he married. Though the conventional spellings of the names in English obscure the relationship, the 'Kenites' are actually 'Cainites', the descendants of Cain, the 'fugitive and wanderer', and of Tubal-Cain, the original smith. For the word 'Cain', in Hebrew (more usefully transliterated as 'qain') is the ordinary word for 'smith'. Now we know that among the nomadic Arabs up to quite modern times such clans of smiths or tinkers have been known. Like

Cain, they were despised and regarded as outcasts. Yet like Cain, they were protected and their persons treated as sacrosanct. Like Cain the wanderer, they did not, as other nomads, travel on more or less fixed circuits, but wandered anywhere where their services were required. It has been suggested that it was such a tribe of 'Cains' that Moses met with, and that from such a tribe he learnt of the God Yahweh. This 'Kenite hypothesis' is, by the nature of the case, unprovable, but it is a suggestive one.

But whatever preparation Moses' mind may have had, and whatever he might have heard about Yahweh 'with the hearing of the ear', the important thing is his own personal encounter with the Lord. This is a passage which we must consider with some care. We have already looked at the ideas about the nature of God and his relationship with man, which are expressed in the 'primeval history' and the patriarchal narratives. Here we must raise the subject again, for when the traditions reach the part of the history which deals with the exodus they have much more to add.

## The nature of God and his relationship with man (2)

According to the OT the ancestors of the Israelites were pastoralists before they became a settled people. In fact, a significant proportion of the population of Palestine never did become settled, but retained the pastoral way of life. Culturally speaking, this pastoral element remained important. From the pastoral sector of the community there emerged at intervals men who challenged the urban values of the settled population. The experience of the shepherd is thus a vital and continuing element in the experience of the people, and some of the most significant old testament figures began as shepherds. Moses does not *begin* as a shepherd. He begins with the advantages (if the biblical tale be true) of an Egyptian education, the education of a member of the Egyptian upper classes. Such an education would be comprehensive. It would be a training in the skills of management, administration and leadership. It would include mathematics, astronomy and navigation, engineering and accounting, the administration of justice, literature and foreign languages. It would include what we should call moral education, with its characteristic Egyptian emphasis on *ma'at*, 'truth', 'faithful-ness', 'reliability', and its inculcation of wisdom. But at a crucial point in his career Moses leaves all this behind, and learns, as all the patriarchs had learnt, to be a shepherd. And he leads his flock to the west of the wilderness, and all unsuspecting to the mount of God. Like Amos later, he could claim: 'And the Lord took me as I followed the flock.'

Note the steps by which Moses is moved. First it is not religious awe, but simply wonder—an attitude not greatly removed from mere curiosity. What he actually sees is a common bush. Doubtless, after the experience was over the bush was still standing there, in the spindly way that desert bushes do, unremarkable. The bush is an object in the visible world, but for Moses it is transfigured. This ordinary object suddenly, for him, becomes significant, takes on meaning. Moses is moved to wonder. All men have such moments, but we do not always allow them to affect us too deeply. We may shrug them off, or reflect on them idly, or turn to something that seems of more practical importance. But Moses *acts on* his feeling of wonder. He turns aside to see this great sight.

And now the wonder is given a religious content. As he lets it take possession of him wonder turns to awe. At first this is simply the feeling that he is in a holy place. This too he *responds* to. He doesn't shake himself and say: 'Aren't I being silly?' He acts as a man should act in the presence of the holy. And so the Holy One becomes real to him. God speaks, and the encounter becomes fully personal.

The final stage is that, having become convinced of the reality of God, he receives a command and a job to do.

It is tempting, when expounding this passage, to concentrate on the words of 3.14, I AM WHO I AM, as if these summed up the revelation. The words are certainly important, but they mark only one element in the revelation of God's character in this passage.

God introduces himself first as 'the God of your father, . . . of Abraham, Isaac and Jacob' (3.6), i.e. as a God of the past. He is not really a new God, though Moses has newly encountered him. He is the old God, who has always been there and has long nurtured this people.

The second thing God does is to announce his will to liberate his people. He is a God who saves (3.7–9). He immediately goes on to invite Moses (and at this stage it *is* an invitation, not a command) to share in his saving enterprise (*3*.10). Both Abraham and Joseph, in their different ways, had been willing to take on their share of the burden of redemption. Moses is reluctant, and like many men who are unwilling to face the hard challenge of God he takes refuge in the raising of theological questions. He asks about the real nature of God. For this is the point of the question in *3*.13. To ask God's name is to ask about his true being. And Moses receives an answer which is yet not an answer.

We can understand the phrase I AM WHO I AM in three ways. And these three ways are not alternatives. We must understand it in all three of them if we are to appreciate what the author is trying to say to us. (See also GBS Chapter 18, a.)

If I were to encounter a stranger, and introduce myself affably, and then invite him to do the same, and say, 'And you are—?' And if he then replied, 'I am who I am'; I should not take his reply as an encouragement to further conversation. Such an answer could only be intended as a rebuff. So it is with God's reply to Moses. The words I AM WHO I AM are not a name, but the withholding of a name. Indeed,the real revelation of God's character in this passage is not in verse 14 but in verse 16, in the command, 'Go . . .' This is God's answer to all who inquire too closely into his nature; namely, a rebuff, and a command. God's nature is grasped best not by those who speculate about him, but by those who obey him.

And yet, secondly, the words I AM WHO I AM do contain a revelation about the nature of God, *in so far as it can be known*. The author is here offering us an explanation of the name 'Yahweh'. The word 'Yahweh' does not, in its form, look like a name at all. It looks for all the world like a Hebrew *verb*, like a third person singular verb. Not altogether implausibly, the writer of our passage represents it as a form of the verb 'to be'. He is hinting that the name means 'He is'. Now at this point we have to be prepared for a little Hebrew grammar. The Hebrew verb, strictly speaking, has no tenses. The particular verbal form here used indicates unfinished action, and is often translated into English as a future. Hence some insist that what Yahweh said to Moses should really be rendered I WILL BE WHAT I WILL BE. Other scholars have further observed that one might equally take the verb

'Yahweh' as a *causative* form of the verb 'to be', and in that case we should have to translate not 'He is' but 'He causes to be' or 'He will cause to be'. Any or all of these meanings might have been in the mind of the biblical author. If they were, what was he trying to convey by them? He seems to be suggesting that the name Yahweh indicates that God is The One who is, the self-existent, the uncreated; or The One who is and will always be, the Eternal, or The One who causes to be all that is, the creator, the uncaused cause of all. (It will now be appreciated why, at the beginning of this section, we queried the characterization of the JE traditions as those of simple, artless storytellers.)

But, thirdly, though the biblical writer gets his theology gloriously right, he almost certainly got his etymology badly wrong. The name 'Yahweh' is not really a verb, though its form may suggest such a conclusion. Almost certainly it is not really connected with the verb 'to be'. 'Yahweh' is a name. Whatever it originally meant its original meaning is now irrecoverable. In the earliest sources in which we meet it it is already a personal name; and long after the author of Exodus chapter 3 had finished his theologizing it was still a personal name. And this is the most important thing of all about it. Yahweh is a person, an individual, as you and I are persons. He can be met, encountered. He is an individual, as you and I are individuals. He can be spoken to, argued with, feared, loved, hated. He can laugh (Ps. *2*.4), be hurt (Hos. *11*.8), be angry (Is. *63*.3) or tender (Ps. *103*.13).

To say such things may be theologically naive, but it is religiously essential, and the OT is not afraid to say them. Yahweh is real, Yahweh is to be reckoned with. Yahweh is to be depended on. Yahweh matters. The intense reality of God as a person, an individual, is conveyed by his possessing a name, this name. It is such a God who in Exodus *3* meets Moses with his command (*3*.16) and his promise (*3*.17).

All this is Moses' own individual, personal experience of God. After the exodus he tries to bring his whole people into the same experience, to share his vision and his conviction, by bringing them to the same mountain.

Between these two events, of course, lies the story of the deliverance itself, of the plagues of Egypt, the institution of the Passover and the passage of the Red Sea. As they have come down to us these stories have all been revised and over-written by the Priestly narrator. Enough of the earlier accounts remains to make it clear that J and E did possess records of these events.

We shall not go into the details of the stories, but only indicate briefly what they are trying to tell us about the character of God. He is a God who *initiates* events. He *makes himself known* to Israel, through Moses. He makes himself known first of all in his acts. He reveals himself as a God who saves. He reveals himself, not in any announcements he makes about his being or nature, but in what he *does*.

What he does demonstrates that he is a God of over-riding power. He defeats the Egyptians (and, as an ancient Israelite would see it, the Egyptian gods) in the land of Egypt itself—on their own ground. It used sometimes to be said that Israel began with a very limited notion of God's power; that they believed that he was limited territorially, to his own country. The exodus event shows this suggestion to be false. From the beginning God is seen to be exercising his power over the strongest countries of the world. He also shows that he controls the forces of nature, the wind and the waves obey him. This he demonstrates at the crossing of the sea itself (Ex. *14*.21).

The account of the crossing of the sea in Ex. *14* is a combination of Yahwistic, Elohistic and Priestly traditions. The statement in *14*.21 that a strong east wind drove back the sea is attributed to J. The statement in *14*.22 that the waters stood up 'like a wall' on either side of the Israelites as they went over is ascribed to P. The modern reader reacts quite differently to these two statements. The Priestly writer's statement looks like a 'miraculous' account of these happenings. The statement by J looks as if it could be interpreted quite non-miraculously. The distinction would never have occurred to the biblical writers themselves. Our idea of a miracle, as an event which transgresses natural law, was not conceived of by the ancient writers, for the whole notion of natural law was foreign to them. Thus the Bible has no word that really corresponds to our word 'miracle'. It often speaks of 'signs'. Signs are significant events, events which have a message. But some of the events which the Bible describes as signs are quite non-miraculous; some are, by our definition, out and out miracles.

Sometimes the Yahwist's statement about the sea blowing back the waters is seized on as offering a naturalistic *explanation* of the crossing of the Red Sea. But the Yahwist himself does not offer it in that spirit. He does not say, 'a strong east wind drove back the waters . . .' He says, '*The Lord* drove back the waters, *by* a strong east wind . . .' Those who feel the need to look for naturalistic explanations of biblical miracles are of course at liberty to take the Yahwist's statement about the east wind as a clue, but they must do so in the recognition that they are *building on* his statement, not merely reproducing what he himself says. Theologically the Yahwist and the Priestly writer are in complete agreement. Both are asserting God's total control over the forces of nature.

This again gives the lie to a commonly held view, that the Israelites only came round rather late to attributing creative power to their God and ascribing to him lordship over the cosmos. Here in these very old traditions of the exodus he is already lord of the cosmos.

Although the JE traditions see it as the object of the exercise to bring Israel back to Sinai, the holy mountain, where the Lord met Moses, they do not confine God's presence to Sinai. It is the place where God reveals himself, but not a place to which he is confined. The JE traditions are insistent that wherever the people are, God's presence goes with them. He is present in the pillar of cloud by day and the pillar of fire by night.

So the people come at last to their own encounter with God, to the meeting place on Sinai.

Though the JE traditions happily speak of God elsewhere as revealing himself almost informally to men, and stress the naturalness with which God may sometimes be approached, in their account of the Sinai experience they demonstrate that God is not to be taken for granted. We said above that the name Yahweh indicates that God is a person, as you and I are persons. That was not quite right. God *is* a person, but there is a difference between his 'personhood' and ours. He is a *holy* person. Throughout the Sinai account we have the overpowering impression of One who can be met, but whom it is dangerous to meet.

This comes out first in the elaborate preparations which have to be made before the meeting. These are described in Ex. *19*.10–15. The people are to consecrate themselves, wash their garments, and abstain from sexual intercourse. The preparations are to take three days. The people are not so much as to touch the holy mountain until the signal is given to them to come forward. To break this command means death.

When God does descend upon the mountain he does not exactly 'appear'. He remains enveloped in thick darkness. There are thunders, and lightning and the sound of a trumpet. The mountain is wrapped in fire and smoke (Ex. *19*.16–19).

The people's reaction is significant (*20*.18 ff.). They have genuinely met God, though at one remove, not as Moses met him. But even that is enough for them, or perhaps too much. The experience of God must not be treated lightly. It is not necessarily something to be desired or hankered after. The man who has met God may acknowledge that meeting to be the most important experience of his life, and yet not have any desire to repeat it. The encounter with God can never be a comfortable encounter.

A further observation which needs to be made is that an experience of God can never be described. Because it is unlike anything else it cannot properly be compared to anything else. Those who have met God can only *hint* at what it is like, in terms that may be recognized by others who have also shared something of the experience. For those who have not, the imagery (of fire and smoke and trumpet blowing) may even sound somewhat ludicrous.

Now most of the Bible's descriptions of such encounters are of *individual* encounters. And we are able more or less readily to respond to these. When Isaiah, for example, describes how he saw the Lord, 'high and lifted up, and his train filled the temple', and describes his feelings and reactions to this vision, we may not be able to claim that we have seen anything quite like that. But if we have felt the presence of God at all then we can make enough sense of his imagery to see 'what he is getting at'.

But the Sinai experience is in a rather different category. It is an attempt to describe a *corporate* encounter with God. It is probably fair to say that most of us have much less experience of the corporate dimension of the religious life, and it may therefore be all the harder for us to appreciate what such descriptions are trying to say. The other great corporate experience which scripture describes, with which the Sinai experience has much in common, and which raises many of the same problems for us, is that of the first Christian Pentecost.

Perhaps it may help us to understand a little of what the Sinai experience meant if we see it as having the same sort of significance in the life of the nation as conversion may have in the life of an individual. It was not that they knew nothing about God before. It was not that they stopped learning about him afterwards. But at that point certain things suddenly made sense to them.

The covenant into which they enter at that point is different from the patriarchal covenant. It does not consist primarily of promises (though the element of promise is not entirely lacking). It focuses what God has already done for them, in bringing them to this place. And it focuses their obligation to respond to him in obedience. At the sea God had already revealed himself in his *acts*; on the mountain he reveals himself in his *commands*.

Now the long series of laws which we find from Exodus *21* onwards, were certainly not in J, though most of the laws are probably very old and certainly pre-deuteronomic. But the earliest account of the meeting on Sinai presumably contained *some* record of the legal requirements of the covenant, probably enshrined in the ten commandments, or something very like them.

The Sinai experience is paradoxical in that it displays the divine in-breaking of the personal God, and at the same time the move away from that towards the institutionalizing of religion. When the people assert that having heard God speak they prefer him in future to communicate through Moses they are stating a preference for the mediation of a priesthood or a priestly figure instead of personal encounter with God for themselves. The God who previously gave his orders as occasion arose has now taken steps to institutionalize his word in permanent form in the law. From now on, Moses only needs to consult him when particular points of dispute arise. And the God who has hitherto been present with his people in the cloud and in the fire will be present from this point onwards in his tabernacle and in the ark, for this is the juncture at which orders are given for the tabernacle and ark to be constructed. (The Priestly tradition describes a very elaborate ark and an even more elaborate tabernacle (Ex. *25*.10–22; 26–27). For JE the tabernacle is a fairly simple tent (Ex. *33*.7 ff.).) Thus at Sinai we see the establishment of the law, the priesthood and the cult. These are the institutions which make the divine encounter more manageable for a people who have not the faith and virtue to talk with God as Abraham talked, or the constitution to stand his speaking out of the smoke and fire as Moses heard him speak. It is important to recognize, however, that these institutional forms of religion do not make the direct encounter with God entirely redundant, for prophets are still needed to whom God can speak in the old ways.

### Mediation and atonement in JE

We have mentioned above the institutional mediators which JE recognizes; the priesthood, personified in Moses and Aaron, and the law, which is not a personal mediator but does nevertheless mediate knowledge of God. But Moses is not only the archetypal priest, he is the archetypal prophet. He speaks to God as no other prophet did, 'face to face, as a man speaks with his friend' (Ex. *34*.11, Num. *12*.8).

Though there is not a great deal of cultic material in J and E there is enough to show us that these traditions do recognize the cultus and the importance of sacrifice as a means of approaching God. The patriarchs offer sacrifices from time to time, and the covenant with Abraham is sealed by sacrifice.

J and E also appreciate the importance of mediatorial intercession. Both Abraham and Moses are great intercessors. Abraham's intercession for the cities of the plain has already been commented on. Moses' intercession in Ex. *32* for the people of Israel after their sin with the golden calf is equally important, but for a different reason. When Moses offers to go again up the mountain he says specifically that it is to make atonement (*32*.30). The Jewish rabbis interpreted his prayer in *32*.32 as a kind of self-sacrifice, an offering of himself as an atonement for the sins of the people. It may be that the rabbis read too much into the words, but even if so, Moses' request to be 'blotted out of the book' of God at least expresses a desire to be *identified* with the sinful people for whom he is interceding, even though he has not shared their sin. This is the importance of the passage, that it recognizes that in true intercession these elements of identification and self-giving must come through.

## The Priestly writing

The Priestly work is dated much later than JE. It took shape in the exile or the immediate post-exilic period, and it reflects the interest of Jews of that era. This was a period when the shock of the exile was still fresh. The exile had shaken the nation's confidence in itself and shaken its complacent belief that God would take care of his people however they might behave. It had proved the great prophets to be right, and Israel had begun, belatedly, to take seriously their condemnations of sin. The new Jewish religion which was forged in the exile was therefore a religion dominated by penitence. It developed a law, which was intended to guard against future corruption and hence any repetition of the exile, and it developed a cultic system rich in provision for expiatory sacrifice, whereby the sins that did inevitably occur could be atoned for. The Priestly work contains that new law, and it devotes a great deal of space to the organization of the cult. Through and through it is filled with the spirit of the new religious order, born in exile.

It seems unlikely that the Priestly work ever existed as an independent, self-contained writing. The Priestly authors took over the existing JE and D traditions. They modified them at some points to suit their own purposes, but for the most part they were content to re-issue them, but in a new framework of their own. The Priestly writings therefore form the framework of the Pentateuch as we now have it. Occasionally P has combined the old material with material of his own. E.g. he seems to have had his own account of the Flood, which he amalgamated with that of the earlier J. He has also added whole new stories, though not very many of them. In Genesis, for example, the only stories which are P material pure and simple are the Gn. *1* account of creation, an alternative account to JE's of the covenant with Abraham (Gn. *17*) and the story of Abraham's buying the field at Hebron (Gn.

*23*). His major additions are the laws which occupy large tracts of the Pentateuch, including virtually the whole of the book of Leviticus.

P's great interest was in *order,* and his own work on the pentateuchal traditions was largely one of ordering. He it is who has added most of the dates, the ages of various individuals, and most of the genealogies. If we look, for example, at the story of the Flood, where P and J material are intermingled, we can see P's interests coming out very clearly. It is P who tells us what Noah's age was; P who contributes the elaborate scheme of dating, so that we know at what time of the year, which month and which day of the month each incident in the story took place. It is P who gives us exact measurements for the ark too.

But above all, it is P who has contributed the *structure* of our existing pentateuch, organizing the whole story round a series of covenants.

The first covenant in P's scheme is that with Noah (Gn. 9.8–17). (J's account of the flood evidently knew nothing of this covenant.) Now Noah is of course the ancestor of all mankind, so the covenant made with him is a universal covenant. The next covenant is the one with Abraham. P's account of this in Gn. *17.* The Abrahamic covenant is more restricted, for Abraham is the father only of one group of peoples. The Sinai covenant is with Israel alone. Most of our surviving material on the Sinai covenant-making is from earlier sources, but there is enough Priestly material incorporated into it to show that P did have his own ideas on the subject. The Priestly writer himself does not use the word 'covenant' in his descriptions of the Sinai event. The material which he has contributed concentrates on the institution of the cultic system, i.e. the giving of plans for the making of the tabernacle and the ordering of sacrificial worship.

### Creation in P

The well-known account of the seven days of creation is a priestly account. In it God proceeds by *ordering*, and indeed, creation is essentially nothing more than an ordering. God begins with chaos. It is there from the start, and God proceeds by imposing order upon it.

The idea of creation out of nothing, which is the traditional Christian doctrine of creation, is doubtless the only understanding of creation which is theologically satisfactory in the long run, but it is important to realize that it is not actually the idea which is present in Gn. *1*, for chaos is presumed to be pre-existent.

God initiates the ordering process by *dividing*, i.e. by distinguishing, making distinctions between one thing and another; distinctions which chaos, left to itself, knows nothing of. He divides light from darkness, water from land, and makes each keep to its own place. He divides what is under the heavens from what is above the heavens. He brings living things into being *by categories,* beginning with the lower forms of life, the plants, then the lower animals, the things that swarm in the sea, the things that fly, and finally the land animals. Each is created *according to its kind,* and is ordered to reproduce according to its own species.

This order is not primarily a scientific but a *religious* order. When the sun, moon and stars are set in the heavens they doubtless served a number of functions, some of which the Priestly writer lists (Gn. *1*.14–15) but the one which interests him most is that they mark out the liturgical year, indicating when the religious festivals fall. And the whole process of creation is represented as taking a *week*, a religious division of time, and culminates in a sabbath, a religious festival.

Incidentally, the picture of the world with which the Priestly writer is working is not one which he has invented for himself. (See GBS, Chapter 8.) There is nothing exclusively biblical or Israelite about the notion of a flat earth, with an over-arching firmament supporting waters above it, and itself standing over a vast abyss of 'waters under the earth'. Most other ancient near eastern peoples pictured the cosmos in more or less similar terms. The biblical writer has simply taken over current ideas about how the world was structured, without questioning them, and he assumes that this is the world whose creation, by God, he has to account for. This is exactly what the present-day theologian does. He does not propose any special, 'Christian' cosmology. He accepts what the scientists tell him about the structure of the solar system and the nature of the rest of the universe; about the way matter came into existence and the manner in which life has

evolved on the earth—he accepts all this as the closest approx-
imation to truth which is currently available, and assumes that
*this* is the world which his doctrine of creation must account
for. Whatever doctrine of creation he ends with will not be the
same as the Bible's, though it will not be unrelated to the
Bible's.

For the Priestly writer the moral order and the cosmic order
are one. Man's duty is to fit into the order where God
intended him to fit; to observe the feasts and the religious
rites, to observe the laws which God has laid down, and to
recognize and preserve the distinctions which God has
ordained. He is not to confuse the holy with the common, nor
man with woman, nor beast with man.

Chaos itself is not seen by the Priestly writer as *evil*. Chaos
is not positively opposed to God. It is not *positively* anything.
It does not actively oppose him or his will. It is simply inert. In
the Babylonian story of creation the creator god has to *fight*
the monster of chaos. But the God of Israel only has to
command. He speaks, and his powerful word imposes order
upon chaos. The remnants of chaos in the created world, most
noticeably seen in the shape of the sea and the desert, are
restrained by being consigned to their restricted places. It is
their nature that they tend to expand, and that disorder tries
to take over the orderly, but God has set boundaries to them
which he commands them not to cross.

Man thus has chaos and order set before him, and his
proper duty is to be on the side of order. Though chaos is not,
in itself, evil, for a being capable of choice actively to *choose*
chaos is certainly evil. For man to *assent* to chaos, and to
prefer it to order, is to deny the orderly nature God has given
him. It is for man, therefore, to obey *law*, for this is the way he
expresses his assent to the order of God.

### Relations between God and man in P

We have said something about this subject under the heading
of 'creation', but much remains to be added. It is to P that we
owe the statement that God created man in his own image
(Gn. *1*.26 f.). The nature of this 'image' has been much
discussed, and there is a very great deal that could be said
about it, but we shall restrict ourselves to the bare essentials.

In the context of Genesis chapter 1 it looks as if the image has something to do with man's lordship over creation. This does not by any means exhaust its significance but it does seem to be the aspect of its meaning which is uppermost in the Priestly writer's mind. Man's relation to the rest of creation is rather like a pale imitation of God's own relationship to creation. Man is set in a position of *power* over the creation ('replenish the earth and subdue it, and have dominion . . .'—Gn. *1*.28) and at the same time responsibility towards it. Man is thus God's own representative on the earth. Israel, as we know, was forbidden to make or to worship images of her God. The Priestly writer is here giving that prohibition an interesting twist by observing that God does have images, but they are not images of wood and stone. His images are responsive human beings.

But P's notion of the image of God points to something deeper still, and something which lies at the basis of all thinking about God, and all attempts to speak about him. We can only think and speak about God *analogically,* i.e. by saying that he is like this, or like that, by using analogies. Now we have to preface all such attempts to talk about him by observing that really, of course, he is not like anything. He is God, the Holy One, and therefore quite different in kind as well as degree from anything else whatever. The Old Testament frequently says exactly this, that God is incomparable. Yet, if we allowed that observation its full weight we should give up hope of saying anything about God at all, and the whole religious enterprise would founder. All the biblical writers however work on the assumption that although God is holy, and therefore infinitely different, infinitely above, and infinitely *other* than his creation, mankind does nevertheless have enough in common with him to enable some sort of start to be made in understanding what God is like. Even in our fallen state there is still something about us sufficiently God-shaped for us to learn something about God by looking at each other. Jesus himself assumes that we can get certain clues about what God is like by seeing what men, at their best, are like. He argues, for instance, that if we look at how human fathers behave we can at least deduce that our Father in heaven must be at least as trustworthy and at least as dominated by love for his children. One of the things that follow

from this is that it is not altogether inappropriate to describe
God by using very human words; we can call him 'father', or
'shepherd', for example, in the confidence that, although
these words are very inadequate, and although there are
many important respects in which God is not at all like human
fathers or human shepherds, they do indicate something
about his nature. In spite of their inadequacies such words do
contain enough truth to make it worth using them rather than
just keeping quiet. We do God more honour by speaking
about him badly than by not speaking at all. Now the usefulness of this whole enterprise of speaking analogically about
God depends on the assumption that there is that within us
which responds, or corresponds, to the divine nature, and this
is what the Priestly writer is asserting with his talk of the
image of God in man.

Though the story of the fall is a J tradition, the Priestly
writer knows about it and it is part of the total structure of the
Pentateuch as it left P's hand. It is important to notice, therefore, that P does not think that at the fall man lost the divine
image, for he is careful to tell us that, after the fall, Adam
begot sons in his image and likeness (Gn. 5.3) passing on to
the rest of humanity the image he had received.

## Sin and expiation in P

The Yahwist, as we saw, is fully conscious of human sin. He
presents the early history of mankind as a slide deeper and
deeper into sinfulness. Yet J is not obsessed by sin. He regrets
it, but accepts it as a fact of life. He is determined to be
cheerful about it, and presents us with a God who, though he
takes sin very seriously, also remains cheerful about it. He
accepts the fact that that is just the way men are (Gn. 8.21).
The Priestly writer, by contrast, perhaps may fairly be
described as being obsessed with sin. As we pointed out
earlier, this obsession is a response to the particular historical
situation in which he wrote. He has seen what the dreadful
results are when Israel persist in disobedience to God, so he
offers them a *law*, so that they know exactly what is expected
of them, and he offers them an elaborate system of sacrifices
and other ceremonies so that when they do offend, they know
what steps to take in order to set things right again.

The detailed laws of Leviticus appear to many Christian readers not to be very interesting. The same readers are likely to find themselves even less sympathetic to the tedious descriptions of peace offerings, whole burnt offerings, sin offerings and guilt offerings, with which the Pentateuch abounds. It is a fair guess that those who find these sacrifices unattractive to read about would have found them even more unattractive to witness. The temple functioned as a slaughterhouse. At least in the post-exilic period (when the Priestly law was in operation) large numbers of animals were slaughtered there daily. Some of these animals were wholly burnt, the rest were burnt in part. The smell of burning flesh and fat is not pleasant, and if large quantities were burnt regularly the smell must have been quite overpowering. In addition to the burning of flesh, fat and bones, there was the blood, which had to be thrown against the side of the altar in some cases, in others poured out at the altar base. It simply ran away down open gutters. According to the Jewish rabbis one of the continuing miracles of God's providence was that there were no flies in the temple precincts. If that was true, it was a miracle indeed. (On the sacrificial system, See GBS, Chapter 27, e.)

But however repulsive some of these cultic practices may have been, the *thinking* behind them is of great importance. The cultic system is a system by means of which *order* is maintained in the universe. By this means uncleanness of all kinds is removed. Things which mar the harmony between God and men are put right. Fellowship between God and man is maintained.

Now the Priestly writer, nor anybody else in the Old Testament for that matter, never explains how or why the sacrificial system has this effect. We are simply assured that it does. It works because God has decided that it should. It is the way which he has chosen for expiation and atonement to be made. We might object that this makes the system essentially an arbitrary one. If we were able to put it to him we might find that the Priestly writer agreed with this estimate, and that he did not find it objectionable. Certainly there were one or two rabbis of the New Testament period who regarded the entire ceremonial law as essentially arbitrary, and who maintained that though there was no real logic in it it ought to be obeyed because God had so decreed.

But note what follows from this. Sacrifice is not something which *man* brings to God, because man happens to think it a good idea. Cultic service is not something man does *for* God, as if God needed anything. Sacrifice is something that *God* has appointed, of his pure grace, so that men may have a way of repairing the damage which their sins and failures do. Sacrifice is a way back, which God offers, into his presence. The key text here is Lv. *17*.11: 'For the life of the flesh is the blood, and *I have given it* upon the altar, to make atonement for yourselves.' Sacrifice, then, for the Priestly writer, is not something which man gives, but which God gives.

It is sometimes objected to the whole institution of sacrifice that it smacks too much of a way of buying God off. It is said that those who offered sacrifices were tempted not to take their sins seriously, because they knew they could bring an offering and the sins would be written off; that they thought their sacrifices would earn God's favour whether they were accompanied by sincere repentance or not. Now we certainly are not in a position to say that no Israelite ever offered sacrifice with such mistaken ideas in his head. What we can say, and say emphatically, is that there is nothing in the Priestly writer's work, or anywhere else in the Old Testament, to give such ideas any encouragement.

Sacrifice, for the Priestly writer in particular and for the Old Testament in general, is not a way of cloaking the seriousness of sin; quite the reverse, it is an *expression* of the seriousness with which sin is taken. Three observations help to confirm this conclusion. First, an obvious point, but one often overlooked; sacrifice is expensive. How much do mutton and beef cost per pound? Estimate, then, if you will, the cost of a whole sheep or a whole bull. Relatively speaking, meat was certainly not less expensive in ancient times than it is now. The man who was so concerned about his sins that he offered up a sheep or a bull can hardly therefore be accused of taking sin lightly.

Secondly: read Lv. 5.14–16 and 6.1–7. These are regulations for the making of guilt offerings, the type of sacrifice which was offered to compensate for specific offences. The former of these two passages concerns purely cultic offences, such as failure to observe the proper rules for offerings to the sanctuary; the second relates to offences against one's neighbour, such as robbery, embezzlement, wrongful appropriation of goods, etc. The vital verses for our purpose are 5.16 and 6.4–5. These make it clear that the *sacrifice is not acceptable until restitution has been made for the wrong committed*. Not only must the offender pay back whatever he had taken or whatever he should have paid in the beginning, but he must 'add a fifth thereunto'. I.e. he has to add an extra twenty per cent. Not until this is done can the sacrifice be brought. The Priestly writer is here making it very clear indeed that sacrifice is not a way of avoiding one's responsibilities. If a man has defrauded his neighbour of £100, to set matters right will cost him £120 plus the price of a ram without blemish.

Thirdly: read Lv. 5.1–13 (and read it carefully, right to the end). These are regulations for the guilt offering too, but the offences in question are of a different kind from those spoken of above. These are the so-called 'unwitting' offences. They mostly concern the contraction of ritual uncleanness of which one may be unaware. When a person finds out, or suspects, that he has contracted such uncleanness he is obliged to offer a sacrifice of a lamb or a goat. (It is worth noting in passing that the 'sins' for which sacrifice avails, in the mind of the Priestly writer, are by no means all of them matters that we should consider blameworthy, or even *moral* matters at all.)

So far so good, but suppose a man cannot afford the price of a lamb or a goat? Must his poverty then keep him in impurity? No, he may offer instead two doves or pigeons. There is no suggestion that such a sacrifice is inferior in its effects; just as in the former case, the priest makes atonement for the offender and he is forgiven.

But suppose he cannot even afford the price of two pigeons? He shall bring a tenth of an ephah of flour (about seven pounds), 'and the priest shall make atonement for him and he shall be forgiven'. There are two significant things here. First, this last offering is bloodless. It is not anything magic about blood that marks the sacrifice as effective. It is effective because God chooses so to regard it. Secondly, its effectiveness is clearly independent of value. The value of the sacrifice is related not to the gravity of the offence but to the means of the worshipper.

All of this confirms the conclusion that for the Priestly writer there is nothing automatic about the way sacrifice operates. God regards it as acceptable not for what it is, but for what it conveys, the desire of the worshipper for forgiveness.

So far we have spoken as if all sacrifice was for sin. This is very far from the truth. If we look at the rest of the Old Testament we see that the vast majority of sacrifices have no explicit or direct connexion with sin at all. Most sacrifices that Israelites offered were peace offerings (so-called—the name is not a good translation of the Hebrew). The sacrifice of a peace offering was simply a joyful occasion, a feast. Most of the sacrifice was eaten by the worshipper himself, and his family and guests. It seems to have been mainly thought of as a fellowship meal, or act of communion, a cheerful 'eating before the Lord'.

Other common sacrifices were thankofferings. They expressed gratitude either for some special deliverance which the worshipper had experienced or simply God's continued blessings of prosperity. Some were offered in fulfilment of vows. A man might promise a sacrifice if the harvest were good, or a journey was accomplished safely.

That is the general picture, but it is fair to say that in the work of the Priestly writer, although all these other sorts of sacrifices are acknowledged, and no doubt continued to be offered, it is the sin offerings and guilt offerings which are the most prominent.

For what kind of sins are sacrifices prescribed? Here we can briefly look over material which we have already brought forward. Some 'sins', as we have seen, are not what we ourselves would call sins. They are various kinds of 'uncleanness', of a ritual sort. Contact with the carcase of an 'unclean' animal, for example, counts as a 'sin' for this sort of purpose. Some kinds of diseases, after they are cured, leave a ritual impurity which has to be removed by sacrifice. The various skin diseases which the Old Testament classifies as 'leprosy' come into this category. (Medical science was not very exact in those days, and what the Bible calls 'leprosy' includes a wide variety of ailments. Lv. *13* describes the symptoms of 'leprosy' in great detail and they are not the symptoms of leprosy as we know it.) Childbirth leaves a ritual impurity too, which has to be 'atoned for' (Lv. *12*). Damp or mildewed patches on the walls of houses also have to have atonement made for them (Lv. *14*.33–53).

We also saw that in Lv. *6* there are a number of specific moral transgressions, such as fraud and embezzlement, for which an atoning sacrifice might be required. But to put this in perspective we need to be aware that these are exceptions. Generally speaking, offences such as theft or fraud would be dealt with by the courts of law. It rather looks as if the offences mentioned in Lv. *6* are not ones which have been brought to light by investigation, but ones which the offender's own uneasy conscience has led him to confess. It is this which brings them into the orbit of the cult rather than the court. All these specific 'sins', whether ritual or moral, are dealt with by the guilt-offering (*asham* in Hebrew).

The sin offering (*hattath*) which is very similiar in its ritual, is not offered for particular offences, but for sin in general, and for communal and corporate sins.

Perhaps the outstanding sacrifice which is offered for this kind of general sin or sinfulness is the great sacrifice on the Day of Atonement (described in Lv. *16*). This is a sacrifice of special solemnity. Its blood is brought into the Holy of Holies itself, as the blood of no other sacrifice was. And the sins for which it atones are described in extremely comprehensive terms. 'Thus he (the priest) shall make atonement for the holy place, because of the uncleannesses of the people of Israel, and because of their transgressions, *all their sins*' (Lv. *16*.16).

All of this may seem to suggest some rather primitive ways of thinking, but it is important to try to understand them, if only because these ideas about sacrifice are taken for granted by the people who wrote the New Testament, and when they come to describe the death of Christ in terms of sacrifice, this is the kind of sacrifice which they have in mind.

The idea that expiation or atonement needs to be made for a patch of mildew on the wall of a house, or for the blood shed in childbirth, or for an attack of acne or ringworm, may not be a helpful one, but the Priestly writer's idea of sacrifice does express some convictions more worthy of notice. He seems to be convinced that when a man has been sorry for and set right all the particular sins which he knows he has committed, and when he has made allowance for the graves he might have walked over unaware and the contamination with which he might unwittingly have been in contact, there is still something unatoned for; not so much sins as Sin, or sinfulness. The priest seems to share the conviction of the prophet (see Is. 6), that however ready he may wish to be to do the divine will, he is an unclean man in the midst of an unclean people, and that he cannot stand before the King, the Lord of Hosts. However primitive and unhelpful, therefore, may be some of the ideas expressed in the cultic system of Israel, it has a contribution to make to the Bible's understanding of sin and of atonement. Above all, it bears witness to the conviction that atonement cannot truly be made by man himself, but only by the means which God provides.

# Section 2

# The Deuteronomic Traditions

In 2 Kings *22–23* we read of how, in the reign of Josiah, 'the book of the law' was found in the temple. It looks as if Josiah had already begun some sort of religious reform when the book was discovered (2 Chr. *34*, a parallel account of the same events, is quite explicit on this point) but the discovery of the law book certainly intensified Josiah's reforming enthusiasm.

What was this law book? It is almost universally agreed that it had much in common with the book of Deuteronomy. We cannot say simply that Josiah's law book *was* Deuteronomy, but it seems to have been a kind of 'first edition' of Deuteronomy. I.e. Josiah's law book was the book of which our Deuteronomy is an expansion and elaboration. (See further, GBS, Chapter 21, f, g, i.)

Why do we conclude that Deuteronomy and the law book are so closely related? It would take a long time to set out the arguments in detail, but they can be quickly summarized. The directions which Josiah's reforms took after the book's discovery are exactly the ones which we should have expected them to take if Deuteronomy (or something very like it) was providing the guiding principles. The principal reform was the closing down of all provincial sanctuaries and the centring of sacrificial worship on one legitimate sanctuary, the Jerusalem temple. At the same time, the worship at the one legitimate sanctuary was reformed. A number of practices which had previously been accepted were now condemned as pagan (2 Kings *23*.4–14). All this marks a very radical revision of Israel's religious ways. It looks as if, up to this point, there had been no really clear idea about what counted as Israelite religious orthodoxy and what did not. The writers of the law book were taking the first big step in defining what was 'orthodox' and acceptable in the way of religious belief and practice.

Let us be clear, before we go any further, about where this discovery fits into the historical pattern. The year is 621 BC. Amos and Hosea had done their work about a century earlier. Isaiah had been dead for about seventy-five years. So the law makers and reformers had their ideas to draw on. Jeremiah had received his call about five years earlier, and seems to have had very mixed feelings about what the reformers were doing. Though the reformers did not know it, the exile and the final collapse of the kingdom were only thirty-five years in the future. The Northern kingdom, of course, had already collapsed, almost exactly a hundred years before. Refugees from the North had doubtless come south at that time, bringing their traditions with them. The law book reflects thorough knowledge of northern traditions, and the reformers who wrote it and Josiah who made use of it both seem to have wished to make it a basis for re-uniting the two halves of the kingdom, as they had not been since the time of Solomon. The Priestly writers' collection of laws was still far away in the future, but the deuteronomic law makers had older collections to draw on, notably the great collection of Ex. *21—23*, the Book of the Covenant.

Who had written this law book, and when? It purports to be a record of speeches delivered by Moses, just before the Israelites entered the Promised Land. But it certainly does not go back to his time. It is *possible* that it was written on Josiah's own instructions, and that its 'finding' was simply a way of claiming it to be authoritative. The Egyptians, when they wished to introduce a new religious book, used to say that it had been 'found in the temple'. It was a convention which was not meant to deceive anyone, but merely to claim authoritative status for the book in question. It is conceivable that Josiah and his advisers were following some similar convention. But most scholars think it more likely that it had been written some time earlier. It might have been written for use in the reform of Hezekiah, which was very similar in its intentions to Josiah's but which was unsuccessful, owing to

Assyrian interference. Or it might have been written by sup-
porters of Hezekiah's reform who were driven underground
during the long reign of his son, the apostate Manasseh. Such
people might have hidden the book away against just such an
eventuality as the rise of another reforming king.

However it came to be written, once Josiah had accepted
the law book as the guiding principle of his reform it became
an immensely influential document. It set the pattern for the
development of Israel's religion from that time onwards.
Josiah was tragically killed while still quite a young man, and
for a while it looked as if his reform might end as abortively as
Hezekiah's had done. But when the people of Judah went into
exile the law book went with them. It was expanded there by
the addition of extra material into our present book of
Deuteronomy. Furthermore, a group of people who shared
its ideals, whom we call the deuteronomic school, took up the
story of the people of Israel where Deuteronomy itself left
off. Deuteronomy recounts the story of the wanderings in the
wilderness up to the entry into the Promised Land. It is in the
context of this story that it sets out its laws. The deuteronomic
school continued the history to cover the conquest, the
settlement, the period of the judges, the founding of the
monarchy, the division of the kingdom, and the history of
the two Israels down to the exile itself. This 'Deuteronomic
History', as we now call it, is set out in four books, the books
of Joshua, Judges, Samuel and Kings (though Samuel and
Kings were at a later time and for purely practical reasons
split into two each). The book of Deuteronomy itself and the
four books which make up the rest of the Deuteronomic
History all share the same basic understanding of God, and
the same ideas about what constitutes right religion.

## The Deuteronomists' understanding of the person of God

There is *one* God. Apart from 2-Isaiah no one in the Old
Testament states this truth of the oneness of God quite so
emphatically as the Deuteronomists. 'Hear, O Israel, the
Lord our God the Lord is one' is a very famous summary of
Israel's faith, and it is found in Deuteronomy (6.4).

The deuteronomic school also make it quite clear that their
idea of God is quite a refined and sophisticated one. In the

prayer of Solomon at the dedication of the temple (1 Kings 8), a prayer which was composed by the deuteronomic editors of the book of Kings, Solomon says: 'But will God indeed dwell upon earth? Behold, the heaven and the heaven of heavens can not contain thee; how much less this house which I have built!' (8.27). This is a very important verse, for here we have a scriptural writer reflecting on the language he himself is using, and making it quite clear that he does not wish that language to be taken literally. The temple is called 'the house of God', 'God's dwelling'. But of course (the writer is saying) we don't mean that in any crude sense. Not only so, but (he goes on) even to talk of God 'dwelling' in heaven is only a manner of speaking. We use such expressions because they help to make God real to us, but to talk of God 'dwelling' anywhere is actually to diminish God, whom even the heavens cannot contain.

And how do we know about this one God? *What* do we know of him? The Deuteronomists acknowledge in many places that knowledge of God comes through his prophets. They assume that we also know about him through his law (which is not necessarily very different, since the law was given by Moses, himself a prophet). But the *first* way in which he made himself known was not through words or commands, but through *acts*. As we have seen, when the writer of Ex. 3 is trying to say who God is he does so in rather difficult, almost philosophical language. He describes God as 'the One who is' (I am what I am). The Deuteronomists define God more concretely (5.6): 'I am the Lord your God, who brought you out of the land of Egypt, out of the house of bondage.' God is being defined, here, by *what he has done*. He is defined as a saviour. This is the first characteristic of him, of which Israel is aware at her very first meeting with him. He is a liberator, a God who brings freedom, one who saves. Before men know anything else about him, he saves them. He *meets* Israel as a saviour.

## The relation of God to man

In trying to speak of the Deuteronomists' understanding of God we have already begun to speak of his relationship with man. This is inevitable, because for the deuteronomic school it is only in his relationship with man that God is known at all.

The classic statement of Dt. 6.4, quoted above, even before it says that God is one, names him as 'our God': 'the Lord *our God*, the Lord is one'.

This relationship with God has a definite beginning. God has not always been Israel's God; or at least, he has not always been known to be Israel's God. The Lord *became* Israel's God, and initiated a relationship with them, by acting on their behalf, even when they did not know him, and delivering them.

God acts on Israel's behalf, and initiates his relationship with them, out of pure grace. There was no question of Israel deserving this special treatment. There was no *reason* why the Lord should choose to make them his own. 'It was not because you were more in number than any other people that the Lord set his love upon you and chose you, for you were the fewest of all people; but it is because the Lord loves you . . .' (Dt. 7.7–8). And 'do not say in your heart . . . . "It is because of my righteousness that the Lord has brought me in to possess this land" . . . Not because of your righteousness or the uprightness of your heart are you going in to possess the land . . .' (Dt. 9.4–5).

One of the Deuteronomists' favourite words is the word which is usually translated as 'to ransom'. It is perhaps better thought of as meaning 'to purchase', 'to make one's own'. Deutero-Isaiah, as we shall see later, is very fond of a parallel word 'redeem'.[1] To 'redeem' something means to restore it to where it belongs, to get it *back*. But the Deuteronomists, in speaking about the rescue from Egypt, do not use the word 'redeem'. God is not getting Israel *back*, because she has never been his. He is making her his own, for the first time. This 'ransoming' or 'purchasing' is not to be taken too literally. It must not be thought that God is obliged to pay anything for Israel, as though anyone else had a legitimate claim on her. God has ransomed Israel by his power, and brought them out of Egypt 'with a mighty hand' (Dt. 9.26).

The relationship of Israel with God is an *exclusive* relationship. It has a peculiarly totalitarian character. There must be no divided loyalties, and anything which threatens to divide Israel's loyalty must be ruthlessly rooted out. There is no toleration of idolatry or the worship of gods other than the

[1] RSV confusingly translates *both* words as 'redeem' in some instances.

Lord. And anyone who tries to seduce Israelites into such worship must be shown no mercy. Dt. *13*, in a series of examples, makes this point very plain. If a prophet appears, and suggests worshipping other gods, then however persuasively he might speak, and however impressive the miracles he might do, he is to be put to death. He may display quite convincingly all the signs of inspiration, but if he contradicts at this crucial point the revelation which has already been given his inspiration is false. Dt. *13* goes on: 'If your brother . . . or your son, or your daughter, or the wife of your bosom, or your friend who is as your own soul, entices you secretly, saying, "Let us go and serve other gods" . . . you shall not yield to him or listen to him, nor shall your eye pity him, nor shall you spare him . . . your hand shall be first against him, to put him to death' (*13*.6–9). Faithfulness to the one God is to be put before even the most sacred of family ties and ties of affection and loyalty. And if these words seem rather ferocious it is worth remembering that in the New Testament too the claims of God are put emphatically before the claims of family loyalty (see, e.g. Mt. *10*.37 and parallels; and cf. Mt. *10*.46–50 and parallels).

Dt. *13* ends by considering the possibility of an entire community within Israel becoming apostate and turning over to the worship of other deities. If there is such a community its people and all their possessions are to be totally destroyed, lest the contagion spread.

After such bloodthirsty examples it may sound rather strange to say that for the Deuteronomists man's response to God is summed up in the command *to love*. To go back once more to Dt. *6*.4, that basic statement of faith, the command to love follows immediately upon the assertion of the oneness of God. 'Hear, O Israel; the Lord our God, the Lord is one; *and you shall love* the Lord your God with all your heart, and with all your soul, and with all your might.' But 'love', for the Deuteronomists, and perhaps for the Old Testament writers as a whole, is not primarily an emotion; it is a matter of will rather than feeling. If a man loves, it is not merely because his feelings move him to do so, but because he has decided to. The biblical writers think of love to God in very much the same way as they think of love to one's parents. And the ancient Israelite loved his parents not simply because nature prompted him to do so, but because it was his duty and obligation. And he saw himself as fulfilling the obligation to love his parents principally by *obeying* them. None of this means that the Israelite was without feeling and emotion, or that he despised such things. Normally, of course, there *would* be a bond of affection between a man and his parents, or between a man and his wife. But no Israelite imagined that if the feeling was *not* there his obligation was in any way diminished.

Though the relationship between God and Israel begins with grace, with God's initiative, once Israel has responded to that grace and accepted God's covenant she is totally bound by it. Once inside the covenant, the demand is for *undeviating* rectitude. 'Righteousness, righteousness you shall pursue, that you may live and inherit the land . . .' (Dt. *16*.20).

Moving outside Deuteronomy itself and into the Deuteronomic History we find this point made very explicit in Jos. *24*. Joshua *24* is an important chapter. The story it tells is an old story but the Deuteronomists have taken it over and interpreted it in such a way as to express their own thinking. It tells how the Israelites, having conquered the land, meet together to re-affirm their covenant with God. Joshua reminds the people of all the great things which God has done for them, and appeals to them (*24*.14–15) to reject other gods and serve the Lord alone. The people readily agree (*24*.16–18) but their assent is evidently too glib for Joshua. He changes tack and appears to be trying to put them off (compare Jesus's response to a rather over-ready avowal in Lk. *9*.57–58). 'But Joshua said to the people: "You cannot serve the Lord; for he is a holy God; he is a jealous God; he will not forgive your transgressions or your sins" ' (*24*.19). He is saying to them: Are you really sure you know what you are taking on? The covenant with God is not something to be accepted lightly. If you enter it and then fail to live up to its demands your situation will be worse than if you had kept clear of it altogether. Once in, there is no going back (cf. Lk. *9*.59–62). There can be no half measures; it must be *total* commitment or no commitment at all.

At several points in our discussion of the relationship of man to God we have spoken of the covenant. The idea of the covenant is prominent in the Old Testament and it is likely that its prominence is very largely due to the work of the Deuteronomists. Doubtless the covenant idea was already there, before the Deuteronomists got to work. It seems to be present in some very old traditions about the patriarchs, and it is probable that both J and E already saw the revelation on Sinai as involving a covenant-making. The pre-exilic prophets, too, seems to presuppose knowledge of it. But it seems to have been the Deuteronomists who exalted the covenant notion into a basic principle of Israel's religious faith. When they re-edited older traditions they seem to have laid extra stress on the covenant, and to have introduced covenant language into traditions where it was not present previously. But whereas earlier thinkers (such as the eighth-century prophets, and the Yahwistic and Elohistic writers) had used a large variety of images for speaking of God's relationship with man, of which the covenant was only one, the Deuteronomists tend to see almost everything in covenantal terms.]

### The relation of man to man

To love God and to obey God means also to love one's fellows. Now the Deuteronomists themselves never express it in quite that fashion (the command, 'Thou shalt love thy neighbour as thyself' is in the Holiness Code—Lv. *19*.18—not in Deuteronomy) but nevertheless that seems to be the principle which guides their thinking. Deuteronomy thus has many humanitarian laws.

That Deuteronomy repeatedly stresses the obligation to care for the poor is not remarkable. All the law codes, as well as the prophets, wisdom writings and psalms, do the same. The Old Testament writers commonly mention several classes of people deserving of charity, the main ones being widows, orphans and the 'sojourner'. 'Sojourner' is the Authorized Version's word. The 'sojourner' was a foreigner, more or less permanently settled in a country other than his own. He had often been driven out of his own land by famine, war, political upheaval or some more personal disaster. He was usually, in origin at least, a refugee. Perhaps the word 'refugee' would be the most accurate modern rendering of the Hebrew word. He was vulnerable because he possessed no land in the country of his adoption. He did not possess any rights as a citizen. He had no family to protect him. The Deuteronomist not only recommends the 'sojourners' repeatedly to the charity of Israelites but adds a very characteristic reason for doing so. He reminds his fellow-countrymen that they themselves were sojourners, in the land of Egypt (*10*.19, cf. *23*.7).

But to the usual list of poor the Deuteronomists add another, the levite. Why should levites be counted among the poor? Whether the levites are best regarded as a tribe or as a professional group is not clear, but be that as it may, they were a priestly class and made their living from exercising their religious functions at sanctuaries up and down the country. There are good reasons for thinking that some of them did possess land, but it is quite certain that many of them did not and that their priestly profession provided their chief or only source of income. Now Deuteronomy is suggesting the closing down of all the provincial sanctuaries and the concentration of sacrificial worship exclusively at Jerusalem. At one point it does say that levites from the provincial shrines are to be allowed to transfer to the central sanctuary and carry out their duties there (Dt. *18*.6–8), but if the legislators were realistic they must have known that this was unlikely to happen, and 2 Kings *23*.9 confirms that when Josiah carried through his reform it did not happen. Doubtless the Jerusalem priests would have resisted any such provision. The numbers of provincial priests must surely have been large enough to swamp the Jerusalem priesthood if they had all been allowed to come. One result of the deuteronomic reform therefore must have been a large number of unemployed levites, hence the Deuteronomists' inclusion of such people among the poor.

Dt. *24*.6–22 is a good sample of Deuteronomy's humanitarian laws. Not all of these laws are new. Some of them are simply repeated from the earlier collection in the Book of the Covenant. They show concern for servants (*24*.14–15), decreeing that a servant or a worker must not be kept waiting for his wages, but must be paid daily (cf. Mt. *20*.8 where the just employer in the parable of the Labourers in the Vineyard does exactly that).

On the subject of servants it is interesting to compare the

ten commandments as they are given in Deuteronomy
(*5*.6–21) with the version of them in Ex. *20*. When it comes to
the command to keep sabbath Deuteronomy of course sets
down the same command as Exodus, but it gives a different
motivation. In Exodus the sabbath is to be kept because 'in six
days the Lord made heaven and earth . . . and rested on the
seventh day'. Israel's sabbath rest is thus an imitation of the
sabbath rest of God. But for Deuteronomy the reason for
sabbath keeping is 'that your manservant and your maidser-
vant may rest as well as you'. The Deuteronomist goes on:
'You shall remember that *you* were a servant in the land of
Egypt . . .'

One extraordinary provision of Deuteronomy (*23*.15 f.) is
that slaves who run away are not to be sent back to their
masters. It may seem at first sight as if this would make
nonsense of the whole institution of slavery, for who would
remain a slave if he could be free simply by running away? But
we have to remember that slavery in Israel and in some other
ancient near eastern societies was not the oppressive institution which we are familiar with from the eighteenth-century
cotton and sugar plantations of the New World. Many Israelite slaves were debt slaves, i.e. they were men who had
become bankrupt and who were temporarily enslaved by
their creditors. What such a debtor was doing, effectively, was
to discharge his debt with his one remaining asset, his labour.
Such slavery had a time limit fixed to it by law (Ex. *21*.1–4;
Dt. *15*.12). While thus discharging the debt the debt slave
was entitled to be fed and housed by his master. But while
giving the debt slave the *right* to go free after six years, both
the Book of the Covenant (Ex. *21*.5 f.) and Deuteronomy
(*15*.16 f.) envisage the possiblity that he may not wish to do
so. For such a man, without resources, freedom was often
merely the freedom to starve. The option of remaining a
slave, in security, was no doubt a very tempting alternative to
the insecurity of freedom.

Slavery was thus, to some extent, a benevolent institution.
The slave was a member of the family and entitled to many of
the privileges of membership. The *exploitation* of slaves,
though we cannot say it never took place, was not the norm.
The Deuteronomists, in decreeing that runaways are not to be
returned, are probably working on the assumption that any

slave who runs away is evidently not being treated properly.

The passages referred to above, Ex. *21*.1–6 and Dt. *15*.12–18, show that in respect of slavery laws the Book of the Covenant and the book of Deuteronomy have much in common. But the differences between them illustrate how far the humanitarianism of Deuteronomy goes beyond that of earlier codes. Ex. *21* allows the slave freedom after six years but seems to make it hard for him to choose it. If during the six years his master has provided him with a wife, and the wife has had children by him, the wife and children remain the master's; to choose freedom for himself will mean leaving them behind. Dt. *15* does not mention this point at all, but it does in another way positively encourage the slave to choose freedom. Instead of being faced with the prospect of going out into the world with nothing, and finding alternative employment and somewhere to live, the Deuteronomists suggest that his master should provide him with some capital to give him a fresh start. This may be idealistic, and doubtless it did not always, or perhaps often, happen, but it shows the direction of the Deuteronomists' thinking.

The Deuteronomists are very sensitive about maintaining human dignity. If a man is in your debt, and you are entitled to take some piece of his property as security, you do not go into his house and seize it. Wait, and let him bring it out to you (Dt. *24*.20 f.) If a man has committed a crime and deserves corporal punishment, by all means administer it, but take care that it be not excessive. Dt. *25*.1–3 limits corporal punishment to forty strokes of the lash or cane. Even this seems quite fierce, but it is the *reasons* for the limitation that are interesting. Punishment is to be limited lest 'your brother be degraded in your sight' (*25*.3). Again the concern is for human dignity.

What emerges from these deuteronomic laws is not merely a humanitarian concern for others but a kind of moderation. The righteous man, as the Deuteronomists picture him, is one who never presses an advantage to the limits; who is not concerned to grab all he can get, or squeeze the last ounce. Having gathered the harvest of his olive trees or his vines he does not go over the trees again a second time. He does not go back to fetch the forgotten sheaf from the field (Dt. *24*.19–22). If there is a percentage ungathered, then the refugee, the fatherless and the widow may have the advantage (24.20). This is not peculiar to Deuteronomy. The Holiness Code displays the same sort of ideals. Lv. 19.9–10 forbids the Israelite to gather the gleanings from his own harvest, or pick up the windfall fruit from his orchard, or to reap every last stalk from the corners and edges of his cornfield. Those to whom God has been good do not honour him by exploiting his gifts for every penny they are worth.

We do have to be a little careful of reading into the provisions of deuteronomic law motives that may not truly be there. The law of Dt. 22.8 is usually quoted among the humanitarian provisions, perhaps wrongly. This is the regulation which insists that parapets be placed round flat roofs, in case people fall off. But the motive actually given is not that of public safety but the avoidance of blood guilt. The Deuteronomists believed that the shedding of blood released malevolent forces which could cause havoc if not appeased. This is illustrated by the regulations in Dt. 21.1–9 for dealing with unsolved murder. If such a murder has happened in open country then measurements have to be taken to see which is the nearest town (21.2). This is because the malevolent forces will naturally attach themselves to the nearest habitable place. If anyone was killed by falling off a roof such forces would attach themselves to the dwelling concerned. Hence the need for protective railings. Here we have a law which is at first sight humanitarian in its intention but whose real motives seem to have more in common with what we should call superstition.

We need to be even more careful in evaluating motives when we look at the laws in which the Deuteronomists show concern not for human beings but for animals. Deuteronomy is exceptional in this respect. No other ancient law code known to us shows such sensitivity to the welfare of animals. The most famous law on the subject is Dt. 25.4: 'You shall not muzzle the ox when it treads out the grain.' The deuteronomic version of the ten commandments explicitly includes the ox and ass in the rule about not working on the sabbath (cf. Ex. 23.12). The instructions to take straying animals back to their owners, however (Dt. 22.1–3, cf. Ex. 23.4) and to give assistance to animals fallen under their load (Dt. 22.4, cf. Ex. 23.5) are to be seen not as examples of kindness to animals but kindness to their owners. And the curious rule that one may take birds' eggs or young birds but must not take the mother bird at the same time (Dt. 22.6 f.) is probably purely superstitious in motivation and has nothing to do with kindness to the bird. In this respect it is similar to the rule in the Book of the Covenant (Ex. 23.19) that one must not boil a kid in the milk of its own mother.

Having said all that we have about the humanitarianism of Deuteronomy we must now observe that there are very strict limits to it. The Deuteronomists can switch off their humanitarianism very abruptly if it conflicts with other interests. This shows that it is not rooted in mere sentiment. If the Deuteronomists deal righteously with their fellow Israelite it is not primarily because they feel sorry for him, but because that is what God wants them to do. Duty to one's fellow man, however high it comes on the list of moral priorities, is always secondary to one's duty to God. The Deuteronomist loves his neighbour *because* he loves God first.

If sympathy for one's fellow man ever *conflicts*, therefore, with duty to God, then sympathy must be put firmly out of mind. We have already seen how this operates in relation to the worship of other gods. In the case of those who counsel such false worship sympathy is positively a sin. 'Your eye shall not pity, neither shall your hand spare.' There must be no sympathy for those whom the Deuteronomists see as a threat to faith.

Perhaps the clearest illustration of the way in which the Deuteronomists set sharp limits to the sphere of sympathy and humanitarian feeling is found in the deuteronomic rules of war. These are set out in Dt. 20. In some respects they are so humane as to be astonishing. Yet they contain apparent inconsistencies. The reason is, when we examine the list carefully, that there are actually two sets of rules, for two different kinds of warfare.

Let us look first at the humane aspects. We have the regulations for conscription (20.5–9), which allow some striking reasons for exemption from military service. Any man who has built a new house but has had no opportunity even for a housewarming is excused. Anyone who has planted a vineyard but not yet enjoyed produce from it is excused. Any man who has betrothed a wife but not yet consummated the marriage is excused. (The similarity of these to the reasons for the guests' refusals in the parable of the Great Feast is not accidental. These are the *legitimate* reasons for refusing or putting off an otherwise imperative call. The parable is telling us that even these are not good enough reasons for putting off the call of Christ.) But the Deuteronomists go on: anyone who is fearful and fainthearted is also excused, i.e. it is a good enough reason for exemption from military duty that a man doesn't feel like fighting. This sounds extraordinary, but it is understandable on two grounds, one practical, the other theological. The practical ground is given by Deuteronomy itself quite explicitly. Such a man is to be excused 'lest the heart of his fellows melt as his heart'. Ancient battles were nearly always won because one side panicked before the armies really got to grips with each other. One might say that the battle was normally won by the side with the strongest nerve. It was therefore not such an impractical idea to confine one's choice of combatants to those who really had stomach for the fight. (For an actual instance of the application of this law, or something very like it, see Jdg. 7.) The theological reason for the exemption is one which echoes through and through the Bible, and is central to the teaching of Jesus, that those who do the work of God (and the Deuteronomists certainly saw Israel's wars as the work of God) must be totally committed. If there is anything about a man that takes the edge off that commitment he had better stay at home.

In the conduct of war itself humane and decent treatment of the enemy is demanded. The enemy must always be offered the opportunity to make terms of peace. If he accepts terms, he may be reduced to servitude but not killed. If the enemy resists, then on winning the war his menfolk may be put to the sword, but not women or children (Dt. *20*.10–15). During the siege of a city its fruit trees are not to be cut down. Other trees may be used for timber or firewood, but the fruit trees, even of an enemy, are to be preserved. (*20*.19 f.) All of this seems very sensible. The Deuteronomists are discouraging *total* war. Even warfare must have its rules, its limits.

Dt. *20*.15 is an important verse, because it makes it clear that all these rules for the conduct of war apply only to *foreign* wars. For wars against the Canaanites, and others who contest possession of the promised land with God's chosen people, quite different rules apply. These are given in 20.16–18. Such enemies are given no opportunity to make terms. They are not allowed the option of servitude. Not even their women or children are to be saved alive. None of their property is to be rescued. This is the other war, the Holy War, because the Canaanites and Amorites and the rest are seen as a threat to Israel's faith (20.18). (These are the rules which Joshua is applying at the capture of Jericho. Jos. 7—8 and cf. Dt. 7.1—6.)

The contrast between the rules for ordinary, foreign war and those for holy war is so sharp as to be startling. There are two quite distinct spheres here; the sphere in which humanity and sympathy, even for a foreign enemy, are encouraged and commanded, and the sphere in which any sympathy is ruled right out as disloyalty to God.

## The places of encounter with God

The older traditions, J and E, spoke of God's presence with Israel in the wilderness in the form of a pillar of cloud by day and a pillar of fire by night (Ex. 13.21 f.; 14.24; Num. 14.14). They were not thinking of the pillar of cloud and fire as merely symbolic of God's guidance, or as a mere indicator of which way to go. The pillar of cloud and fire conveys God's real presence, as is made clear in Ex. 14.24.

The Deuteronomists know and accept this older idea, for they refer in Dt. 1.33 to 'the Lord your God, who went before you in the way to seek out a place to pitch your tents, in fire by night, to show you by what way you should go, and in the cloud by day'.

But quite apart from the pillar of fire which led Israel through the wilderness, Deuteronomy regularly associates God's presence with fire. The Deuteronomists are not of course alone in this, but they do stress the notion quite heavily. When they refer back to the meeting with God on Sinai (which they call by its alternative name of Horeb) they repeatedly refer to God's speaking 'out of the midst of the fire' (see chapters 4, 5 and 9). And in Dt. 9.3 they speak of God going ahead of his people, over the Jordan, in the form of 'a consuming fire', to drive out the enemy, (cf. 4.24).

The presence of God 'in the fire', however, is a very uncomfortable presence. Already on Sinai/Horeb the Israelites are unwilling to meet God in this way. Dt. *5*.24–27 picks up from Ex. *20*.18–20 the people's request that God should not insist on speaking to them thus directly. They ask that Moses should meet God on their behalf and pass on to them God's words, so that they do not have to face the divine presence for themselves. The Deuteronomists therefore confine talk of God's presence in fire to the period of the exodus, the wanderings and the conquest. Once Israel is settled in her land God's grace provides a more bearable way of meeting with him, and a form of his presence with his people which is less intimidating. Once they are settled in the land, God is present with his people in his Name.

It is crucial to the Deuteronomists' religious outlook that the Name is centred in one particular holy place. They speak again and again of 'the place which the Lord your God will choose, to set his name there', or 'to make his name dwell there'. The book of Deuteronomy never actually tells us what this 'place' is. Josiah and those who supported his reform did not doubt that it intended to be understood as meaning Jerusalem. The reason why Deuteronomy does not name Jerusalem is a very simple one. Deuteronomy is set out as if it was a speech delivered by Moses, before the conquest of the land. It would have been rather anachronistic for Moses to be represented as referring by name to cities which were not yet in Israel's possession. Even when the land *was* conquered, under Joshua, Jerusalem did not fall, and remained in Jebusite hands until the time of David. Jerusalem did not become an Israelite centre until the time of the monarchy, therefore, and its importance stemmed from the fact that it was the seat of the kings. So the Deuteronomists put into Moses' mouth words which do not refer explicitly to Jerusalem, but simply drop very strong hints about the 'place' which was to become important to Israel only some hundreds of years after Moses' death.

For the Deuteronomists the identity of the one place is probably less important than its function. It is the place where the Name, 'this glorious and awe-ful name, the Lord your God' is set (Dt. *28*.58). It is therefore the place where God's people can come and meet him, not in fire and terror, but in the ordered, solemn and joyful celebration of the great festivals, and the offering of their prayers, gifts and sacrifices.

## Sacrifice in Deuteronomy

Deuteronomy has not a great deal to say about sacrifice. This is not because the Deuteronomists did not consider sacrifice important. They must have considered it important because they go to a lot of trouble to propose the reform of centralizing all sacrifice in one place (*12*.10–14) and to work out the consequent changes that will need to be made to Israel's religious and secular life. Yet they have very little to say about the different kinds of sacrifice which are to be offered, or about the manner of offering them. There is nothing in Deuteronomy corresponding to the detailed legislation of the Priestly writer in Lv. *1–7*.

There is really nothing strange about concluding that the Deuteronomists regard sacrifice as important but have little to say about it. The Deuteronomists *take the importance of sacrifice for granted.* It does not occur to them that its importance could be in dispute. But there are two additional reasons for their relative silence on the subject. First, Deuteronomy has been called a 'lay document'. What is meant by this is that it appears to be aimed at a lay audience. The kind of information it offers is what the lay worshipper would need to know. Things which only the priests would need to know it does not bother to record. The lay nature of Deuteronomy stands out clearly if we compare it with the later Priestly writing. P contains a good deal of fairly detailed legislation about the offering of sacrifices, about the ordination rituals for priests, and about various other matters which only the priests themselves would really need to be familiar with. Lv. *13*, for example, contains detailed notes on the symptoms of 'leprosy' which would enable the priest to diagnose this complaint and to prescribe the appropriate rituals. Only the priest himself would need this careful guidance.

Deuteronomy, by contrast, sticks for the most part to broad statements reminding the lay worshipper of his obligations, and goes into details only at those points at which the layman needs them. It reminds Israelites that sacrifices *are* expected and is emphatic that they must be offered only in 'the place which the Lord your God chooses' (*12*.11). It is explicit about the other sorts of offerings which worshippers are expected to bring, such as the produce of the harvest (*26*.1 ff.) and the offerings for the support of the priesthood (*18*.1–5). It goes into detail only on such questions as secular slaughter (*12*.15–28), and the distinction between clean and unclean animals (Chapter 14.)

The matter of secular slaughter needed to be raised because up to the time of Josiah's reform all slaughter of domestic animals had counted as sacrifice. If an Israelite wished to eat meat (and unless he was rich he could not afford to do so very often) he offered a sacrifice at his local shrine. The Deuteronomists want to abolish the local shrines. One result of this would have been to turn all those of their countrymen who were not within easy reach of Jerusalem into virtual vegetarians. Their answer to this problem is to institute secular slaughter. Characteristically they insist that this is not really a new idea. They point out that animals killed in hunting never have been regarded as sacrifices. They are thus only extending to domestic animals a practice which had always applied to wild ones. The Deuteronomists therefore prescribe quite carefully the ritual (for it *is* a ritual) for secular slaughter, for even though the slaughter is non-sacrificial the blood is still sacred and has to be disposed of in a proper manner (*12*.20–24), and they go on to distinguish it from the ritual of sacrifice (*12*.26–28). The details are necessary because this is a ritual which the layman himself will need to carry out.

So this is the first reason for the Deuteronomists' relative silence about sacrifice; they concentrate on what the layman needs. The second reason is also illustrated by the rules for secular slaughter: the Deuteronomists only go into detail on matters in which they are *altering* the rules. Secular slaughter was a new idea, so the legislators need to spell out what it involves. But they are not proposing any alteration to normal sacrificial ritual, so they just assume that it continues in the accepted way. The one point of change about sacrifice is its confinement to the single sanctuary.

## Deuteronomy and the festivals

The Deuteronomists' legislation on the festivals is found in Chapter 16. Here again we find them concentrating on information for laymen. The details of the rituals are for the most part not set out. The reader is told simply that he must appear for the three major feasts; that they are pilgrimage feasts, i.e. they are to be celebrated at the central sanctuary, not at home; that he must bring his offerings with him, and that the feast must be shared with his servants and with the poor.

The only point at which any details at all are given is in connexion with the feast of Passover/Unleavened Bread. This is because some new features are being introduced. According to 2 Kings 23.21–23 Josiah's reform culminated in a celebration of Passover. And it says that 'no such Passover had been kept since the days of the judges'. There was evidently something new and striking about Josiah's Passover. What was it? Some scholars have suggested that the festival had fallen into disuse and that Josiah was reviving it. The striking thing about Josiah's Passover therefore was that he was celebrating it at all. Though we cannot go into the arguments here, a good case can be made out for this interpretation. Nevertheless, we *can* find a satisfactory explanation for the statement in 2 Kings 23.22 without supposing that Josiah was re-instituting a festival which had totally lapsed.

We have argued that Josiah was basing his reform on Deuteronomy, or a book substantially like it, and Deuteronomy's legislation on the feast of Passover/Unleavened Bread does contain an important new feature. Passover had always been, it seems, a domestic festival. It was celebrated in the home. The accounts of it in Ex. 12 presuppose this. Each household kills its own sacrificial lamb; its blood is smeared on doorposts and lintels. Deuteronomy is laying it down that only in the central sanctuary can sacrifice legitimately be offered, and this means that it has got to alter the character of the Passover. No longer can people be allowed to kill their own sacrificial lamb and eat it at home. Passover must become a pilgrimage festival, and be celebrated in the one sanctuary. Possibly this is what 2 Kings is alluding to when it says that no such Passover had been held since the days of the judges. The writer of Kings (himself, of course, a member of the deuteronomic school) thinks that Deuteronomy was uttered by Moses, and that Josiah's change in the pattern of the festival was a reversion to ancient practice. In fact it was an innovation.

Though the Deuteronomists do not give us more than brief

outlines of the festivals the celebration of the feasts is important to them. They simply assume that for the most part the festival system continues as it was before the reform. (For further information on the festival system see GBS, Chapter 7, g–o,)

## Deuteronomy and piety

The effects of Deuteronomy on the cult are paradoxical. First, and most obviously, by centralizing worship in the temple and by controlling it in the way they do the deuteronomic school seem to lay great stress on the cult and to exalt its importance. It becomes no longer a series of homely and local celebrations, but the focus of *national* life. If Israel wishes to prosper; if she means to remain in covenant with her saviour God, she must not only continue to uphold the cult but she must get it right. Mistakes will not be tolerated.

So for the Deuteronomists the proper observance of the cult is vital, and an essential part of Israel's response to God. And yet by confining sacrifice and the celebration of the major feasts to Jerusalem they cut most of the population off from the cult for most of the year. This is where the paradox comes in. They tell people to take religion more seriously, and at the same time they abolish their local places of worship. Did they really expect their fellow countrymen to sustain a proper spiritual and devotional life on the basis of three visits a year to the central sanctuary?

They were evidently not unaware of the problem they were setting, for they do take steps to suggest some kind of replacement for the worship of the provincial shrines. They try to encourage the development of a family piety. By their own rules this domestic religion cannot involve sacrifices or offerings. It finds its centre *in the study of the law itself*. The key passage is 6.6–9. 'And these words which I command you this day shall be upon your heart; and you shall teach them diligently to your children, and shall talk of them when you sit in your house, and when you walk by the way, and when you lie down, and when you rise.' Deuteronomy goes on to say that the Israelite is to bind the words as a sign upon his hand and as frontlets between his eyes, and to write them on his doorposts and his gates. Devotion now centres on the law itself, and on the teaching and handing on of the law. It also involves passing on the story of salvation. For 'when your child asks you in time to come, "What is the meaning of the testimonies and the statutes and the ordinances . . .?" then you shall say . . . "We were Pharaoh's slaves in Egypt . . ." ' (6.20 f.). Compare also Dt. *11*.18–20.

From this point onwards Israel's worship takes two forms, which diverge but do not oppose each other. There is the worship in the temple, where sacrifices are offered and the great festivals celebrated and other rituals carried out. And there is the devotion to the law, the keeping of it and the study of it and the recital of it, centred in the home, or in purely private meditation, or (in later times) in the synagogue.

In instituting this second kind of piety the Deuteronomists were doing better than they knew. In 621 the book of the law was published. In 597, and then again in 586, not a generation later, Judah's leading people were taken into exile. The sanctuary in which their religious life had been centred was eight hundred miles away and quite inaccessible. But Deuteronomy had not only exalted the temple and its worship, it had also shown people how to do without it. The exiles were able to build on the hints that Deuteronomy had given them and develop a religious life which could sustain them and which did not need the temple. In the generations that followed, more and more Jews came to live outside the homeland. For them, it was not a question of visiting the temple three times a year, but perhaps once in a lifetime. By the time the final catastrophe took place, in AD 70, and the temple was destroyed once and for all, although it would not be fair to say that the Jews hardly noticed, it was only the Palestinian Jews, and especially the Jerusalem Jews, whose life style was seriously affected. The rest carried on as they had learnt to do for generations. Thus did the Deuteronomists accomplish these two contradictory things: they put the temple at the centre of Jewish religion, and they took the first steps in creating a Jewish religion which did not need the temple at its centre.

### The rest of the Deuteronomic History—Joshua to Kings

The books of Joshua, Judges, Samuel and Kings carry on the story of Israel from where Deuteronomy itself leaves off, at the entry into Palestine. They recount the conquest, the settlement, the period of the judges, the establishment of the monarchy, and the history of the kingdom (which quickly became two kingdoms) down to the exile in 586. The deuteronomic editors of these books were putting together older material, and putting it together in such a way that it made a pattern. This overall pattern expresses the deuteronomic school's own religious convictions (See GBS, Chapter 22, a, b.)

We need to be aware of two features of this history if we are to appreciate it properly. First, the older material which the Deuteronomists are working with often expresses ideas of its own which are not precisely in harmony with those of the Deuteronomists themselves. The Deuteronomists have pressed into service some fairly unlikely material, usually without obliterating the original character of the stories they are using. For example, we have the stories about Samson in the book of Judges. The deuteronomic editors represent Samson as one of the major judges. They fit him into a series, that is to say, of national figures, military leaders who delivered Israel from national enemies. If we look at the stories themselves, out of their deuteronomic context, we quickly see that they do not present Samson as any such thing. Samson never actually leads anybody anywhere, or raises any army. He *provokes* the Philistines, sometimes with silly practical jokes and sometimes with outright atrocities, but at no time does he actually deliver Israel from them as a judge was expected to do. Samson is a clown, but at the end a tragic figure, because he has God-given gifts which he doesn't know how to use.

A very different example is the material which occupies most of the second book of Samuel. These are the stories about the reign of David which together we often call the Court History of David, or the Succession Narrative.[2] They are fine stories, subtly and sensitively told. The deuteronomic editors seem hardly to have modified them at all. They let them stand as they are. Yet the writer of these stories worked with a very different purpose from that of the Deuteronomists themselves. The Deuteronomists work with a very clearcut theory of history. They divide people very sharply into

[2] The Succession Narrative is broadly the material of 2 Sam. *8—21:24*, and 1 Kings *1–3*.

'goodies' and 'baddies'. They see God as rewarding faithfulness and religious propriety, and punishing unfaithfulness; and they see this system of rewards and punishments as working out in quite simple ways. The author of the Succession Narrative is just as strongly convinced as his deuteronomic editors that God is firmly in control of all that happens, but he presents a much less simple picture. God does not merely reward faithfulness, but sometimes works his saving will in spite of the *un*faithfulness of his chosen ones. And far from dividing his characters into 'goodies' and 'baddies' he presents even David, the archetypal king, God's anointed, as a by no means exemplary personality.

Here again, therefore, the deuteronomic historians have preserved stories which do not express their own viewpoint. The historians' own ideas have to be sought, not in the materials which they made use of, but in the framework into which they set them, and in the occasional editorial comment or other insertions which they make. A good example of editorial insertion is found in the historians' account of Solomon. The editors have used quite a variety of material bearing on Solomon's reign. They seem to have had access to some official court records of Solomon's reign, which have given them basic facts about events, buildings constructed, foreign policies pursued, state visits, government organizations, trading ventures, etc. They have had a fairly detailed record of the construction of the temple. They have also used popular tales, like the story of Solomon and the two harlots, and the story of the king's dream (Chapter 3). The Deuteronomists' own hand, however, is clearly visible. It is visible especially in the comments on Solomon's *religious* policies and attitudes which are sprinkled through the account of his reign, e.g. 1 Kings *3*.2–3 and *11*.1–13. And it is visible in the prayer of Solomon at the dedication of the temple (1 Kings *8*), which is a deuteronomic composition and full of deuteronomic expressions and deuteronomic thinking.

This, then, is the first point to watch, that not everything in the Deuteronomic History expresses the deuteronomic viewpoint. The second is that the Deuteronomic History is not uniform; the editors do not always handle their source material in the same way. In Judges and Kings it is for the most part very tightly organized, and pushed into a fairly rigid scheme. In Samuel, as we have already seen, the editors are content to let their sources tell their own story, with editorial comment reduced to a minimum.

What are the positive ideas which the deuteronomic historians are putting across? They are very simple, and have already been mentioned. The Deuteronomists are convinced that God rewards faithfulness, national faithfulness. Faithfulness consists first of all in worshipping the Lord alone. Idolatry and the worship of gods other than the Lord are the most grievous sins, and are grievously punished. Faithfulness also consists in keeping the rest of the laws, the statutes and the ordinances which God has laid down for Israel to keep. It further involves refusal to sacrifice at the 'high places': i.e. thoroughgoing faithfulness to God means confining sacrificial worship to the one central sanctuary. These are the conditions of the covenant with God. This last provision is not, of course, operative until the central sanctuary has actually been built. Israel in the time of the judges is not condemned for sacrificing at the high places (i.e. the provincial sanctuaries), because at that period there was nowhere else to worship. 1 Kings 3.2–3, which we have just referred to, allows that early in Solomon's reign, before he had dedicated the temple, it was still quite proper to resort to the high places.

It will readily be seen how the list of ideas set out above corresponds to those expressed in the book of Deuteronomy. We shall now look briefly at the books of Judges and Kings to see how the deuteronomic editorial scheme brings out these ideas.

The scheme in Judges is highly artificial. There are twelve judges, six major and six minor (to correspond with the number of the tribes). Jdg. 2.11–23 sets out the pattern that is followed. The people of Israel do what is evil in the sight of the Lord. They are led astray into the worship of baal and other deities. So the Lord hands them over to their enemies and they are plundered and destroyed. When they appeal to him in their trouble he raises up for them a judge, who re-establishes the worship of Israel's true God and then delivers them from their oppressors. The people remain faithful while the judge lives, but after he dies they turn away again and the whole cycle recommences. Within this framework many colourful stories are told, but the framework itself is very prominent.

A careful study of the history of the period and of the Bible's own chronology shows that the deuteronomic editors have adapted the historical facts quite considerably to make them fit the scheme. The judges are presented as national leaders. The stories themselves make it clear that none of them actually led an army of all twelve tribes or exercised authority over the entire area of Palestine. The judges are presented as *successive* leaders, following each other in series. Almost certainly they were local leaders whose careers at some points overlapped each other. But historical accuracy is not the historians' main aim. The Deuteronomists see it as their job to teach a lesson, and the lesson has the practical object of keeping their people faithful to God. This history is presented in such a way as to teach the necessary lesson.

In the book of Kings the deuteronomic viewpoint is brought out rather differently. Again there is a pattern to the way in which the reigns of the various kings are presented. There is a stereotyped formula by which the reign of each king is introduced and another by which the account of his reign is closed. But the deuteronomic point of view is brought out chiefly in the moral and religious judgments on the kings which these formulae regularly contain. In each case we are told whether the king 'did that which was evil in the sight of the Lord' or whether 'he did that which was right'. In the body of the account of each king the editors often point to the events or the policies which justify their judgment, but the main criteria are in any case very clear and very simple. The kings are judged first by whether they promote idolatry or confine themselves to the worship of Israel's one God, and second by whether they tolerate the 'high places'. By these criteria most of the kings fail. All the northern kings, without exception, 'did that which is evil in the sight of the Lord'. This is because they maintained rival sanctuaries to Jerusalem. One or two southern kings get a qualified approval. They did that which was right in the eyes of the Lord, nevertheless they did not remove the high places. Unqualified approval is given only to two, Hezekiah and Josiah. These were the reforming kings who did remove the high places and attempt to centralize worship.

Here too the artificiality of the judgment is obvious. In the first place, kings before the time of Hezekiah and Josiah can scarcely be blamed for not enforcing the law of the single sanctuary, since it had not been published in their day. But the Deuteronomists hold that they ought to have known about it, because they believe that the law of the single sanctuary went back to the time of Moses.

In the second place, the deuteronomic theory does not fit the facts as the Deuteromonists themselves record them. If faithfulness was always rewarded and unfaithfulness punished we should expect the kings who did what was right in the eyes of the Lord to have long and prosperous reigns, and the ones who did evil to be unsuccessful. But Josiah, after carrying through his reform, died while still a young man at the hands of Pharaoh Necho who had invaded his land; whereas Manasseh, the wickedest king of all, who undid his father Hezekiah's reforms and persecuted loyal worshippers of God, reigned for forty years quite untroubled.

Thirdly, the narrowness of the deuteronomic criteria is evident. Using their standards of religious judgment the deuteronomic historians are obliged to write off as wicked, or to dismiss as insignificant, kings who by any normal standards were good kings with solid achievements to their credit. Omri, one of the ninth century northern kings, built up Israel into something like the centre of an empire. He kept his country stable and strong in difficult times. We know this from Assyrian records which speak of him with great respect. The deuteronomic historians dismiss him in seven verses. Ahab his son is dealt with at length, but seen by the deuteronomists as a symbol of all that is wicked. He clashed with the prophets. He is presented as one who promoted baal worship. Yet his achievements too were considerable. Not only did he hold his father's empire together, but he led a coalition which managed to stop Assyrian advance at the battle of Qarqar and keep the Assyrians out of western Asia for a century. Furthermore, the book of Kings itself (1 Kings 20, 22) preserves stories which show him to have been both a heroic and a humane man.

In reading the Deuteronomic History therefore we must be constantly aware that its judgments are often ones which we ourselves would not subscribe to, or not in any other context.

It is a large part of the Deuteronomists' aim to explain why the exile took place. They show that the history of Israel was

largely a history of unfaithfulness. God restrained his punishment of them, hoping for repentance and conformity to the
covenant. When that turning eventually came however,
under Josiah, it was already too late. But the Deuteronomists
do look beyond the exile. 2 Kings ends with the release of the
king Jehoyakin from prison. It is only a little thing, but it is a
straw in the wind, a symbol, a sign of hope.

But more substantially, if we go back yet again to
Solomon's prayer at the dedication of the temple, we find it
ends with a reference to the exile (1 Kings 8.46–53) and with a
hope. 'If they repent with all their mind and with all their
heart in the land of their enemies . . . and pray towards their
land . . . and the house which I have built for thy name, then
hear thou in heaven thy dwelling place their prayer and their
supplication, and maintain their cause.'

The Deuteronomists' preaching doubtless had its good
effects. Their lesson that the only hope for Israel lay in fidelity
to her national God was well learnt by the exiles, and in
response to it they drew up plans for a new, post-exilic order
in which the infidelities of the past would not be able to repeat
themselves. The Priestly writing, which we have already
looked at, embodies some of these plans.

But in another respect the Deuteronomists created a problem. Their simple theory of rewards and punishments did not
really fit all the facts. It certainly did not fit the facts of the
post-exilic age. For when Israel was restored to her land and
the new order was instituted; when the temple was rebuilt and
its worship was purified and the law of God made central to
the nation's life, she did not prosper. She did not regain her
political independence; her king was not restored; she was
dominated by foreigners. Economic recovery seemed to be
permanently beyond her reach. Acceptance of the
deuteronomic theory that saw prosperity as the inevitable
reward of faithfulness made it very hard for Israelites to make
sense of their continued national sufferings. Not only so, but
when the deuteronomic theory of rewards and punishments
was applied not to nations but to individuals it raised the
problem of righteous suffering in a very acute form. And this
is a problem which dominates the thinking of some of Israel's
best minds in the post-exilic period.

# Section 3

## The Prophetic Traditions (1)

PROPHETS are prominent in the narrative literature of the Old Testament. Moses himself is described as a prophet. Around the time of the beginning of the kingdom Samuel, and a little later, Nathan, play important parts. In the next century, in the Northern kingdom, Elijah and Elisha are active.

All these were important prophets, yet the Bible offers us no substantial record of their oracles. Rarely are we given their actual words. Instead, we have stories about what they did. Elijah and Elisha belonged to the ninth century, but from the eighth century onwards we have prophetic records of a different kind. The books bearing the names of Amos, Hosea, Isaiah, Jeremiah, etc. not only give us some account of what those prophets did, they purport to give us at some length a record of what the prophets said. When we talk about prophecy in Israel we have to remember that we are talking about both these groups, the earlier and the later. They belong to the same movement, though the kind of information we happen to have available about them is quite different. (The old label for the second group, 'the writing prophets', is a misleading one, for it suggests that these prophets wrote down their words themselves, which most of them probably did not.)

When we look at this range of prophets, spanning at least seven or eight hundred years, and possibly more, we cannot but be struck by its diversity. Not all prophets looked alike. Not all prophets fulfilled exactly the same functions. Not all prophets agreed with each other, for we have several accounts of prophetic disagreements (e.g. 1 Kings *22*; Jer. *28*). This

diversity among the prophets was probably greater in real life
than appears from our Old Testament, for the Old Testament
gives us accounts of no more than a handful of prophets, while
the others, who have left no record at all, must have numbered thousands. In 1 Kings *22*.6 the king of Israel seems to
have no difficulty in mustering 400 prophets at one time, and
this was from the northern territory alone.

The behaviour of at least some of the prophets would strike
a modern spectator as bizarre. It is worth noting that the
Hebrew verb which means 'to prophesy' also means 'to rave',
'to act like a madman'. The band of prophets whom Saul met
in 1 Sam. *10* were indulging in this sort of excited behaviour
and speech. Saul found their ravings so infectious that he
began to act like them.

These prophesyings seem to have required musical accom-
paniment, for the prophets whom Saul met were a 'band' in
more senses than one, for they had 'harp, tambourine, flute
and lyre before them'. They probably looked rather like a pop
group.

It is sometimes argued that this sort of behaviour was
confined to the earliest prophets, or to false prophets, or to
the less respectable fringes of the profession. But Elisha
seems respectable enough. He is certainly taken seriously by
whoever wrote the book of Kings. But when in 2 Kings *3* he
rather grumpily allows himself to be persuaded by the king of
Israel to deliver an oracle, he gives in with the words, 'All
right, bring me a minstrel' (*3*.15).

There is no direct evidence that later prophets such as
Amos or Jeremiah needed such aids, or indulged in the 'rav-
ing' type of prophecy at all, but we have no certain guarantee
that they did not do so. It may just be accident that our
records do not mention it. The writers of those records may
simply have taken it for granted that that was how prophetic
oracles were normally received.

Some prophets seem to have worked in groups and lived as
communities. The prophets just mentioned, of 1 Sam. *10*,
were evidently such a group. Elisha is frequently associated
with groups called 'the sons of the prophets'. According to 2
Kings *2* there were communities of these sons of the prophets
living at Bethel, and some at Jericho. Isaiah at one point (Is.
*8*.16) refers to his disciples.

Yet others seem to have been lone figures. Apart from his successor Elisha who accompanied him at the end of his career, Elijah appears to have no associates. Amos denies that he has any connexion with the sons of the prophets (Amos 7.14). Jeremiah, by all accounts, was at loggerheads with such prophetic communities as existed in his day.

Some prophets had attachments to sanctuaries. Samuel served his apprenticeship at a sanctuary (Shiloh), and frequently appears at 'high places' thereafter. If Isaiah really did see his vision, inside the Holy Place of the Jerusalem temple, as the description in Is. 6 implies, then he can hardly have been a member of the general public, but must have been on the staff of the sanctuary. It is usually concluded that there may have been considerable numbers of prophets who had official positions at places of worship, and perhaps others who fulfilled occasional duties there.

Yet other prophets seem to have been attached to the king's court. The four hundred whom the king of Israel called on in 1 Kings 22 have already been mentioned. In 1 Kings 18–19 Ahab and Jezebel have several hundred court prophets too, albeit baal prophets. (Prophecy was a phenomenon by no means confined to Israel or to the religion of Yahweh.) Going back to an earlier period, Nathan gives every impression of having some official position at the court of David.

Along with all these variations in lifestyle goes a wide range of functions. There used to be a saying that 'the prophets were not foretellers but forthtellers'. This is a half truth. The prophets were certainly more than foretellers, but none of them seems to have despised the job of foretelling the future. Or if they are not exactly foretelling the future they are often acting in some other clairvoyant capacity, giving information about events at a distance, or revealing what is not apparent to the senses. When Saul first encounters Samuel he is merely seeking information about some lost asses (and proposes to pay him about ten pence for his trouble). Samuel, as it turns out, has rather more momentous things to say to Saul, but he does tell him what has happened to the asses (1 Sam. 9.20). Elisha, in the episode already referred to (2 King 3) is able to tell the distressed armies of Israel and Judah how to find water in the desert. Elisha at one period of his career, indeed, seems to have specialized in military intelligence, for in 2

Kings 6.8 ff. we find him acting as a sort of prophetic spy by using his powers to detect where ambushes had been set. All the classical prophets make predictions of one sort or another, and Ezekiel when in Babylonia claims to be able to see exactly what is going on in Jerusalem. Dt. 18.2 f. regards accurate prediction of the future as a reliable test of whether a prophet is genuinely inspired by God. Though such clairvoyant gifts, therefore, may seem to us rather marginal to the more serious functions of the prophets, they were evidently not so regarded in Old Testament times themselves. (On all of the foregoing, see GBS, Chapter 19, a–h.)

But the prophet's basic function is to act as a channel of communication between God and man. He is a two-way channel. He not only communicates God's word to men, but he puts men's case to God. It is often overlooked just how prominent in prophetic activities is the job of making intercession. Now of course, anyone can pray. The Bible everywhere assumes that all men *can* pray and that all men *ought* to pray. But the Old Testament, at least, further assumes that not all are equally good at it, and that if one wants any serious praying done it is best to call in an expert.

The evidence that the prophets were specialists in intercession is massive, and we shall only mention a few salient texts. The classic instance of Moses' intercession is Ex. 32.30–34. After the sin of the golden calf, Moses says, 'Perhaps I can make atonement for your sin.' But how does he actually attempt this? Simply by praying. The power of Samuel's intercession is demonstrated in 1 Sam. 7. And later, even after the people have rejected his advice about the kingship, and Samuel feels that he himself has been rejected by them, he still says (1 Sam. 12.23), 'Far be it from me that I should sin against the Lord by ceasing to pray for you.' Amos, though he denies that he is a prophet at all in the accepted sense of the word, nevertheless not only speaks the word of the Lord but exercises the prophetic function of intercession too (Amos 7.1–6). In the time of Hezekiah the king there was a grave national crisis. The country had been overrun and the besieging armies surrounded Jerusalem. It was a time, one might think, for desperate measures. Hezekiah sends a deputation of the most senior officers of government to the prophet Isaiah. They put the position before him and then make their request: 'Therefore, lift up your prayer . . .' (Is. *37*.4). That's all. When we come to Jeremiah, it is a measure of the totality of God's withdrawal from his people that he will no longer listen to prayer (*11*.11), 'Though they cry to me, I will not listen to them.' The prophet himself is forbidden to pray for them (*11*.14). And in *15*.1 it is said that even the most potent prophetic intercessors of the past would be able to do nothing if they had faced the circumstances of the present. 'Though Moses and Samuel stood before me, yet my heart would not turn toward this people.' Nothing could demonstrate more dramatically that normally this was one of the most vital of prophetic functions. (See also the interesting text of Gn. *20*.7.)

But above all, of course, the prophet is one who speaks the divine word. He is possessed by it, and cannot help but speak what he is given to say. This we learn from two such disparate characters as the gentile Balaam (Num. *22–24*) who would dearly like to earn his prophet's fee by uttering oracles of disaster against Israel, but cannot; and Jeremiah, who has other reasons for not wanting to speak the word he is given, but finds it like a burning fire shut up in his bones, so that he cannot hold it in (Jer. *20*.9).

Sometimes the prophet's word is given to him in a dream. Sometimes, especially among the later prophets, it is said to be mediated to him by an angel. But most often, where we are given any indication at all about the mechanism of inspiration, God speaks to the prophet directly. Astonishingly, we are in at least two places told that the prophet has access to the inmost secrets of the divine council, when the Lord takes counsel from his heavenly court. In 1 Kings 22 Micaiah describes what he sees going on in the heavenly audience chamber. And Jeremiah (*23*.22) assumes that any prophet worthy of the name has a seat in God's cabinet, and he dismisses his prophetic opponents contemptuously because they have not.

While we are on the subject of such large claims, this is an appropriate point to mention one of the most important features of prophecy. It is an open profession. Anyone can be a prophet. How striking this feature is can be seen if we contrast prophecy with its sister institution of priesthood. Priesthood in the Old Testament is limited to members of certain families. It is limited to males of those families: there are in Israel no women priests. It is limited to males who are physically sound and healthy: i.e. no one who is deformed or mutilated may exercise priesthood.

There is no evidence that physical imperfections or ritual impurity were barriers to prophecy. Sex was no barrier. We know that women could prophesy. There may not have been great numbers of women prophets but there were certainly some, and some important ones at that. Age was no barrier. A child could be a prophet. We have all heard the story of the call of the child Samuel; and Jeremiah, if not exactly a child at the time of his call, was certainly very young (Jer. *1*.6. The use of the word 'child' here by AV and RV is not very exact. 'Youth' is better).

It is possible that in practice the job of prophet often 'ran in families', prophet sons following in the footsteps of prophetic fathers. The 'sons of the prophets' referred to above may have been to some extent family groups, though the Hebrew word for 'sons' does not *necessarily* imply that. They may have been simply guilds or professional associations, part of whose job was to teach their younger members the trade. Either way, they bear witness to the fact that prophecy was to some extent—and perhaps a very considerable extent—institutionalized. *But it was not completely so.* Though the prophetic call might normally come to someone like Samuel, who was already undergoing a religious apprenticeship, as it were, it could also come to Amos, who was neither a prophet nor a prophet's son, but a herdsman, with a sideline in mulberry-figs.

A most important statement of this principle of open entry to the prophetic ranks is the story in Num. *11*.16–30. (It makes an emphatic contrast with the parallel story in Num. *16*, which tells what horrible things happen to unauthorized people who try to act as priests.) In Num. *11* Moses appoints seventy elders to help him. He takes them outside the camp to the tent sanctuary, and there, as it were, ordains them, and they prophesy. This is institutional religion at work. Meanwhile, back at the camp, Eldad and Medad, who were not among the seventy, also prophesy. Moses is informed, and invited to forbid these upstart prophets. He flatly refuses, and says rather that he wishes there were more like them. 'Would that all the Lord's people were prophets' (Num. *11*.29).

It is doubtful whether a doctrine of the priesthood of all believers can be firmly anchored in the Old Testament (indeed, that very doctrine seems to be what Korah, Dathan and Abiram are arguing for in Num. *16*.3), but the doctrine of the prophethood of all believers is emphatically stated and everywhere adhered to.

The prophet's *authority,* the authentication of his claim to be speaking God's word, rests largely on his call. We have accounts of the call of quite a number of the prophets, though not of all. Amos, for example, does not tell us what happened at his call, though he does assert very forcefully that he had one (Amos 7.15). The call usually takes place in a vision. It is an interesting exercise to compare the various accounts of prophetic calls which we do have. They differ in many ways, from the brief assertion of Amos in 7.15, to the description at almost tedious length in Ezek. *1–3.* The prophets in their visions see quite different things. Some see God himself. Isaiah says bluntly, 'I saw the Lord . . .' (Is. *6.*1). Ezekiel cannot bring himself to say anything so bold, but admits only to seeing 'the appearance of the likeness of the glory of the Lord' (Ezek. *1.*28). Jeremiah's call comes through the sight of very ordinary things, a twig bursting into flower, a pan boiling over (Jer. *1*). Samuel apparently sees nothing at all. Like St. Paul later, he hears a voice, and sees no one (1 Sam. *3*).

Yet there are common features too. Most of those called are overcome with awe. Most express reluctance. All seem to feel that they have no choice. They are not the choosers, but the chosen.

The call is important as the prophet's authorization, because his authority is so frequently challenged. Our canonical prophets were often in a minority, sometimes, apparently, a minority of one.[1] Not only did their hearers doubt them but *their prophetic colleagues* contradicted them. When prophets disagreed, who was to decide which were the true and which the false? The prophet himself might even doubt whether the words given to him to speak were true.[2] Jeremiah expresses such doubts in a very outspoken way (Jer. *20.*7 f.).

[1] 1 Kings *19.*10, 14; 1 Kings *22.*1–28.
[2] It was believed that God might, for his own purposes, deliberately give his prophets a false message on occasion. See 1 Kings *22.*20–23; Dt. *13.*1–3. Compare also the strange story in 1 Kings *13.*

Deuteronomy suggests, rather naively (Dt. *18*.21 f.), that the best test is to wait and see. If the things which a prophet predicts come true, then he was right. If not, then he was wrong. By this test many of our canonical prophets would have failed, for nearly every prophetic book contains predictions, some of them quite important ones, which were falsified by events. *In the long run* the deuteronomic test is valid, and our canonical prophets *are* in the canon precisely because the burden of their message was vindicated by history, but for the prophet's contemporaries the test must have had its limitations.

In chapter *13* the book of Deuteronomy makes another point. A prophet can be tested, to a certain extent, by asking whether what he says is in line with truth already delivered and received. If a prophet comes along, works a miracle, and then advises people to worship idols, they are not to listen to that prophet, but instead put him to death. Miracles prove nothing. Fidelity proves everything.

Yet even the test of fidelity is not easily applied. The prophets undoubtedly *saw themselves* as recalling Israel to established truths, to acknowledged standards of conduct, to old laws and 'ancient paths' (Jer. *6*.16). And yet to others they must often have looked like innovators. What they were doing was something that was both intensely radical and extremely conservative. They were recalling people to what they already knew, of God and of his demands. But at the same time they insisted that people face up to what those demands meant *now*. They reminded their hearers of God's great acts of salvation in the past, and yet asserted that God was doing 'new things'.

## The preliterary prophets

We are using the term 'preliterary prophets' to designate those older prophets who have left no record of their oracles; prophets such as Samuel, Nathan, Elijah and Elisha, and others of that period. Moses is a special case. Much is attributed to him, but for that very reason it is difficult to be sure what the historical Moses said or thought. Most scholars would be happy to assert that he is the chief architect of Israel's religion, and indeed of the Israelite nation. This reminds us that Israel's faith and nationhood are themselves *rooted* in prophecy. But Moses is unique and we shall therefore not consider him further in this section on the prophets.

About the other preliterary prophets something has already been said in passing. It needs to be said once more that we have not much information about them that would enable us to guess at their *ideas* or their thinking. The information we have relates mostly to their political activities. This is dealt with fully in books bearing on Old Testament history. Here we shall content ourselves with a brief summary of the directions which that political activity took, in an attempt to see what conclusions can be drawn from it about the prophets' religious convictions.

The prophets' political activities are largely bound up with the monarchy. All the biblical sources agree that Samuel was instrumental in *establishing* the monarchy, though they do not agree whether he did so willingly or grudgingly. Prophecy therefore validated kingship, and seems to have seen itself as responsible for the direction which the monarchy took. Much of the books of Samuel and Kings is taken up with the story of how prophets tried to keep a guiding hand on the institution they had created.

The establishment of the monarchy already demonstrates one thing about the way the prophets thought. They are not merely a conservative force. Kingship is undeniably an innovation. By helping to introduce it the prophets are showing their people how to adapt to new situations, to meet the unprecedented. They are showing them what is the will of God for his people *now,* and they are acknowledging that his will demands radical changes and a new style of national life.

But whereas their fellow countrymen were inclined to see the adoption of the monarchy as a simple question of comforming to the ways of the world, that was not the way the prophets looked at it. It was God's will that Israel should take over an institution which the nations had developed. It was not his will that they should do so *uncritically.* The prophets therefore constantly interfered (though 'interfere' is a word they would have objected to) in an endeavour to make the monarchy the *kind* of monarchy which they believed God wanted.

The story of Nathan's rebuke to David over his sin with

Bathsheba is an important one. It is meant to demonstrate what the relationship between kings and prophets ought, in the opinion of the prophets themselves, to be. A king here acts unrighteously. A prophet condemns his action. The king accepts his condemnation humbly and penitently and behaves himself better in future (2 Sam. *11–12*).

The prophets not only criticized unrighteous kings, they took a hand in deciding the succession. Samuel by his own authority could replace Saul by David. Nathan is partly instrumental in replacing David by Solomon, though he can only do it by helping to organize a *coup d'état* (the prophets' authority already seems to be weakening). At the end of Solomon's reign a prophet again intervenes in the succession, in the person of Ahijah (1 Kings *11*.26–*12*.24). The result is the division of the kingdom.

All of this is done in an attempt to shape the monarchy in accordance with prophetic ideas, by ensuring that the throne was occupied by someone of whom the prophets approved. Unfortunately, once on the throne the prophets' nominees did not necessarily behave in the way which the prophets wished.

The prophets were constantly trying to deny their kings rights which kings of other nations took for granted. In 1 Sam. *13*.5–15 Samuel objects to Saul's offering of sacrifice. The king of any other nation would have assumed that he was entitled to act as his people's high priest. Nathan, in his rebuke to David, is denying the king's rights to make his own rules of conduct. Among other nations the kings made the laws. The job of a king in Israel is to *keep* the laws. Israel's laws are made only by God and they are not made to suit any man's convenience. Elijah is denying Ahab the right to appropriate or re-allocate land, (1 Kings *21*). This was a basic right of feudal monarchs. But Israel's land belonged to God, and at the conquest he had allocated it to the tribes, and among the tribes it was allocated to families and was inalienable. For a king to act righteously, as the prophets saw it, was for him to acknowledge these limitations on his power. The true king was God, and the earthly king acted only as his regent or representative.

We see then that behind the activities of the preliterary prophets is at least one strong idea, the idea of righteousness.

The notion of righteousness is a very rich one and we have here only touched on one or two aspects of it. To the prophets' way of thinking this standard of righteousness is the standard by which all men are to be judged, but especially kings and rulers, for it is in their hands to determine to a large extent the righteousness of the nation. From the start, therefore, the prophets are not concerned solely, or even primarily, with private, individual religious convictions or with private morality. They are concerned with public affairs.

God's will for his people involves the demand for righteousness. It also involves the offer of *salvation*. The preliterary prophets assume this rather than state it. They understand the idea of salvation in a very positive, concrete and largely political sense. God's great act, by which he initiated the relationship with his people, and indeed, by which he called them into being, was an act of liberation. He freed them from bondage to the Egyptians. This liberty which God gave them is the entitlement of every Israelite. They are no longer slaves, but sons. It is a liberty which must not be bargained or filched away.

The prophets (generally speaking: there may have been exceptions) acquiesced in the introduction of the monarchy because a king was needed in order to preserve Israel's liberty; to rescue them from foreign domination. To put it in the Bible's own language, it was the king's job *to save* his people. (Cf. 1 Sam. *10*.27 where some men refuse to acknowledge Saul as king because they doubt his power *to save*.) But the prophets saw that a king was not only a potential guarantor of liberty for his people, he was himself a potential *threat* to that liberty (1 Sam. *8*.10–18 is the clearest articulation of this possibility). Israelites must not be allowed to become slaves *to* the king. The division of the kingdom is precipitated because Rehoboam wants to make them exactly that (1 Kings *12*, especially vv. 9–15).

Thus, though few of the actual words of the preliterary prophets have come down to us, behind their activities we may detect these two great concerns, for the salvation of Israel, which means her freedom, and for her righteousness.

## The possession of the land

We have had occasion to refer to the subject of landownership in connexion with the incident of Naboth's vine-yard and it might be useful here to draw together one or two threads relating to this important theme.

Possession of the land was the substance of the ancient promises to the patriarchs. When God led Israel out of Egypt it was to fulfil these promises by giving them the land. The land was to be held in possession by the families of Israel. The kings were raised up by God to make sure that Israel retained her land and was not deprived of it by aliens (which is why it is the gravest reversal of his responsibility for a king to engage in robbing an Israelite of his land, as Ahab did). The most drastic punishment which could be threatened, and which was eventually inflicted at the time of the exile, was for Israel to be driven from her land. And God's restoration of his people to favour, his forgiveness of them, is expressed by his restoration of them to their ancient territory.

Christians have occasionally taken over this idea, but only at the cost of spiritualizing it almost beyond recognition. This process is at least as old as the New Testament itself, for the writer to the Hebrews contrasts the achievement of Joshua unfavourably with that of Jesus (*4*.8), and suggests that the promises to the patriarchs are only really fulfilled when God's people find 'a better country, that is, a heavenly one' (*11*.16). 1 Peter (*1*.3) likewise takes the notion of the 'inheritance', which in the Old Testament refers to the promised land, and uses it to refer to the benefits which Christ has won for us, 'an inheritance which is undefiled and unfading, kept in heaven . . .'

Christian hymns have taken the adaptation further, and often see the 'promised land' as referring simply to heaven. See, for example, MHB 824 (compare Jos. *3*) and MHB 649. It is not that this process of re-interpretation is inadmissible, but we must not be misled by it when reading the Old Testament. For within the pages of the Old Testament itself, though the possession of the land does signify divine favour, it is a very ordinary, practical, political and earthy expression of that favour, not at all a spiritual one.

## Messianism and the preliterary prophets

There were some prophets at least who saw God's promises

for the future as being closely bound up not only with the monarchy but with one particular line of monarchs, the house of David, and with Jerusalem, where the Davidic king had his throne, and where also the temple came to be built. Nathan's announcement of the covenant with David (2 Sam. 7) ties all these things together. Not all the prophets were to take such a positive view either of the Davidic kings or of the sanctity of Jerusalem and its temple; nevertheless, what we call messianism has its roots here, in the conviction that it is through the house of David that God wills to bring about the salvation of his people.

## The prophetic books

We need to be a little careful in saying just what we mean by 'the prophetic books', because this phrase is used in different ways by different people. In the Jewish Bible the books of Joshua, Judges, Samuel and Kings are counted as 'The Former Prophets'. There are good reasons for describing the books from Joshua to Kings as 'prophetic', but it has not been a Christian tradition to do so and many Christian students find the usage confusing, so we shall not employ it in this book. By 'the prophetic books' we shall mean what the Jews call more restrictively 'The Latter Prophets'. The Jewish canon counts four 'latter prophets', Isaiah, Jeremiah, Ezekiel and 'The Twelve'. This phrase 'The Twelve' comprises what Christians usually call 'The Minor Prophets'. The title 'Minor Prophets' is firmly established in Christian usage, and there is no reason why we should not go on employing it, as long as we remember that 'minor' was never meant to suggest that these books are of minor importance. It only means that they are shorter. Some of the 'minor' prophets, such as Amos, Hosea and Micah, are of quite *major* significance.

So for the moment we are considering Isaiah, Jeremiah, Ezekiel and The Twelve, though we shall in fact have very little to say about most of The Twelve, apart from the three mentioned above. Note that the book of Daniel is not one of The Twelve. In Christian tradition Daniel has come to be treated as a prophet, and in the Christian canon the book of Daniel has been inserted after Ezekiel. This can certainly be defended on several grounds, but for study purposes there is a good deal to be gained by allowing Jewish custom to guide us at this point. The Jews do not reckon Daniel among the prophets. In many respects Daniel is very *like* a prophet, but the book which bears his name is much more closely related to another class of literature, which we call Apocalyptic. The reasons for this will appear when we look at Daniel in detail in another chapter.

We shall not go into details about the literary analysis of the prophetic books, but in order to understand these books accurately at all it is necessary to know a little about how they have taken shape. What follows is an indication of some of the principal conclusions to which literary scholars have come. There is no space here to go into the sometimes complex arguments on which the conclusions are based. These arguments, and the evidence from which they proceed, can be followed up in the textbooks on Old Testament introduction.

It is unlikely that any of the prophetic books were written, in their present form, by the prophets themselves. There is nothing to suggest that Amos or Hosea wrote down any of their own words at all. Isaiah is said to have written a brief (and rather cryptic) oracle on a clay tablet on one particular occasion (Is. 8.1 f.), which suggests that recording his words in writing was not normally a concern of his. Jeremiah did communicate in writing. He wrote down his oracles for Baruch to deliver for him in the temple, on an occasion when he could not go to the temple himself (the reasons are not specified but it may have been a matter of ritual impurity) (Jer. 36). And when this record was deliberately destroyed he did go to the trouble of making another copy. He also communicated by letter with his countrymen who had been deported to Babylon (Jer. 29). So here we have what looks like the beginning of prophetic writing down of oracles, but there is a great deal of material in the book of Jeremiah as we now have it which could not have formed part of Baruch's scroll. It does not seem possible that Jeremiah wrote the book that bears his name, though most scholars assume that the oracles written down by Baruch have found their way into the book. Ezekiel very likely did write considerable portions of the book of Ezekiel. He may conceivably have issued, himself, a collection of his prophecies. But the book as it stands shows clear signs of having been edited by someone else.

Chapters *40–55* of the book of Isaiah are usually called
Deutero-Isaiah or Second Isaiah, because they clearly come
from a much later date than most of chapters *1–39*, and seem
to belong together in style and thought. The nameless prophet who was responsible for these chapters may well have
written them himself, and perhaps even in substantially the
form in which we have them.

What this amounts to is that the prophetic books *contain*
*the words of the prophets* whose names they bear, but they
may contain a good deal else besides. The amount of writing
done by the prophet himself increases (generally speaking) as
we go from the earlier to the later books. This is not accident.
The earlier prophets could stand in the sanctuary court on a
feast day and their words would be retailed by the pilgrims to
every part of the country. Once the exile had taken place the
people were scattered. There were several widely dispersed
communities in Babylonia, and some in Egypt, as well as
those in the homeland. Any prophet who wished to be heard
by all of these was obliged to take to writing.

Much of the material which survives, therefore, survived at
first because it was *remembered*. The prophet's disciples, and
perhaps other people too, remembered what he had said, and
what he had done, and only at a later stage did someone
reduce this material to writing. The prophet's disciples may
sometimes have re-issued the original prophet's words, possibly with alterations to bring them up to date, re-applying
them in situations different from the ones in which they were
first spoken. This happened because the prophet's followers
believed that, even after his own day, God still had something
to say through those original words. The same oracle could be
given a succession of meanings at different times. In doing
this, the prophet's disciples were not doing anything
altogether different from what we ourselves do when we
preach from a prophetic text. We can only preach from the
prophets, or indeed, find usefulness in reading the prophets, if
we share the disciples' conviction that God is still speaking
through the old words. Those words can become the Word
again in every generation. The prophets' disciples, of course,
were themselves prophets. To re-apply an old prophetic word
to a new situation is itself a prophetic activity. The interpreters of the prophets must themselves share something of the

prophetic inspiration if they are to do their job. To say what the prophets' words *meant*, in their own generation, is a job for scholars. But to say what the prophets' words *mean*, in our generation, can be a job only for prophets and preachers.

The book of Isaiah, which has had a very long and very complicated history, shows many examples of oracles being re-issued and oracles having new meaning found in them in different situations. But perhaps the simplest example with which to illustrate the point is found in a different book, that of Hosea. Hosea was a northerner, and spoke to the Northern Kingdom. After that kingdom had lost its independence and its leaders had been carried off into captivity, never to return, Hosea's words were collected and published. The nation he had addressed was no longer there to hear, but the people of the *Southern* Kingdom, Judah, were convinced that the message he had delivered to their northern fellow countrymen (in vain, as it happened) was a message also for them. The book as we now have it betrays at a number of points the fact that the audience which the editor is thinking of is not the audience which the prophet was thinking of.

The prophetic books contain different kinds of material. We have stories *about* the prophet. These are of two kinds; first, stories in the third person, i.e. stories told about him by someone other than the prophet; and secondly, stories in the first person, i.e. told as if by the prophet himself. A good pair of examples can be found in Hosea chapters *1* and *3*. Both are accounts of episodes in Hosea's matrimonial life. They *may* be descriptions of the same events, though this is far from certain. Chapter *3* is recorded as if in the prophet's own words. Chapter *1* looks like an account by somebody else.

The way in which such stories are shaped depends to some extent on the purpose for which they were recorded, i.e. on the point which the story was being used to make. Jer. chapters *7* and *26* are both third person accounts of how the prophet went up to the temple court to deliver an address. They appear to refer to the same occasion, but they are very differently constructed. In chapter *7* the storyteller is interested primarily in what Jeremiah actually said on that occasion. The narrative is reduced to a bare introduction about how Jeremiah came to deliver the speech where he did. In chapter *26* the balance of the account is quite different, because here the storyteller is interested not so much in what the prophet said as in the trouble he got into for saying it. The content of the speech itself is therefore given in summary form in about five verses.

But the bulk of the prophetic books is taken up not with stories but with oracles, records of the prophets' words. These too are of two kinds. We have poetic oracles and we have prose. When the Bible is translated into English the distinction between poetry and prose is usually blurred. Poetry is only apparent to the reader if it is *printed* as poetry. Not all editions of the English Bible do this, but the RSV, NEB and the Jerusalem Bible are very careful about it. To flick through the prophetic books in any of these editions will confirm the fact that very large portions of them are in poetry. The prophets were poets. The poetic form seems to have been the *normal* form of a prophetic oracle. But prophetic oracles share the characteristics of much other poetry in that they are often compressed, allusive, cryptic. The prose oracles are usually plainer in meaning.

Some of the prose oracles may have been delivered by the prophets themselves, to explain or apply the poetic ones. Some may be explanations or summaries added by the people who handed down or edited the original prophet's words.

Occasionally we have examples of a prose oracle and a poetic oracle appearing to cover much the same ground. Ezek. *24*.3b–5 is a poetic oracle about boiling a pot with meat in it. Taken by itself its meaning would be far from transparent, but fortunately the introduction to the oracle in *24*.1–3a tells us that it was uttered during the Babylonians' siege of Jerusalem, which gives us a clue to its meaning. More interestingly, for our present purpose, it is followed in *24*.6–14 by a prose oracle which says much the same thing but which also contains comments on the interpretation of the imagery. The pot is the city; the contents, which are to be given such a roasting, are the citizens.

The collectors and editors of the prophetic literature had much less interest than we have in chronology. We must not expect to read a prophetic book as if it were a biography of the prophet, set down in order. We must not assume that the oracles which are set down first in the book were necessarily delivered earlier than those which come further on. There is a general tendency of the editors and collectors to group together first of all the oracles critical of the prophet's own nation. Oracles against foreign nations tend to be grouped together by themselves, and prophecies of hope tend to be grouped together on their own too. This is, however, not a rigid scheme.

## AMOS

### Amos's background

We know only the barest of facts about Amos's background. But those bare facts are very important. He prophesied in the Northern Kingdom and seems to have addressed the northerners almost exclusively. Yet he himself came from Judah, from an area a few miles south of Jerusalem.

Much of the land of Israel is not suitable for agriculture, and if it is to be exploited at all it can only be by pastoralists. Throughout her history Israel's population therefore consisted of two distinct parts, with different, though closely interdependent lifestyles. There were the relatively mobile keepers of flocks, and the settled peasants and city-dwellers. The pastoralists seem to have been more conservative in their religious and political thinking, and to have been more anxious to preserve the old traditions of Israel. Amos was one of these.

Amos is the earliest prophet whose words have been recorded for us in any extensive way, and he lived round about the middle of the eighth century. Both Israel (the Northern Kingdom) and her sister kingdom of Judah had just enjoyed about half a century of prosperity and freedom from outside domination. This was about to come to an end. Assyria, after a period of weakness, was gathering strength and looking to expand her empire again. The historian can see that this resurgence of Assyria was bound to spell the end of Israel's quiet life.

Amos prophesies destruction for the nation, and exile 'beyond Damascus'. But he does not do this because he has read the newspapers and made political deductions. Amos is a prophet, and his deductions are not those of the political commentator but of the man of faith. He does not argue that

Israel will be destroyed by Assyria because the Assyrians will be seeking to extend their sphere of influence in western Asia. He argues that Israel is a corrupt society and therefore it will be destroyed by God. Amos never in fact mentions Assyria. Doubtless, he could have made as good a guess as the next man as to the likeliest means of Israel's destruction, but to him the Assyrians were simply the tool that happened to be nearest to God's hand.

## The nature of God and his relationship with man

Amos has a very clear, sharply defined picture of God. Amos has met God. He knows him quite intimately. He knows what God thinks. He knows what God wants of him. Amos's God is a very decisive God who lays down clear conditions and leaves people in no doubt as to what they are. He acts on principles which are well understood, because he has made no secret of them.

For Amos assumes that the knowledge he has of God is equally available to everybody. He regards himself as 'no prophet, nor a prophet's son', but merely a man who states the obvious.

The opening words of the book (1.1–2.3) set the tone. Amos is here not even addressing Israel, but the world at large. He castigates a long series of nations for various atrocities. All men, he is saying, know what is right. All of them know what God requires of them. If there are those who do not know it is because they *choose* not to know. Therefore they are without excuse, whoever they are. (The first three chapters of Amos and the first three chapters of Paul's Letter to the Romans run interestingly parallel.)

In 2.4–3.2 we continue with oracles addressed to Judah and Israel. Amos is saying that all people should have known, but his own people should have known better. God demands righteousness. He demands it from the gentiles. He demands it from Israel. The only difference is that Israel has less excuse.

Then what advantage has the Jew? Much in every way. God has a special relationship with Israel. 'You only have I known of all the families of the earth' (Amos 3.2). Amos does not speak explicitly of God's *covenant* with Israel, but he does seem to presuppose knowledge of such a covenant. And the covenant whose existence he takes for granted is the conditional covenant of Sinai. Amos everywhere assumes that God's relationship with Israel depends on conditions that are known and understood, and that if the conditions are not kept, then the relationship will necessarily end.

Amos's God, then, is quite inflexible. Righteousness he has demanded, righteousness he will have. The advantage of Israel's special relationship with him is that they have unparalleled opportunities to learn his will. But if they choose not to keep to the conditions, then that advantage will be turned to disadvantage. The greater their opportunities to learn God's will, the greater the guilt if they disregard it. 'You only have I known of all the families of the earth; *therefore I will punish you* for all your iniquities.'

## The nature of righteousness

Amos actually spends very little of his time (if the book which bears his name fairly represents him) talking about religion. Most of what he has to say is about society and the way people conduct themselves towards each other. The righteousness which he talks about is expected to work itself out in the relations between man and man. And yet, Amos is not simply a social reformer. Religious presuppositions underlie everything he says. The righteousness which he calls on his people to display is a reflection of the righteousness of God himself. He goes into some detail about the righteousness which God demands. He goes into far less detail about the righteousness of God's own character, because this is something which he assumes his hearers know about. Here we see that the chief part of a prophet's or a preacher's job is to remind people of what they know already, and to challenge them to act as if it were true.

The righteousness of God is displayed first of all in his acts of salvation, and secondly in his acts of judgment. To say that God's righteousness or justice is displayed in acts of *salvation* may sound an odd statement. But many of the Bible's statements about righteousness, justice and justification sound odd in English because the Hebrew words for righteousness, etc. do not correspond exactly in meaning to their nearest

English equivalents. N. H. Snaith expresses this by saying that for the biblical writers there is always a tendency for righteousness 'to topple over into benevolence'. We might put it another way by saying that for the Hebrew speaker the idea of benevolence is already *included in* the notion of right-eousness or justice. For us, justice and mercy can be readily contrasted. We could say of a particular decision: 'It wasn't very merciful, but it was just.' A Hebrew speaker would probably have found that a very odd statement indeed, because to his way of thinking, a man who had failed to show mercy would *by that very token* have failed to act justly.

God's righteousness, then, has manifested itself in acts of deliverance. If men persistently fail to respond to those acts with righteous behaviour of their own, by safeguarding the vulnerable and delivering the oppressed and disadvantaged, only his acts of judgment remain.

The particular social circumstances which form the background to Amos's demand were created by the continued growth of that feudalism which the earlier prophets had unsuccessfully resisted. The words of Amos reflect a sharply stratified society, where some lead lives of indolence and luxury (6.4–6) and sustain that position at the expense of the poor. As Amos sees it, their wealth is not the legitimate reward of enterprise, but is built up by exploitation, by corrupt business methods (8.5 f.) and by bribery and perverting justice in the courts of law (5.12–15).

## Repentance and forgiveness

Amos's God insists on righteousness (5.24) and demands that Israel stick to the conditions of his covenant with them. But he is not hasty. He does not immediately abrogate his covenant at the first lapse. In 4.6–12 Amos makes it clear that God has given Israel every chance. There have already been disasters, warning disasters, whose message should have been plain and ought to have been heeded. Since these lesser disasters had no effect the great disaster, destruction of the nation, must now come. The people's behaviour has left God with no option. On a similar theme, 7.1–6 speaks of disasters which God had threatened, but which never materialized, thanks to the prophet's intercession. But Israel made no use of this time for amendment of life, which God's forbearance allowed them. God has therefore measured them according to the strictest standards of rectitude and no longer allows margin for error. 'Behold, I am setting a plumbline in the midst of my people Israel; *I will never again* pass by them.' There are to be no more chances (7.8).

Amos assumes, throughout all this, God's readiness to forgive, if his demands are met. A fresh start is always possible, but the onus is on men to turn, and to lead new lives, following the commandments of God and walking in his holy ways. It is men who must take the initiative. Then God will respond. If Amos sometimes talks as if punishment, final punishment, is absolutely inevitable, it is not because he doubts God's forgiving response to repentance, but because he is eventually convinced that the repentance is not to be forthcoming.

It is significant that Amos has no time for sacrifice or for organized worship. The key passage is 5.18–25. The celebrations that go on on 'the Lord's day' serve the cause of darkness rather than light (5.18). The enactment of the great festivals, far from making the people acceptable to God, fills him with positive distaste (5.21). The singing in public worship repels him (5.23) and sacrifices are a waste of time and money (5.22) (cf. the sarcastic words of 4.4 f.).

It is sometimes claimed that Amos rejected such worship only because it was insincere and hypocritical, and because it was divorced from righteousness of life. But he seems to be saying something more radical than that. It is conceivable that as a man of Judah he regards only the cult of Jerusalem as legitimate, but even this suggestion does not explain his words in 5.25. Here he denies that sacrifice ever has been any proper part of genuine Israelite religion. The pentateuch asserts that Israel's sacrificial and festival systems were instituted by Moses, in the wilderness period. Amos evidently subscribes to a religious tradition which believes no such thing.

All this is instructive. It not only confirms that there was some variety in Israel's religious traditions at this period, i.e. that not all Israelites believed the same things. It also gives us an insight into the way Amos thinks. Others may see God as accommodating himself to human weakness by offering men a means whereby their inevitable shortcomings can be atoned for. Amos does not. Amos's God makes his demands, and if men will not, or cannot, meet them, he has nothing left but the ultimate deterrent.

## The place of hope

It seems likely that, once he was convinced that repentance would not be forthcoming, Amos had no hope to offer. Those who edited his book or those who passed on his words, found this lack of hope intolerable, and someone, somewhere, added the last five verses of our present book to make up the lack. The book of Amos, like that of Hosea mentioned above (p. 90) was eventually edited for the people of Judah. They needed hope, and their hope was fulfilled. But Amos himself had spoken primarily to Northern Israel. And there was no hope for *them*. They were carried into exile by the Assyrians in 722 and lost their identity among the people in whose lands they were settled.

Books about the Old Testament often speak of the exile and its significance, about its refining and purifying effect, and about Israel's eventual restoration, with all the assurance of grace which that event provides. It is sometimes forgotten that there were *two* Israel's. Both went into exile. Only one was restored. St. Augustine somewhere, in another connexion, offers the nice reminder: 'Do not despair, one of the thieves was saved: do not presume, one of the thieves was damned.'

What Amos offers us, then, is something less than a gospel. He can speak with the tongues of men and of angels, and his faith is second to none other's. But he offers no hope, and perhaps, in the end, little love either. Of those born of woman there have been few greater, yet the least preacher of Christ will take precedence of him.

## HOSEA

### Hosea's background

Hosea, like Amos, addressed the Northern Kingdom. Unlike Amos he was himself a northerner. He seems to have been active a little later (but only a little) than Amos. When Amos predicted ruin for the country very few others could see it coming, for outwardly the nation was still prosperous. By Hosea's time the threats had begun to materialize. During Hosea's ministry Israelite kings followed each other in rapid succession, some being victims of *coups d'état* and assassination. There was an almost permanent state of political crisis. Israel's final destruction by the Assyrians in 722/21 probably occurred after Hosea's active career had ended, for none of his recorded words reflect knowledge of it.

About Hosea's personal life we know very little. This ignorance needs to be stressed. Some writers and preachers manage to give the impression of being well informed about the prophet's private life. But much of the 'information' is mere guesswork. It is often said, for example, that he was a baker. There is no evidence for this other than the fact that he uses the word 'oven' three times.

Neither do we know very much for certain about Hosea's domestic life. Such information as we have is important, because the metaphor of the divine marriage is prominent in his thinking, and it is interesting to have some clues as to how this relates to his own experience. But the book of Hosea nowhere gives us a complete picture of his private affairs and there is much that remains obscure. Almost all the information we have is contained in Hos. *1*.1–*3*.5, and the materials are cryptic, difficult to interpret, and not easy to reconcile with each other.

The passage in *1*.1–*3*.5 is speaking sometimes about what is ostensibly the prophet's own experience, and sometimes about the relationship between Israel and her God. The one is used as the image of the other. But it is not always clear at what points the prophet's focus changes from the personal to the theological or back again. For this and other reasons we cannot reliably reconstruct the prophet's biography from these verses. Anyone who wishes to follow up the details of the arguments should consult the commentaries. All that can be done here is to indicate what questions remain open. This is done so that the student may be aware of the limitations of our knowledge. Hosea is a marvellous subject for preaching, but he is not well served by preachers who pretend to know more about his private life than can genuinely be known.

The principal doubts concern the relation between the

events spoken of in chapter *1* and those of chapter *3*. We do not know whether the 'wife of harlotry' mentioned in *1*.2, who is named as 'Gomer, daughter of Diblaim', is the same as the 'adulteress' of *3*.1. Some interpreters think that two quite different relationships with two different women are being spoken of. If she *is* the same woman, we do not know whether the book is giving us two accounts of the same event, Hosea's marriage to the woman, or accounts of two successive events. If they are successive events then it is likely that one account describes Hosea's original acquiring of the woman, the other his buying back of the woman after she had been unfaithful to him and the marriage had broken up.

We cannot be certain, indeed, that the prophet is describing real events at all. Some have concluded that the story (or stories) of a broken marriage was simply a parable that the prophet told. In this case, Hos. *1–3* would have nothing at all to tell us about the prophet's own life story. We have a good parallel to this in the prophet Ezekiel. In chapter *16* Ezekiel tells a long story of a relationship with a foundling girl. In chapter *23* he has a similarly long account of a double marriage (a polygamous marriage, that is) to two sisters called Oholah and Oholibah. He tells both stories in the first person, though as it happens he makes it clear at the beginning of each that the speaker is meant to be God. If it were not for this circumstance, and the fact that elsewhere he speaks of his real wife, and of his grief at her death, we might have imagined that this prophet, too, had an interesting matrimonial history.

If we reject the parable interpretation and conclude that Hosea genuinely is alluding to his own personal experience a further question of interpretation arises. Did he marry a wife in good faith and only later discover that she was promiscuous, or did he, as *2*.1 and *3*.1 on the surface seem to suggest, marry a woman *whom he knew at the time* to be of doubtful character? Most preachers opt for the former possibility, and conclude that his unlooked for experience of a broken marriage led him into a deeper appreciation of God's relations with his people, i.e. that he learnt his theology from his experience of life. This is doubtless the more congenial interpretation to most twentieth-century Christians, but it is not therefore necessarily true. The alternative is that the prophet had already arrived at his understanding of Israel's unfaithfulness to her marriage covenant with God, and chose to demonstrate it very forcefully in an enacted prophecy by deliberately marrying a prostitute.

In spite of the doubts that remain on all the above points, Hosea's *message* still comes across remarkably clearly.

### The nature of God and his relationship with man

The bulk of Hosea's message is about divine judgment. It is common to contrast Amos and Hosea by saying that Amos is the prophet of judgment whereas Hosea speaks about divine forgiveness. It is true that Hosea does bring divine mercy into view in a way that Amos never does, but it is important to recognize that nevertheless he is in most of his oracles saying things very similar to Amos. Note, for example, his metaphor in *13*.7 f., where he represents God as a ferocious wild animal. This is not the sort of imagery one would expect of a prophet of pure mercy.

Hosea perceives the *tension* between the judgment of God and his love. Amos appears to think in terms of the conditional covenant and argues quite straightforwardly that if Israel steadfastly refuses to honour her side of the bargain then the bargain will be at an end. For God to allow his righteousness to be compromised by a disobedient people would be an intolerable defeat. Hosea sees that if God allows his covenant to come to an end, for whatever justifiable reason, that is also a defeat. If the people persist in wrongdoing, therefore, God *must*, and yet *cannot*, put an end to the relationship. To be true to himself he has to insist on rectitude. Yet to be true to himself he cannot let go a people to whom he is committed.

Both Amos and Hosea have an intensely strong feeling of God as a *person*, someone whom they know and can talk to. But whereas for Amos God is an individual, who can encounter a man as he follows his flock and say 'Go, prophesy . . .', or who can encounter a nation in its high sanctuary, standing by the altar and saying 'Smite . . .', for Hosea God is always seen in community. Hosea sees him as the head of a family, as a husband and a father.

We shall grievously misinterpret Hosea's imagery if we

forget that the father in ancient Israel was by our standards an extremely authoritarian figure, with wide powers of discipline over both wife and children. This is why Hosea can use the same 'family' images to convey judgment as well as love.

Let us look at the parent/child aspect of these relationships first. Are there limits to parental love? If a child is persistently recalcitrant, is there a point at which the parent may say, 'Enough! This relationship is at an end'? Israelite law says: yes, such a point may be reached, and this eventuality must be provided for. Dt. *21*.18–21 describes, unemotionally, the horrifying procedure. But can we imagine any parent ever actually resorting to such a law? Amos is saying, in effect, that this is the point which *has* been reached in Israel's relationship with God. Hosea seems to share our conviction that in real life no father could bring himself to it, and that the divine father is no exception. He says on God's behalf (*11*.8 f.): 'How can I give you up, O Ephraim? How can I hand you over, O Israel? . . . My heart recoils within me, my compassion grows warm and tender. I will not execute my fierce anger, I will not again destroy Ephraim.'

If this is the notion of the covenant then it has been so deepened that the word 'covenant' no longer seems appropriate to it. Israel is not merely some stranger with whom God happens to have struck a bargain. Such a bargain may be abrogated by either party if its terms are not kept by the other. But Israel is God's *son*.

This image of sonship is by no means unique in the Old Testament, but by no means common. The Old Testament writers were reticent about using it because such imagery *was* used among the pagans, and occasionally interpreted by them in rather gross ways. Some nations did think of themselves as being physically descended from their gods. No Israelite would have tolerated such an idea. Israel is an adopted son, a chosen son, though it is only the New Testament and not the Old that explicitly uses the language of adoption. But it is characteristic of Hosea not to be embarrassed by the pagan associations of his imagery. He develops the notion of sonship in a very intimate and human way, representing God as the father who taught the toddler Israel to walk, putting a toddler's reins on him; lifting him up when he got tired (*11*.3–4).

The pagan associations of the images of the wife and bride of God are very strong indeed. The idea of the divine marriage was an old and well-established one in the near east. The marriage of the god to his land, when he impregnates it and makes it fertile, was celebrated regularly in Canaanite shrines, celebrated with sexual rites which the prophets complain of constantly. (This is why they regularly describe religious infidelity as 'whoring after the baals'.) In Babylonia and Assyria the same was true, to the extent that the temples were the largest owners of slave prostitutes in those countries. For a prophet to appropriate pagan language about God and his bride was therefore a bold thing to do.

Hosea does not describe God's marriage to Israel as a covenant, though the idea was probably in his mind. When he speaks, in 2.14 ff., of the renewal of the marriage, he speaks of a return to the wilderness, hinting that this was where the marriage first began. God and Israel are to relive their honeymoon. A parallel between the marriage and the Sinai covenant-making is being at least suggested here. Marriage in any case *is* a covenant relationship. It is founded on a legal contract. Looked at in that light, it can be seen that if a wife is unfaithful to her husband then the husband has the right to terminate the marriage (in Old Testament law the converse does not apply). But a marriage, though it has a necessary basis in law, is much *more than* a legal contract. It is an emotional relationship. It cannot simply be ended by the stroke of a pen. It is this aspect of the matter which Hosea stresses. God has an attachment to his people, which means that he cannot simply cast them off without denying something in his own nature.

There is a law in the Old Testament which prescribes the death penalty for adultery. The only two texts in which it is stated are slightly later than Hosea's time. Certainly Hosea reflects no knowledge of such a penalty. He does in chapter 2 speak of divorce. The phrase, 'She is not my wife and I am not her husband' in 2.2 is said to be a divorce formula. Whether he is only threatening divorce or referring to the fact that he actually did divorce his own wife we cannot be sure. He refers in the same chapter to the use of an unpleasant divorce procedure (known to us from other ancient near eastern legal systems and echoed in several non-legal biblical texts) whereby a woman who had disgraced her husband was publicly stripped of her clothing and sent away naked (2.3, 10). The prophet does therefore contemplate an end of the relationship, or at least a break in it.

But he does also speak of the restoration of the relationship. Throughout this passage (2.14–23) the marriage of the prophet himself and the marriage of God to Israel are so intertwined that it is not always clear which is uppermost in the writer's mind at any given point.

Whereas Amos had relatively little to say about religion as such, Hosea says a great deal. For Hosea, the great threat is baal worship, which he sees his people as falling into. It has been suggested (though this is just a guess) that his wife was herself a baal-worshipper, and that her unfaithfulness was connected with the sexual rites of baalism. It has been suggested that she may herself have been a temple prostitute. If this was so, then Hosea's knowledge of baalism was knowledge at first hand. Be that as it may, Hosea has not only borrowed much of his imagery from his opponents, he also seems to have learnt something from their ideas. Israel's traditional God was the stern God of Amos, whom one must obey or perish. The god of the baal worshippers was one who had an indissoluble relationship with his land. And he too was a saviour god, who yearly fought his battles with the forces of chaos and infertility on his people's behalf. Hosea perceives that when the baal worshippers asserted that god is love, even though they were inclined to interpret that insight in reprehensible ways, it was a real insight into the divine nature; and that when they assumed that their god's love bound him inalienably to his people, so that the thought of abandoning them could not arise, they might not be altogether wrong.

For though Canaanite religion had its cruder aspects, it was by no means wholly to be condemned. It offered a real alternative view of the world, and it had genuine insights into the nature of God and his relations with men. Its high god was thought of as the creator of all things, and called 'Father of gods and men'. And the high god had a son, who fought with death and seemed to have been vanquished, but rose again, and through his death and resurrection give life to the world. The career of Baal, god and son of god, expresses the conviction that suffering is a divine activity, and that the world cannot be saved, except a god should die.

Canaanite religion is by now well documented and repays study. Those who are prepared to consider it sympathetically may well come to the conclusion that, for all its crudities, there are more things to admire in it than to despise.

It is interesting that though Hosea has so much to say about the possibility of divine forgiveness, he is one with Amos in having no faith in the cult, or in the institution of sacrifice. He sees sacrifice as an *alternative* to true faithfulness and to genuine knowledge of God. See the famous text of Hos. 6.5. It does not seem to occur to Hosea that sacrifice might be *an expression of* knowledge of God and of real repentance. One of Hosea's key words is 'respond', or 'answer'. What God is looking for is a response. What he offers, if his people will make only the slightest move towards him, is a response. Yet Hosea does not see sacrifice and worship as expressions of such a response to God. The response which Hosea sees as desirable is the response of love, and above all, love express-ing itself in obedience and loyalty.

It may be partly for this reason that Hosea leaves us with the tension between God's righteousness and his steadfast love unresolved. The perception that God must punish, and yet cannot, is Hosea's last word. Hosea grasps the humanity of God. Hosea's God has real feelings. Yet in the last resort perhaps he is all too human. He certainly does not know all the answers. Perhaps that is unimportant beside the fact that he faces the same questions.

## Hope in Hosea

Because Hosea leaves us with an unresolved tension, he has little to offer us in the way of a *positive assurance* of salvation. He cannot deny hope, because he has such a strong grasp of love. He cannot believe that God can bring himself finally to destroy, as Amos had threatened. Neither does he seem able to believe that Israel can forever fail to respond to the God who will 'allure her . . . and speak to her heart'. God will take her back to the wilderness, where he met her first (2.14) and from the wilderness he will lead her, not to the certainty of salvation, but to its possibility, to 'a door of hope' (2.15).

# ISAIAH OF JERUSALEM

## Isaiah's background

We refer to the eighth-century Isaiah as 'Isaiah of Jerusalem' in order to distinguish him from the prophet whose words are preserved in Is. *40–55*, whom we call Deutero-Isaiah (or Second Isaiah), and from the author or authors of the material in Is. *56–66*, Trito-Isaiah. The materials relating to Isaiah of Jerusalem are to be found, therefore, only in the first part of the book which bears his name, i.e. chapters *1–39*. However, by no means all, even of chapters *1–39*, is regarded as original eighth-century material. Chapters which contain much of the most important genuinely Isaianic material are *1–12* and *28–31*. In addition, chapters *36–39* contain historical narratives involving Isaiah, mostly duplicated in the book of Kings.

Isaiah dates his call 'in the year that king Uzziah died' (*6.1*), i.e. 746 BC. He therefore began his prophetic career in Judah at roughly the same time as Amos prophesied (probably very briefly) in the North. He certainly overlapped considerably with Hosea, for the two prophets refer to a number of the same events. But his ministry was very long. He not only prophesied about the fall of the Northern Kingdom (722/1) which Hosea reflects no knowledge of, but was still active right at the end of the century, in the reign of Hezekiah. According to legend, indeed, he did not die until the time of Manasseh. Even if we discount the legend, Isaiah's career must have lasted about fifty years. If the legend is to be trusted then the figure must be more like sixty, at least. (The legend is not entirely without scriptural attestation, for the words 'they were sawn asunder' in Heb. *9.37* reflect knowledge of the story of Isaiah's martyrdom.)

We thus know a *few* more personal details about his life than in the case of Amos and Hosea. He refers, apparently, to his wife (*8.3*) calling her 'the prophetess'. He also mentions two of his children, who, like Hosea's children, were given prophetic names (Shear Yashub—*7.3*, and Maher Shalal Hash Baz—*8.3*). Isaiah appears to have lived in Jerusalem, and is associated with the court and the temple. There is no evidence whatever for the oft-repeated statement that he was

of artistocratic birth. He also seems to have been connected
with a prophetic *community,* which is often assumed to have
played an important part in preserving his oracles. His 'disciples' are mentioned in *8.16.*

Isaiah lived through three great national crises. We have
several narratives relating incidents in his life, some of which
are connected with these crises. Since they also illustrate
some aspects of his thinking it will be worth looking at them in
a little more detail.

The first great crisis was the occasion of what is called the
Syro-Ephraimite coalition. This was in 734/33. See Is.
*7.1–8.8,* and cf. 2 Kings *16.* It was an attempt by Syria and
Northern Israel (Ephraim) to get Judah to join them in
resisting the Assyrians. When she refused, they attacked her
(or threatened to do so) to make her join by force. King
Ahaz's refusal to join the resistance to Assyria was almost
certainly wise, and Isaiah thoroughly approves the policy.
But under threat of attack from the two allies Ahaz takes
fright and appeals to the Assyrians themselves for help. He
had to pay heavily for the assistance, both in financial terms
and in terms of political subservience. This Isaiah does *not*
approve.

Isaiah's view appears to be that God's people should not
depend on political and military alliances of *any* sort. Neither
resistance to Assyria nor active appeal to her for help is at all
necessary. As long as the nation steadfastly does the will of
God he will protect them. His advice is summed up in *7.9:* 'If
you will not *believe,* surely you shall not be established.' Cf.
his words in another context (*28.16*): 'He who believes will
not be in haste.' He is appealing for *faith.*

Now the word 'faith' is relatively rare in the Old Testament.
Where it does appear it usually means something more like
'faithfulness'. But the quality for which Isaiah is asking is faith
in a sense very close to that of the New Testament. The ideas
expressed in Is. *7.9b* and *28.16,* quoted above, are not very
far removed from those of Matt. *6.25–34.*

To say that the word 'faith' is rare in the Old Testament
must not be taken to mean that faith is not an Old Testament
virtue. Old Testament characters frequently display the *quality* of faith. They tend not to use the *word.* The Old Testament
generally favours other words when describing man's proper

attitude to God. In the Old Testament the proper response of man to God is most frequently described as *love*. 'You shall *love* the Lord your God . . .' (Dt. *6*.5). We are so familiar with this idea of loving God that we often overlook the fact that it is not at all an idea characteristic of the New Testament. The New Testament *never* speaks of loving God, except where it happens to be quoting Dt. *6*.5; i.e. the New Testament writers never choose the word for themselves when describing man's attitude to God. They employ it only when it is offered them by the Old Testament. The word they choose for themselves is 'faith'.

None of this means that the Old Testament and the New are very far apart, because when we ask what is the *content* of the words 'love' and 'faith' as the two testaments use them, i.e. when we ask *what it means in practice* to love God or to have faith in him, we discover that the answers lie quite close together. In the Old Testament, love expresses itself primarily in obedience. In the New Testament the test of faith, too, is obedience. For if someone says 'Lord, Lord' (that is, he claims to have faith in Christ), but does not do the things that Christ says, his profession of faith is meaningless (Matt. *7*.21, Lk. *6*.46).

The second national crisis of Isaiah's lifetime was when the Assyrians came west once more in the seven-twenties, in military campaigns which eventually led to the overthrow of the Northern Kingdom and the deportation of many of its people. In chapter *28*, probably delivered a little before the final catastrophe to the North, the prophet depicts the pride of the 'drunkards of Ephraim', the northern leaders whose irresponsibility and corruption are leading, he asserts, to disaster. He goes on to use the events in the North as a warning to his own people. They must not think that they are immune to the divine wrath.

The third great crisis was caused by Hezekiah's attempts towards the end of the century to throw off the Assyrian yoke, and the punitive Assyrian attacks which ensued. See Is. *36–37*, cf. 2 Kings *18–19*. Here again Isaiah's advice is to trust God. Neither diplomatic posturings nor military resistance is the way. Though Isaiah condemned Hezekiah's scheming with other anti-Assyrians, when the attack did come he counselled confidence, and promised that Jerusalem would not be captured. This conviction of his about Jerusalem's inviolability we shall refer to again shortly.

However, not everything is clear about Isaiah's reaction to this last episode. Hezekiah's attempts to liberate himself from the Assyrians involved also a quite extensive religious reform. Though the prophet clearly disapproved of some of the political aspects of Hezekiah's policies he can hardly have objected to some of their religious consequences.

### The nature of God and his relationship with man

Any study of Isaiah's understanding of God must begin with the account of his call in chapter 6. The vision is said to take place in the temple, and the prophet is overcome by his awareness of the *holiness* of God.

Now holiness is not, as originally conceived, a *moral* quality. It has *acquired* a moral connotation, and indeed, Isaiah is partly responsible for the fact that it has done so. Holiness cannot be defined. It cannot be translated into terms of anything else. Holy is what God is. It is the name we give to that which sets him apart from his creation. It is the name for the difference between God and all else. Holiness is the gulf which marks off God from ourselves and the world. It is, as it were, the 'godness' of God. In this sense of the word, only God may be properly described as 'holy'.

Yet there is also a derivative sense in which it may be applied to things which are not God. It is applied to things which in a peculiar way *belong* to him, which stand near to his person. Thus, the temple can be described as holy. Its furniture and fittings, the tongs and firepans on its altar are holy. The prophets are holy. Yet to call these things and people 'holy' is not intended to say anything about their moral or aesthetic character at all. It merely signals the fact that they are peculiarly God's.

The temple is not holy because it is a more beautiful building than other buildings; because the worship that goes on in it is less insincere, its priesthood less rapacious than is the case with other temples. It is not holy because it has fewer flies and less stench in its courts than other places of sacrifice. It is holy *only* because it is *his* temple and he has caused his name to dwell there.

Likewise his holy prophets are not holy because they live more beautiful lives than other men; because they are cleaner in their habits, have fewer rows with their wives or are better at bringing up their children. They are holy because, and only because, they are *his* prophets, and he has set his word in their mouths and they cannot refrain.

Isaiah did not of course *discover* the holiness of God. Five hundred years earlier Moses had been overcome by it in his encounter at the bush. Five hundred years earlier again, in dread and great darkness, Abraham had been overpowered by it too (Gn. *15*). And indeed, mankind has always known of it, because without awareness of God's holiness there is no real awareness of God.

Awareness of God's holiness makes Isaiah aware of his own *un*holiness; 'uncleanness' the text calls it. In his vision Isaiah is 'cleansed', made holy, in what I have called the derivative sense. He becomes God's man in a way he was not before.

The experience of Isaiah in the temple offers us a pattern for religious experience in general. God is always there. He was always there in the temple, seated upon his throne, high and lifted up. The person who allows himself to become aware of the reality of that presence becomes at the same time aware of his own impurity. And the person who accepts God's offer of purification and forgiveness is immediately challenged to a task.

But it is part of Isaiah's achievement that he does see his 'uncleanness' as sinfulness, and his purification as forgiveness. For him, holiness becomes inextricably bound together with righteousness. It was stated above that holiness, in itself, cannot be defined; but what it issues in, or expresses itself in, is very readily definable, namely righteousness. The key text here is Is. 5.16: 'The holy God *shows himself holy* in righteousness' (RSV translation). We might put it another way and say that holiness is what God *is*, righteousness is what he *does*.

Isaiah's demand for righteousness is framed in similar terms to that of Amos. Perhaps the most attractive, as well as a very forceful, way of setting out this demand is in chapter 5. This 'song of the vineyard' is important partly because it expounds an image which the NT later takes up. Like Amos, Isaiah thrusts the responsibility for self-reform firmly on to men themselves. *1*.10–20 established this clearly, with its demand to 'Wash yourselves, make yourselves clean' (*1*.16). Forgiveness is offered, on strict conditions, that men become 'willing and obedient'. The same passage appears to see little point in the offering of sacrifices and indeed in public worship generally (*1*.11–15). Yet, be it said in parenthesis, the view of sacrifice here seems less negative than that expressed in Amos. Isaiah does not assert that sacrifice is not a proper part of Israel's religion. He criticizes the Israelites' sacrifices no more fiercely than he condemns their prayers (*1*.15), and is fairly explicit that his real objection is not to the prayers or the sacrifices themselves but to the inconsistency of the worship with the moral behaviour of the worshippers.

And elsewhere, as we have already observed, Isaiah's attitude to temple and cult is more positive. His call does take place in the temple. It does include purif'cation by an expiatory ritual, albeit a not very regular one. And the purification there is not by self-reform but by divine initiative.

Isaiah, then, like Hosea, is equally aware of the divine mercy, or at least, the divine commitment to his people which cannot simply abandon them. Whereas Hosea seems to have come to this conviction through his own individual experience of love, Isaiah's vision of the divine commitment seems to have come to him from a very different direction. Isaiah is a Jerusalem prophet, and he belongs to a tradition which attached great significance to the covenant with the house of David, and to the royal sanctuary where God's presence was. He cannot envisage God totally abandoning his people, for that would be to break his own promise to David.

In another form, therefore, Isaiah faces Hosea's dilemma. How can God insist on his demand for righteousness and at the same time remain faithful to his own promises? He solves it by means of his doctrine of the remnant.

It may be that Isaiah's use of the remnant idea went through two phases. It looks as if he may initially have used the idea negatively, as Amos does in *3*.12. He prophesied, that is to say, that after the punishing disaster which God would inflict there would be *only* a remnant left, i.e. nothing worth saving. But he certainly came to use the idea positively, to say that the surviving remnant, poor as it might be, could yet be the seed of renewal. It is possible that the prophet's disciples, responding to this positive note, have re-interpreted some of his earlier, more negative sayings. A likely instance is at the end of chapter six. Here the message which the prophet is commanded to speak looks entirely negative. In verse 13 he uses the image of the felled tree, which men are not just content to cut down but then go on to try and burn the stump. The final comment, 'The holy seed is its stump', is inconsistent with this line of thought. It is suggesting that even the hacked and blackened stump may yet sprout again. This looks as if it had been added to bring the passage into line with the later, more positive use of the remnant idea by the prophet and his followers.

## Hope in Isaiah

Isaiah expresses a more positive hope than any of the canonical prophets who came before him. This hope seems to spring from confidence in God's covenant with David. Isaiah seems to be convinced that the house of David is the means through which God will save his people. The 'messianic' passages for which Isaiah is famous, are expressions of this conviction. It is important to realize that whatever *extra* significance Christians may wish to see in these passages, for the prophet himself they were essentially short-term predictions. He was talking about the reigning king, or about the crown prince, or at least about some member of the royal house shortly to take power. It is probably fair to say that for Isaiah the 'messiah' is not so much an individual as a dynasty.

In the interpretation of the messianic passages, however, critical questions loom quite large. There have been scholars who have judged that most of these passages are not by Isaiah at all but by a later hand. Even if they are really by Isaiah himself, the passages may have been added to or re-interpreted at a later stage. *11*.1–9 is a good example of this possibility. *11*.1–5 describe the coming of a just king, whose virtues are described in quite this-worldly terms. There is nothing here which could not have been said about the reigning king or his shortly-to-be-expected successor, and nothing that would seem inappropriate in the mouth of an eighth-century prophet. But in verse 6 the scene abruptly changes, and in the description of the coming good times we have

miraculous features. A return to paradisal conditions is envisaged, in which animals no longer eat each other and the
carnivores revert to vegetarianism. This is the kind of thing
that was being written much later in the OT period. It looks
very much as if Isaiah's political expectations have been
retouched and given a more radical twist. The passage is now
no longer talking about the hoped for virtues of the next
government but about the last days and the kingdom of God.

But Isaiah's hope lay not only in the messianic house, but in
the holy city. Jerusalem was not only the place where God's
anointed had his throne, but where God's temple was, and
where he himself dwelt. Again there is controversy about
what the original Isaiah actually did preach, for the words that
have come down to us are partly contradictory (e.g. *39.6*
appears to imply that Jerusalem will be overthrown). But
there are strong indications that Isaiah believed that
Jerusalem was inviolable. God's own seat was there, and he
could not therefore allow it to be taken. Whether or not the
real Isaiah believed this, he was certainly credited with the
belief by later generations. The description in *1.1–8* of
the devastation of the land portrays a devastation which stops
at Jerusalem. And at the time of the Assyrian attacks Isaiah is
said to have expressed the confidence that, whatever else
happened, the invaders would not subdue Jerusalem. When
Sennacherib did withdraw, having failed (for whatever
reason) to take the city, Isaiah's faith appeared to have been
justified by events.

Doubtless Isaiah did not invent the notion of the inviolable
sacred city, but he gave the development of the idea a powerful impetus. Jerusalem becomes a very potent symbol from
this point onwards. In the later apocalyptic literature, which
describes the coming of the glorious age, it is not, as is often
supposed, the messiah who is usually the central figure.
Often, in such literature, the messiah is absent, or plays only a
minor role. The real hero (or rather heroine) is Jerusalem, the
holy city. She holds the centre of the stage. Jerusalem represents the ideal, God-directed, civilized life of mankind.
Ezekiel thinks there is a plan laid up in heaven of what
Jerusalem is meant to be like. Later writers see this ideal,
heavenly Jerusalem as waiting, ready to be revealed at the last
time, when she will come down out of heaven like a bride. She

is the goal to which the whole plan of salvation moves, where God's presence is, and in which his holy ones will dwell forever. By Christians she is taken as a symbol of the church, and the prophecies about Jerusalem were only to be fulfilled when they came to fruition in the church.

None of this, of course, is articulated by Isaiah, but what he does say about Jerusalem contained the seeds of many of these later developments.

# Section 4

## The Prophetic Traditions (2)

AFTER the great flowering period of prophecy in the second half of the eighth century there was a sort of prophetic 'dark age'. Hezekiah's attempts to free the country from Assyrian domination had had the opposite effect to the one intended and had left Judah more firmly under Assyrian control than before. Hezekiah's son, Manasseh, who reigned for most of the first half of the seventh century, was resolved to learn from his father's mistakes. He accepted Assyrian rule and was careful to obey his masters in all things. This involved accepting some aspects of Assyrian religion, and Manasseh appears to have suppressed rather fiercely those elements in Judah's religious leadership who found this objectionable. No prophet of independent mind could speak publicly during this period. (GBS, Chapter 10, h.)

Manasseh's son and successor, Amon, pursued the same policies but did not reign long. The heir to the throne was an eight-year-old child, Josiah. His education was taken in hand by people determined to imbue him with the traditions of his national faith. This Josiah was eventually to carry out a most important reform in 621 BC. By this time Assyria was weakening and could no longer control her empire, so the sort of reform which Josiah had in mind, which had both religious and political dimensions to it, had become politically possible. (GBS, Chapter 21. j.)

It was during Josiah's reign that Jeremiah appeared. He received his call some years before the reform. He witnessed Josiah's attempts to give his country political independence and religious renewal, and his ultimate political failure and death. He lived on through the turbulent reigns of his successors, Jehoyaqim, Jehoyakin and Zedekiah, and saw the fall of Jerusalem, the destruction of the temple, and the end of the monarchy. (GBS, Chapter 23, d.)

## JEREMIAH

### The life of Jeremiah

We shall begin with a brief sketch of Jeremiah's career. It falls into four main periods.

(1) Jeremiah's call took place in 626. He was very young at the time, probably a young teenager. He belonged to an old priestly family, but not to the Jerusalem priesthood associated with the temple. His message in these first few years between his call and the great reform of 621 seems to have been chiefly one of judgment and destruction. (For all of the foregoing see Jer. *1*.)

(2) The next period runs from the reform itself (621) to Josiah's death in 609, a span of twelve years. There is virtually nothing in the book of Jeremiah which can reliably be assigned to this period. This in itself is extraordinary. A prophet lives through one of the most significant religious events in his country's history and apparently has nothing to say about it. We cannot even say for certain what Jeremiah's attitude to the reform was.

We can, however, make some intelligent guesses. Jeremiah's silence is itself important evidence. It suggests that he was in two minds about it; that he could not wholeheartedly approve it, but did not wish to condemn it. In so far as the reform did much to purify Israel's worship, and got rid of the Assyrian elements and some forms of idolatry, Jeremiah can scarcely have found it objectionable. But it did focus religious life more emphatically than ever before on temple worship, and as we shall see, Jeremiah had serious reservations about temple-centred devotion. It would not be surprising therefore if he was in two minds about the reform as a whole, and if he was willing to keep quiet and give it a chance, but without offering any active support. He does later deliver a scathing attack on Josiah's son, Jehoyaqim, who undid many of Josiah's reforms, and contrasts him unfavourably with his father, who 'did justice and righteousness' (22.13–19). He could hardly have said this if he had been altogether opposed to Josiah's policies.

(3) From the death of Josiah to the fall of Jerusalem in 586 was a stormy period for Jeremiah. Josiah's successor, Jehoya-qim, did not uphold the principles of his father's reform. In foreign policy he was inclined to appeal to the Egyptians for help against the new power in the east, which had overthrown and replaced the Assyrians, namely Babylon. Jeremiah regarded this policy as wrongheaded. His view was that Baby-lon was God's chosen instrument for the punishment of his people, and that the proper attitude was not to resist the Babylonians at all. See, e.g. 21.1–10; 25.1–16; and see chap-ter 27 where he is still making the same point in Zedekiah's reign. Neither this nor his other criticisms of the government endeared Jeremiah to the authorities. He was persecuted and laughed at, especially because his prophecies of doom did not appear to be fulfilled.

Eventually, however, in 597, the Babylonians did over-throw Judah and take some of her people into exile, among them the king Jehoyakin (who had replaced his father when the Babylonian army was virtually on the doorstep). The Babylonians put their own nominee, Zedekiah, on the throne. Jeremiah's message now was that God had not yet finished his punishment; there was worse to come. (See chap-ter 27, already referred to.) Zedekiah was more inclined to listen to Jeremiah than his predecessors had been, but he seems to have been a weak personality, easily swayed by other advisers and with little will of his own. As Jeremiah had predicted, the end came in 586, when the Babylonians deported more people, destroyed the temple, and brought the monarchy to an end. Instead of a king they appointed a governor, Gedaliah, and set up a court for him at Mizpah. They were about to take Jeremiah into exile with the rest when it was pointed out to them that he had consistently advocated pro-Babylonian policies and might be a good per-son to leave behind. He was thus instructed to remain at Gedaliah's court to advise him (Jer. 38.14–40.12).

(4) All seems to have gone well until Gedaliah was mur-dered. The rest of the Jewish leaders, fearing reprisals from the Babylonians for the murder of their governor, resolved to

flee to Egypt. Jeremiah opposed this, but they went, nevertheless, and took Jeremiah with them (*41*.1–*43*.7). He eventually died in Egypt. We have some few prophecies from this Egyptian period (e.g. *43*.8–*44*.30).

## Jeremiah's experience of God

In the book of Jeremiah we have a number of passages which are usually called the 'confessions of Jeremiah'. They are records of his prayers and conversations with God. In them he voices his doubts and his inner struggles. They are indeed not so much prayers as arguments with God, sometimes even verging on the blasphemous. The passages in question are *11*.18–23; *12*.1–6; *15*.10–21; *17*.12–18; *18*.18–23; *20*.7–18, and they are unique in prophetic literature.

We must be very careful, however, what conclusions we draw from this uniqueness. There are some who conclude that other prophets did not have such intimate, personal experience of God. We are not entitled to say this. We can only say that other prophets *do not tell us* in detail about such intimate personal experiences. To say that the *accounts* are unique is not to say that the *experience* was unique.

Although there is nothing quite like the confessions of Jeremiah there are hints elsewhere in prophetic literature that other prophets (and perhaps not only prophets) were familiar with personal struggles and doubts, and that they met God in the intimacy of their own hearts. A classic instance is the story of Elijah's flight to Horeb and his vision there in the cave (1 Kings *19*). Elijah there voices doubts about the usefulness of his own mission, persistent doubts, like Jeremiah's. And like Jeremiah he comes to recognize the true voice of God in the 'still small voice' that speaks in his loneliness. Even if we dismiss all this as legend, and assert that we have no way of knowing what the genuine, historical Elijah thought and felt, this does not affect the argument. For *whoever wrote the story* clearly knew about such direct, personal experience of God, and expected his readers to understand it too.

The personal encounter with God can be paralleled in all the prophetic call visions. The hesitations and doubts of the prophet can be paralleled in most of them. The argument or controversy with God can be paralleled in the cases of

Abraham and Moses (Gn. *18* and Ex. *32*, respectively). None of these are as detailed or as personally revealing as Jeremiah's confessions, but they are enough to show that Jeremiah's experiences are not in themselves unique, and that Jeremiah did not, as sometimes used to be implied, invent, singlehanded, the whole idea of a personal, individual relationship with God.

The fact that we have these confessions from Jeremiah and nothing quite like them from other prophets may be largely accident. Jeremiah's friend and secretary Baruch figures quite prominently in the book. He was evidently very close to Jeremiah and is usually assumed to have had a large hand in the collecting of the prophet's oracles. (Some of this is put beyond doubt by the story in Jer. *36*.) It may well be from Baruch that we have these very personal 'confessions', which were doubtless not originally meant by the prophet for publication. It seems likely that the reason we have no such confessions from other prophets is that none of them had a Baruch standing by to preserve them.

What, then, of the content of the confessions? They consist almost entirely of poetry, and are very like psalms. They express the prophet's dislike of his task, or at least of the trouble and controversy it causes. He has become 'a man of strife and contention to the whole land' (*15*.10). They convey his fear of the plots to murder him (e.g. *11*.19, 21) and nearly all of them pray for vengeance on his enemies and those who oppose him. Most of the confession passages contain God's words of comfort, not excusing him from the task, but strengthening him. This 'comfort' is sometimes of a rather harsh kind, as in *12*.5: 'If you have run with the footmen and they have wearied you, how will you contend with horses?'

But the most important passage is the final one, *20*.7–18. The hint in *15*.18 that God is deceiving him is in *20*.7 made into a clear accusation, and the prophet rebels altogether against his task. God has given him false words to say, which then are not fulfilled. He prophesies doom and destruction, but it does not happen. Yet if he attempts to keep silent, because he no longer believes his own message, God forces him to speak. He ends by cursing the day he was born, in a manner strongly reminiscent of Job.

There is thus an enormous discrepancy between the character of the prophet and the character of the message which he is called on to proclaim. Jeremiah is a diffident, gentle person. He says of himself, 'I was as a gentle lamb'. He loves joyous occasions, 'the voice of the bridegroom and the voice of the bride', and simple domestic things, like 'the sound of millstones and the light of a lamp'. Yet it is thrust on him to preach an unpopular and violently controversial message, so that he must become 'an iron pillar and brazen walls against the whole land'. There are preachers and prophets who betray a certain relish when they announce doom and judgment. Jeremiah was not one of them. He grieves deeply for his people. 'O that my head were waters, and my eyes a fountain of tears, that I might weep day and night for the slain of the daughter of my people' (9.1).

## Jeremiah's understanding of sin

Jeremiah repeats the standard prophetic teaching, that God will forgive if only people will turn to him, and he appeals for repentance, and appeals very movingly. (See, for example, 3.14, 22 f.; 4.1–4; 7.5–7.)

Yet at other points Jeremiah seems to contradict himself. In the manner of Amos, he pronounces judgment as if there was no possibility of averting it. He ends a prophecy of judgment in 4.23–28 with the words: '. . . for I have spoken, I have purposed; I have not relented nor will I turn back.' Chapter 5 expands the theme of judgment and sets out some of the reasons why there can be no remission. The people have failed to respond to earlier punishments; 'they have refused to take correction' (5.3). 'They have refused to repent' (5.3, again, and cf. 8.5). And this state of affairs is universal. There are no exceptions. Abraham failed to find ten righteous persons for whose sake Sodom might be rescued, but Jeremiah cannot find even one for whose sake God might pardon Jerusalem (5.1).

Over and over again Jeremiah stresses the *unnaturalness* of Israel's sin. It is so shocking and outrageous just because Israel was the very nation that ought to have known better. He is picking up a thought here from Amos, and from Isaiah who in Is. 1.3 compares his people unfavourably with dumb animals. Even a dumb ox, says Isaiah, knows where it belongs and who its master is, yet Israel ignores its own lord. Jeremiah has a similar comparison in *8.7*. Even the migrating birds have enough sense to keep the rules which God has laid down for them. They arrive when he says they should arrive, and build their nests as prescribed, and depart in their season. But Israel cannot be bothered to keep the rules that govern her existence.

He likewise refers back to Isaiah's parable of the thankless vineyard (Is. *5*), by comparing Israel in *2.21* to a choice vine, grown from pure seed, which the grower had every right to expect would produce good grapes. Yet unaccountably it turned wild and produced nothing worth picking.

Israel's behaviour is simply incredible, like a bride who displays no interest in her bridal dress or her jewellery (*2.32*). Unthinkable! They not only prefer the foul, standing water of the storage cistern to the clear running water of the spring, but they haven't even the sense to make the cisterns themselves watertight (*2.13*). Even the idolatrous nations stick to their gods. Israel, who has a real God, can't even be loyal to him (*2.11–12*): 'Be appalled, O heavens, at this, be shocked, be utterly desolate, says the Lord.'

For God to forgive such monstrous behaviour is not only impossible, it would be downright improper. It would be like a man taking back a wife whom he had once divorced and who had in the interim been married to someone else (*3.1*), an idea which Israelites apparently found grossly offensive (cf. Dt. *24.1–4*).

Israel's sin is thus indelible, not to be wiped out. God says to them (*2.22*), 'Though you wash yourselves with lye (the most powerful cleansing agent known) and use much soap, the stain of your guilt is still before me.' And even more strongly, he says, 'The sin of Judah is written with a pen of iron; with a point of diamond it is engraved on the tablet of their heart' (*17.1*).

Yet none of this is meant to call in question God's willingness to forgive. The inevitability of punishment and the ineradicability of sin are due rather to Israel's failure to repent. As we saw above, Jeremiah sometimes speaks like Amos, as if Israel *would not* repent (*4.23–28*; *5.3*; *8.5*). Occasionally, however, he goes further, and suggests that Israel *cannot* repent. This comes out in the one or two texts in

which he compares sin with lust. In 3.2 he speaks, as several
prophets do, especially Hosea, of Israel's sin as harlotry. But
he draws something out of this image which no one else does.
When Jeremiah speaks of lust he points to its *over-powering*
nature. In 2.23 f. the image is of *animal* lust. The nation is like
a young camel or a wild ass on heat. Such creatures in their
season are totally intractable and uncontrollable. They have
only one thing on their minds. Lust takes over. So when
Jeremiah refers back at the end of this little passage to the
harlot (2.25) he has established in our minds this feature of
lust, its uncontrollability. The prostitute Jeremiah speaks of
in 2.25 is saying: 'It is hopeless.' She has already been taken
over. She cannot pull out. 'I have loved strangers, and after
them I will go.' It is the only way of life she knows, and no
other is any longer possible for her. Israel's sin, the prophet is
saying, is like that. It has become ingrained, habitual,
controlling.

This is where Jeremiah goes beyond Amos, and indeed
beyond all the other prophets before him. The others always
assume that Israel has a choice. She can repent, if she chooses.
But Jeremiah, at some moments, perceives that Israel no
longer has a choice. He is very close to St. Augustine's perception of sin as a corruption of the will, so that the sinner no
longer knows when he is sinning or is capable of choosing
rightly. He sums this up in 17.9 with his statement that 'the
heart is deceitful above all things, and desperately corrupt'.

Now this may look remarkably like the Christian doctrine
of original sin. It is certainly a large step on the way to such a
doctrine, but there is an important difference between
Jeremiah's notion of sin and the doctrine of original sin as set
out by St. Paul and later Christian writers. The doctrine of
original sin is a *universal* doctrine. It tells us about the propen-
sity to sin which is in *all men*. It says that all of us, merely by
virtue of being human, are incapable, left to ourselves, of
refraining from sin. Jeremiah is not saying this. He is only
saying that *some* people are in this condition of being no
longer able to avoid sinning. He is saying that it is possible so
to give way to sin that it corrupts one's vision. Such people no
longer know what they are really doing, and are no longer
able by repentance to pull themselves back to sensibility and
virtue.

Specifically, of course, Jeremiah believes that his contemporaries had become thus corrupt. Only such complete corruption could explain the utter irrationality of their behaviour, its 'unnaturalness', as we described it above. In tracing the history of Israel's corruption Jeremiah is, as often, very close to Hosea. Like Hosea, he believes that the corruption goes back a long way. Hosea traces much of it back to the ancestor Jacob; Jeremiah, 2.1–8, is content to see it going back at least to the settlement in the promised land. Since that time Israel has been consistently unfaithful. Yet Jeremiah and Hosea both agree that there *was* a time of faithfulness, in the far past. They agree in describing it in terms of a honeymoon, in the wilderness. 'I remember', says God to Israel, 'the devotion of your youth, your love as a bride, how you followed me in the wilderness, in a land not sown. Israel was holy to the Lord' (*2.2 f.*; cf. Hos. *2.14–15*).

But since that time there has been a steady slide into faithlessness. Jeremiah alludes briefly to Hosea's image of the adulterous wife (*3.20*). This faithlessness has become endemic. Israel has lost the capacity for self-help. It is, of course, their own fault that they have got into that condition, but having got into it, they cannot get out of it unaided. A prophet with Jeremiah's view of sin could only end in total pessimism unless he had an equally strong doctrine of grace.

## Hope in Jeremiah

Whatever Jeremiah is, he is not a pessimist. Whatever his despair, he never loses faith. Hope is built into his message from the beginning. The commission he is given at the time of his call (*1.10*) is not only '. . . to pluck up and to break down, to destroy and to overthrow', but *'to build and to plant'*. And though for most of his ministry the plucking up and breaking down, the destroying and the overthrowing are the most prominent part of his mission and message, he never loses sight of the other side of his work. When the siege of Jerusalem was at its height—a siege which he had prophesied, and which he asserted was bound to end in Jerusalem's capture and destruction—he was caught attempting to leave the city. But he was not, as the authorities thought, simply deserting, or going over to the enemy. He was going back to his village to buy a field (Jer. *32*). To do this in the middle of a war, when the country had been ravaged, and when the conquerors were likely to redistribute land as they thought fit, might seem to be the height of folly. Jeremiah does it as an assertion of his faith in the future, and he is backing his faith with hard cash, for 'fields shall be bought in this land of which you are saying, "It is a desolation" . . . Fields shall be bought for money, and deeds shall be signed and sealed and witnessed' (*32*.43 f.).

Once the exile has actually happened, he writes encouragingly to the exiles, telling them not to despair, for God has a future for them. He tells them that they, who have been carried off, are not the rejects, the failures. It is rather the reverse. It is those left at home who are the rejects, and the exiles are the ones with whom the future lies. They are to settle down, build houses, plant gardens, and raise families, because the return will not be soon, but eventually they will return. All this is in chapter *29*.

But how does this prospect of restoration relate to Jeremiah's notion of endemic sin? If his people are really as corrupt as he has been saying, why should there be any more hope for the future than there has been in the past? If they persistently failed to obey God before, what reason is there to think that they will obey him now? The answer lies in Jer. *31*, and in the idea of the new covenant. The key verses are *31*.31–33.

Jeremiah explicitly contrasts this new covenant with the covenant of Sinai. It is 'not like the covenant which I made with their fathers when I . . . brought them out of the land of Egypt' (*31*.32). Where does the difference between the two covenants lie? To put it another way: What is new about the new covenant? There is nothing new in the actual terms or content of the covenant. Jeremiah sums up its content as: 'I will be their God and they shall be my people' (*31*.33). This is exactly the content of the old covenant. Neither can we contrast them by saying that the old covenant was a covenant of *law*, whereas the new covenant has some other basis. For under the new covenant Jeremiah says: 'I will put *my law* within them' (*31*.33), and there is no suggestion that this is a new or a different law. It is simply 'my law', the same, recognizable law which has always been the basis of God's relation with his people. Neither can we contrast the two covenants (as some have occasionally tried to do) by saying that the old covenant was a covenant with the nation, whereas the new covenant is made with individuals. For Jeremiah says that the new covenant is to be made 'with the house of Israel and with the house of Judah' (*31*.31), i.e. with the two halves of the nation. Like the former covenant, it is a national affair.

The one difference between the covenants to which Jeremiah points concerns the place where the law is written. In the old covenant the law was written on tablets of stone. In the new covenant the law is to be written 'within them . . . on their hearts' (*31*.33). What is the prophet trying to say here? It is customary to say that the old covenant was 'external', whereas the new covenant is 'inward'. But what exactly does such a statement *mean*?

Here we have to remember that for the Hebrew speaker the word 'heart' did not have the associations which it has for us. The English tradition generally associates the heart with feeling and emotion. The Hebrew did not. For the Hebrew speaker the seat of the emotions was the bowels (a notion not totally unfamiliar to us, for we do hear the expression 'gut reaction', meaning an apparently instinctive emotional response). The heart, for Hebrew speakers, was the organ of thought and will. So when a prophet speaks of a law 'written upon the heart' he is speaking of a law delivered in such a manner that *the will to keep it is changed*. Instead of a heart 'deceitful above all things and desperately corrupt' (*17*.9) Israel is to be given a heart controlled, programmed, by divine law. Instead of *sin* being written there 'with a point of diamond' (*17*.1) *the law* will be written indelibly. The outcome will be that the new covenant will differ from the old in that *it will not be broken*. When Jeremiah refers back to the old covenant the one characteristic of it which he picks out for mention is that it was broken ('which covenant of mine they broke . . . says the Lord'—*31*.32). In *31*.35–36 Jeremiah refers back, rather in the manner of the Priestly writer in Gn. *8*.22, to the order of creation. The new covenant with his people will be as fixed as the cosmic order. Jeremiah does not quite go as far as Ezekiel, who speaks of the giving of a new heart, but his language suggesting the remaking of the will, and his association of the new covenant with the fixity of the created order, is the beginning of an interesting tradition, which sees God's act of grace in forgiveness (*31*.34) as a new creative act, and which leads ultimately to such statements as 2 Cor. 5.17, that 'if anyone is in Christ, he is a new creation'.

## The place of encounter with God

Jeremiah's ideas about forgiveness and renewal are not brought into any association with sacrifice or the temple. In spite of his own priestly origins Jeremiah does not see the cultic system as offering any effective way back to God, or providing any useful expression of divine grace. In 6.20 he says that incense offerings are a waste of time, and 'your burnt offerings are not acceptable, nor your sacrifices pleasing to me'. In 7.21 he asserts that the burnt offering, which was the most solemn kind of offering, wholly burnt on the altar, might as well be simply eaten by the worshippers themselves. It is just meat, like any other. He goes on to say, as Amos said in Am. 5.25, that sacrifice is no proper part of Israel's religion. The original law delivered to Moses in the wilderness did not command it. This is in flat contradiction to what is said in the pentateuch, but in Jeremiah's time, of course, the pentateuch did not yet exist, and there were evidently those who did not regard as authoritative those traditions which traced the sacrificial system back to Moses.

Jeremiah's opposition is not merely to the sacrificial system, but to the temple as such. Isaiah, though he too could be critical of the sacrificial system as it actually operated in his day, had a very positive attitude to the temple, and received his own call there. He saw the temple, if not exactly as a guarantee of divine favour, at least as a strong sign of God's grace. Jeremiah belongs in quite a different camp, and sees the temple as a positive snare. Isaiah himself may unwittingly have prompted some of his countrymen to place quite the wrong kind of faith in the temple. His preaching of Zion's inviolability made it much harder for Jeremiah's prophecies of doom against the temple to get a hearing. People who say: 'The temple of the Lord, the temple of the Lord, the temple of Lord' (Jer. 7.4) believing that God cannot allow his house to perish, are 'trusting in lying words'.

Jeremiah at one point in his career made a powerful speech

against the temple, and made it in the temple court itself. He prophesied that God would make this sanctuary 'like Shiloh', the old sanctuary of the time of Eli, which is presumed to have fallen to the Philistines when they captured the ark, and which was never a sanctuary again. We have two accounts of this speech, in chapter 7 and again in chapter 26. The speech got Jeremiah into very considerable trouble, and there were those who wished to have him put to death for it (26.16–24).

There is a well-established tradition in the Old Testament which sees the temple as a strong signal of God's presence and grace; as the place where he dwells, or where his name dwells, in the midst of his people; as a place where God can be met, and where atonement can be made for sin. Jeremiah belongs to quite a different tradition, but one which has several worthy representatives. One of the latest was St. Stephen, who also made a speech against the temple, retelling the history of his people in such a way as to represent the building of the temple as the great act of apostasy. In Jeremiah's case, reasoned arguments from precedents led to his acquittal. In Stephen's there were no reasoned arguments, only rage.

For Jeremiah, then, the temple is not a place of encounter with God. Yet there is a place of encounter which he recognizes. At this point those who stress Jeremiah's individualism and his sponsorship of 'inward religion' come close to the truth. The place of encounter is within everyman.

## Enacted prophecy

One oddity about the prophets which we have not so far mentioned is that they were not always content simply to *speak* the word that God had given them, but felt compelled to dramatize it, as it were, to act it out. This used to be given the name 'prophetic symbolism' but it is better called 'enacted prophecy'. A very familiar instance from early prophecy is the incident in 1 Kings 11.29–38, where Ahijah tears his robe into twelve pieces and hands ten to Jeroboam, signifying that God is to take ten of the tribes from the control of Solomon's heir and give them to Jeroboam to rule. In 1 Kings 22.11 a false prophet, Zedekiah ben Chenaanah, puts horns on his head and charges about to show what Israel's army is to do to the Syrians. Isaiah demonstrates a prophecy about the conquest of Egypt and Ethiopia by going about dressed (or undressed) as a captive (Is. 20). And Hosea's marriage is another possible example of an enacted prophecy, if we see the prophet as deliberately marrying a harlot in order to make his point.

With the possible exception of Ezekiel, no prophet makes so much use of prophetic enactment as Jeremiah. His parable of the potter's house (18.1–11) is not quite an enacted prophecy, but is a halfway step towards one. Jeremiah does not do the action himself, but he seeks out the pottery, where he knows perfectly well what will be going on, in order to demonstrate his message. God can make and remake his nation as easily as the potter makes and remakes pots, scrapping one if it isn't working out right, and making the collapsed lump of clay into a new shape.

His use of the Rechabites in chapter 35 is rather similar. The Rechabites were total abstainers, in obedience to a command given by their ancestor. Jeremiah invites some of them to the temple, and there he offers them wine. Predictably, they refuse. 'There!' says the prophet, 'if these men can be so faithful to the merely human command of their forefather, cannot Judah manage to be faithful to the far weightier command of God?'

In chapter 19 there is a description of the ceremonial breaking of a flask as a prophecy of destruction. This was a very traditional act, attested at many places and many periods in the ancient near east. In 13.1–11 we have a more bizarre enactment with a loin-cloth, taken to the bank of the Euphrates and hidden there, and later dug up again. As an enacted parable or prophecy this one is probably the least compelling to the modern reader of all Jeremiah's actions.

Chapters 27–28 offer us the spectacle of a sort of competition in enacted prophecy. Jeremiah appears wearing a wooden yoke, of the type worn by oxen, as a sign that the people are to be brought under the yoke of the Babylonians. An opponent, Hananiah, breaks the yoke, signifying that Jeremiah is wrong, and that Babylon's rule will be quickly broken. Jeremiah happily expresses the hope that Hananiah is right (28.6). Nevertheless, he shortly reappears, wearing a yoke of iron, unbreakable.

Yet not all enacted prophecy is mere play-acting. It is not

necessarily superficial demonstration. The action used may be something that affects the prophet deeply and personally. If Hosea's marriage really comes into the category of prophetic enactment then we can see that such actions are not lightly undertaken. Jeremiah's buying of the field, in chapter *32*, is such an action. It does not merely *symbolize* confidence in the future, it is a real and active *expression* of such confidence. The prophet is 'putting his money where his mouth is', showing that he really means what he is saying about the prospects for the future.

And just as Hosea's marriage is making a prophetic point, so Jeremiah's refusal to marry makes a prophetic point likewise (*16*.1–4). As his buying of the field expresses his optimism when disaster finally strikes, his refusal to marry expresses his much earlier conviction about the inevitability of that disaster. So sure is he, in the early part of his career, that destruction must come, that he refrains from marriage on the grounds that a wife and children would only be destined for trouble and death.

Here we are going beyond enacted prophecy as a simple matter of dramatic symbolism; the prophet's unmarried state is a permanent reminder of his convictions. The prophet's convictions are controlling not just his utterances but his whole life. The man has become the message.

Even more than is the case with Hosea, Jeremiah's entire life and character are a parable, a living out of the message he proclaims. He not only announces his people's destruction, he suffers that destruction in his own person. 'For the wound of the daughter of my people is my heart wounded' (*8*.21). He not only speaks of their rejection of God, he experiences that rejection in his own soul. No one listened to Jeremiah until it was much too late. 'He was despised and rejected of men, a man of sorrows and acquainted with grief; and as one from whom men hide their faces he was despised, and we esteemed him not.' Yet at last they realized that he had been right. His words are only here in the Bible because he was vindicated by events. 'Out of the travail of his soul he saw light, and was satisfied.' (On the possible connexion between Jeremiah and Is. *53*, see below, p. 153.)

Perhaps this is why Jeremiah sees no need of expiatory sacrifice, that he sees his own sufferings as in some way expiatory, 'making his soul an offering for sin'. If he has nothing to say about mediators this may be because he is himself a mediator, bearing in his own body the tension between God and his world. Of all Christ's forerunners, perhaps it is in Jeremiah that the word most nearly becomes flesh.

## EZEKIEL

### Historical background

Ezekiel's career began before Jeremiah's ended. According to his book Ezekiel was among the people carried into captivity after Jerusalem's *first* fall to the Babylonians, i.e. in 597. It was there, in exile, that he received his call to be a prophet, and he exercised his ministry entirely from Babylonia. (GBS, Chapter 10, i and Chapter 23, e.)

In fact, some scholars have doubted the accuracy of the book on this point. Many of Ezekiel's prophecies are directed not to his fellow exiles but to the community of Jews left at home, and in making these prophecies Ezekiel seems to exhibit a remarkably detailed knowledge of what was happening in Jerusalem. So detailed is his knowledge, claim some, that he must really have been there in Jerusalem. Either he did not go to Babylon as early as 597 or he must have been allowed to make a return visit.

Whether we find this argument convincing or not, the fact remains that Ezekiel's attention is directed very much towards the community in Jerusalem. Between 597 and 586, the two deportations, he speaks like an old-fashioned prophet of doom. The events of 597 have not exhausted God's wrath, and the people in any case have learnt nothing from them. The real disaster is still to come. Jeremiah was saying something very similar at the same time.

After 586 he changes his tune completely. There was evidence that the people *had* learnt something at last. Indeed, they had taken the prophetic message so much to heart, belatedly, that they were inclined to despair. Ezekiel's message is now one of comfort and restoration.

### Ezekiel the man

Ezekiel therefore stands astride the exile. He looks both

forward and backward. He is first a pre-exilic prophet, delivering the same sort of message as other pre-exilic prophets. But in the latter half of his career he is a prophet of the exilic period itself, and his new message sets the tone for the prophets who were to come after him.

In some ways he is not only quite typical of pre-exilic prophets, but his work displays some of prophecy's most primitive features. There is little mention of prophetic ecstasy in Amos, Hosea, Isaiah or Jeremiah, but Ezekiel goes into prophetic trances like an old-fashioned seer. Enacted prophecy, which had already made something of a comeback under Jeremiah, is frequently, and elaborately, exhibited by Ezekiel. He indulges in all sorts of odd behaviour.

In chapter 4 we have a very extended piece of play-acting in which the prophet first of all does something like playing toy soldiers, using a brick to represent the city, and then laying siege to it with ramps and battering rams. He then lies down on his left side for three hundred and ninety days, and on his right side for forty days, to signify the number of years of the punishment of Israel and Judah respectively. All this time he lives on the kind of food to which a besieged people might be reduced, and rations himself strictly, as a besieged people must do.

In chapter 5 we have another strange action, in which the prophet cuts off all his hair. Some of the hair he burns; some he slashes with a sword, and some he scatters to the wind. A very little of the hair he takes carefully and sews into the hem of his coat. All this is to represent the fate of the people of Judah.

But as an exilic prophet Ezekiel has characteristics not shared with any of his predecessors. He strongly emphasizes the cult; the temple and its sacrificial ritual are very important to him. He also stresses the law, especially the ritual law, as the basis of God's relations with his people. His visions also display features foreshadowing even later developments, for they have something in common with the visions of the apocalyptic writers.

Ezekiel is a dual character in another respect. Much of his interest in law and cult can be explained by the fact that he is not only a prophet but a priest. Now Jeremiah, too, was a priest, but his work reflects little of priestly interests. Ezekiel, unlike Jeremiah, belonged to the Jerusalem priesthood, and priestly interests affect his thinking in very important ways.

## Ezekiel as a communicator

Ezekiel is perhaps the least popular of the major prophets. Most modern readers of the Bible react unsympathetically to him. There are several reasons for this. Ezekiel's style does not endear him to most of us. Earlier prophets tend to express themselves crisply, in fairly short oracles and vivid images. In Ezekiel the images are there, but he often elaborates them in ways that for the modern reader make them less, and not more compelling. And the short, direct oracle is often replaced by rather wordy argument.

His preoccupations, too, are not ones which attract many of us to him. Many readers are unsympathetic to his interest in the cult and in religious rules, especially the rules of 'uncleanness'. He is indeed so strongly repelled by uncleanness that he cannot stop talking about it.

Ezekiel seems to have difficulty in communicating emotion and feeling. To this extent his written words must seriously misrepresent him, for he is clearly a man of very strong emotions. His manner and his language alienate us at every turn, which is a pity, because the content of what he has to say is of enormous importance.

As an example of the differences between Ezekiel and his prophetic colleagues let us look at the way he handles a typical prophetic theme, that of the unfaithful wife. Hosea's treatment of the theme, as we saw, is full of difficulties and obscurities. And yet, remarkably, its impact is powerful. What comes across is Hosea's emotional *involvement* with his wife, and God's with his people; the anger, as well as the hurt at the betrayal; the tenderness of desire to restore her; the aching for some sign of response to the husband's love.

Ezekiel's use of the same theme is based fairly closely on Jeremiah's. Jeremiah, in chapter 3, has a collection of oracles around the theme of the family, looking at the notion of Israel the adulteress and the faithless children from different angles. The main point is condemnatory, and yet in spite of this, something other than the feeling of condemnation shines through. There is the same yearning for a response which we found in Hosea.

Ezekiel's chapter *23* is basically an expansion of the short oracle in Jer. *3*.6–11, about the Lord's love for his two wives, Israel and Judah. From the point of view of the modern reader it is a pity that the parable is about a polygamous marriage, for our tradition makes it hard at the outset to envisage the feelings of a man with a genuine and legitimate sexual relationship with two women at once. But apart from this, the whole tone of Ezekiel's description is cold. The divine husband in chapter 23 may show *concern* for his delinquent wives, but there is little sign of *affection*. And the whole point of the passage is that it prophesies the judgment of the adulteresses, not their redemption.

It is interesting to compare this with the very brief mention which we have of Ezekiel's own marriage. We are told simply that when his wife died, 'the delight of his eyes', he was forbidden by God to mourn for her. This was another piece of enacted prophecy. Yet in the very bare words with which Ezekiel describes the incident we glimpse a man who knows what love is, and whose grief is greater because he cannot weep (*24*.15–18).

In Ezek. *16* we have perhaps Ezekiel's most impressive piece of sustained writing. This is a remarkable extended parable, which manages to combine both the theme of the erring wife and that of the delinquent child. It is a parable about a foundling girl, new born and abandoned, discovered by the roadside and given a home by the Lord. The child is taken and cared for, and grows up to be a beautiful girl. The Lord then marries her and lavishes on her everything she could want. But she betrays him and turns to harlotry. About half the chapter is taken up with accounts of the girl's condemnation and punishment.

There are several points to note here, all of which are highly significant for our understanding of Ezekiel and his message. Ezekiel makes it clear that the relationship between the child and the father is an adoptive, not a natural one. The child is alien (she comes from Canaan, and has an Amorite for a father and a Hittite for a mother—*16*.2). She has no worth and nothing to commend her. The prophet stresses how the foundling was lying there, unwashed from its birth, its

afterbirth still attached. In us these details excite pity.
Ezekiel probably meant them to excite revulsion. He wants
to stress that the girl is unattractive from the very beginning,
and that if the Lord takes her and lets her live it is an act of
pure grace.

But between the child and her rescuer there is no natural
bond. In spite of all he does for her there is little evidence in
the prophet's words of any *affection* which the Lord feels for
her. And when the time comes for punishment there is no sign
of tension in the mind of the father/husband/judge. There is
nothing corresponding to Hosea's cry: 'How can I give you
up, O Ephraim?' (Hos. *11*.8–9). Jeremiah makes rather small
use of the father-child image, but when he does do so he
exploits it in the same way as Hosea, to show how the father's
feelings are torn in two by the need to punish. Jer. *31*.20 is
almost uncanny in its resemblance to the words of Hosea: 'Is
Ephraim my dear son? Is he my darling child? For as often as I
speak against him, I do remember him still. Therefore my
heart yearns for him; I will surely have mercy on him.' If the
Lord in Ezekiel's parable has such feelings he keeps them
very well under control.

The girl later *becomes* attractive, but the prophet goes out
of his way to emphasize that her beauty is not something
which she has acquired naturally. She owes it to the fact that
the Lord has fed her on fine food and endowed her with
beautiful clothes and jewellery. The foundling never at any
time possessed anything of worth, or any attraction, that she
had not been given.

Neither was there ever a time when she was faithful. Hosea
and Jeremiah, when they use the image of the divine marriage, look back to a blissful honeymoon period. They
remember the devotion of Israel's youth, her love as a bride
(Jer. *2*.2; cf. Hos. *2*.14–15). Ezekiel mentions no such period.
The girl was never anything but corrupt. This fits in with his
other accounts of Israel's spiritual history. It is throughout,
according to Ezekiel, a history of failure and betrayal (cf.
chapter *20*).

Ezekiel therefore, even when he is employing these most
tender of images, does not employ them to express tenderness. He stresses the divine grace; but even grace, as he
presents it, has a hard edge to it. He may not be a man

incapable of feeling, but he is certainly a man who does not readily *express* feeling; or at any rate, not in his writing.

## Ezekiel's view of God

Ezekiel offers us a God somewhat in his own image. He may have men's interests at heart, but he is remote. Ezekiel emphasizes his grace, but it is the grace of condescending majesty rather than of love. The clearest indications of Ezekiel's view of God are found in the account of his call, in chapters *1–3*.

Our first impression of this account, and the vision which accompanies it, is that it is quite different from anything else in prophetic literature. But let us be quite clear where the differences lie. What Ezekiel describes is a vision of the Lord enthroned. But does not Isaiah in Is. *6* describe exactly the same? But whereas Isaiah is content to say 'I saw the Lord, high and lifted up, seated upon a throne', and goes on to sketch some impression of how his train filled the temple and what his seraphic attendants looked like, Ezekiel tries to set down *in detail* exactly how the throne was constructed and what the cherubim were like. His attempt at accuracy in fact only leads to obscurity, though not all of this is the prophet's fault. It is partly due to our ignorance of the rather technical vocabulary in which he describes the machinery of the throne which is also a chariot. The difference, we conclude, between Isaiah and Ezekiel may not be in the nature of the vision, but in the nature of the description.

Be that as it may, the element of awe in Ezekiel's experience of God is unmistakable, though whether Ezekiel's wordy attempt to convey it is more successful than Isaiah's more succinct one is debatable.

Men's view of God is inevitably coloured by the human institutions with which they are familiar. The Yahwistic writer (J) lived in the early days of Israel's monarchy, when her king was still little more than a tribal sheikh, not at all intimidating and fairly approachable by his subjects. And though the Yahwist is not unacquainted with the terror of holiness, for the most part he describes a God who is not unlike a tribal sheikh either, and who may drop in on a man in the cool of the evening, and share his hospitality.

Ezekiel lives in Babylonia, and his acquaintance with kingship is quite different. He knows of the Great King, the King of kings, the king of Babylon, who cannot be approached in person by his subjects. Even a determined man with plenty of money for bribes who wished to speak with him might get no further than his under-secretary's forty-third assistant secretary. Such a Great King was rarely seen at all by his people, except when he might hold audience, surrounded by hundreds of his attendants, or when at the great festivals he exercised his divine office and was carried in procession on his throne.

It is such kingship that provides Ezekiel's model for the kingship of God, and it is the processions, when the gods were carried in great splendour around the city, and ensconced again in their sanctuaries, surrounded and guarded by 'cherubs' (winged compound beasts with human faces), which have provided him with much of the imagery of his call vision.

Note that the call itself takes place in Babylonia. God is quite capable of calling a man to prophesy when he is not in his own land of Palestine. And the throne of God itself is mobile. It is chariot as well as throne. Isaiah saw God's glory in the temple at Jerusalem. And later in Ezekiel's book the glory of the Lord returns from the east, and again fills that temple (43.1–3). But for the time being the glory is in Babylonia, and no whit diminished.

Note also the devices which Ezekiel uses to 'distance' God. Isaiah and Amos say, 'I saw the Lord'. They, and many other prophets, say bluntly that the Lord spoke to them. Ezekiel uses much more roundabout language. Ezekiel admits only to seeing 'the appearance of the likeness of the Lord's glory', and he will be no more precise than that he 'heard the sound of one speaking' (1.28). Here again we have a feature in Ezekiel which points forward to later things, for in later Judaism this indirectness of speech became characteristic. So much apart was God from men that it was felt improper to speak of him more directly.

Perhaps this need to 'distance' God helps to explain another feature of Ezekiel's visions. Although at his call he hears 'the sound of one speaking', and we take it that the 'one' was actually the deity himself (though Ezekiel doesn't like to say so), in his other visions there is usually an intermediary.

He does not converse with God directly, but with someone 'who had the appearance of a man' (*8*.2); or with 'a man clothed in linen' (*10*.6); or, 'a man whose appearance was like brass' (*40*.3). The idea that God might communicate with his prophets through an angel was not a new one (we find it, for example, in the Elijah stories; 1 Kings *19*.4–8), but it was not common before Ezekiel's time. The prophets' contact with God is thought of as being too direct to need such mediators. But in post-exilic prophecy and in the apocalyptic writings it becomes a standard device. The prophet may see the vision for himself, but he usually has to have a heavenly interpreter to tell him what it means.

### Sin and grace in Ezekiel

One of the first things that is likely to strike the modern reader about Ezekiel's ideas on sin is that he makes no distinction between moral and ritual offences. He is not, of course, unusual in this. Old Testament law codes in general, including the ten commandments, mix moral and religious commands together with apparently no thought of incongruity. But Ezekiel does it in a more striking way, throwing together, as if they were of equal seriousness, accusations of murder, robbery, failure to be charitable to the poor, idolatry, and lack of care about contact with ritual 'uncleanness'.

Although there are parallels in the *laws* to this lack of discriminiation it is by no means characteristic of other *prophets*. It is doubtless to Ezekiel's priestly background that we must ascribe the weight he gives to ritual offences.

It is likely that if we were able to put the question to him Ezekiel would agree that murder and the perversion of justice really are more important and reprehensible than sleeping with one's wife at the time of her menstrual flow. The reason for his apparent failure to discriminate between different sins is that he has such a powerful doctrine of God's holiness. If man is to stand before the holy God then *no* impurity, however trivial, can be tolerated. *Any* defilement, small or great, renders a man unfit for God's service, so to that extent all defilements are serious.

In the first part of his career Ezekiel faced the same problem as the other pre-exilic prophets, that people would not

listen, that they would not take his condemnations of sin
seriously enough. But after the catastrophe of 586 he faces
the opposite difficulty. Events have so convinced them of the
gravity of their sins that they find it hard to believe the offer of
salvation.

The reaction is understandable. Prophets at least from the
eighth century onwards had been castigating the nation for its
unfaithfulness and had been predicting disaster. When the
disaster at last happened the people were convinced that they
were suffering not only for their own sins but for those of their
fathers. Ezekiel himself had added force to this feeling by
stressing that Israel never had been faithful. Sin had, as it
were, been piling up for generations. On the head of this
particular generation it had chosen to come crashing down.
They were ready enough to repent of their own sins. The
problem was, how could their repentance wipe out that great
backlog of wrongdoing carried over from former generations? The fathers had eaten sour grapes, but it was the
children's teeth that were set on edge. This was a proverb
current at the time, Jeremiah refers to it as well as Ezekiel. It
sums up the attitude outlined above (Ezek. *18*.2; Jer. *31*.29).

Ezekiel replies to this objection very carefully and at some
length. His answer is in chapter 18. He traces the history of
three generations of men, from father, to son, to grandson,
and asserts that each gets the reward or punishment of his
own virtues or misdeeds. The wicked son gets no credit for his
father's virtues. The son's wrongdoing is not held against the
grandson. It is often said that Ezekiel is stressing *individual*
responsibility here, but that is not quite true. He frames his
illustration in terms of the lives of individuals, but the point he
is making is about *generations*. Each *generation* must stand on
its own moral feet, and take responsibility for its own actions.

And no generation is entitled to despair and to say, 'We
have made our mistakes, we must accept the consequences',
for repentance is always possible. 'When the wicked man
turns away from the wickedness that he has committed, and
does that which is lawful and right, he shall surely live' (Ezek.
*18*.21).

Now there can be no doubt that if we take Ezekiel's words
at their face value they amount to an overstatement of his
case. He seems to be suggesting that no one ever suffers for

the sins of someone else; that parents' mistakes do not have any ill effect on their children, and that children's wrongdoing does not hurt their parents. All of us know that this is far from the truth. No man is an island. We suffer for each other's sins all the time, and also benefit from each other's virtues. If we had put it to him, there is no doubt that Ezekiel would not have denied this. But God from of old has given his preachers licence to overstate their case where they think necessary. And never is it more justified than when it is needed to give men hope, and to assure them of the possibility of salvation. Ezekiel's contemporaries needed hope; they needed to be assured that if they repented of their own sins, that was enough for God.

The teaching of Ezek. *18* cannot therefore be universalized, not just as it stands. Nothing could illustrate better the necessity of seeing a prophet's teaching against the background of his own times. The truth of Ezek. *18* was the truth that that particular set of people, at that particular time, needed to hear. If it were put to other people, at another time, it might have to be put very differently. Indeed, Ezekiel himself, preaching to the same people only a very few years earlier was giving them a very different message.

In fact, when God does forgive, it is not at all evident that he waits for repentance. The end of chapter *16*, the parable of the foundling, comes round to the subject of restoration and forgiveness of the unfaithful girl, and Ezekiel expresses himself in a rather curious way. On the one hand he makes the forgiveness look rather grudging, and in the final verse of the chapter seems to suggest that its sole object is to make the recipient feel even more ashamed of herself. And yet it is clear that restoration happens first, and the response is hoped for later. It is also clear, in *16.59–60*, that God is keeping his half of the covenant even though Israel has broken hers.

At other places Ezekiel keeps emphasizing that when God saves he does so 'for his own sake', or 'for the sake of his name'. Again, the way Ezekiel puts it tends to make a bad impression on the reader. He *seems* to be saying that God only saves Israel in order to protect his own reputation, but that may not be what he really means. More probably, he is trying to tell us that God saves Israel not because of what *she* is, but because of what *he* is. He saves, not because Israel even yet deserves salvation, but because he is that sort of God.

Though Ezekiel does not, like Jeremiah, speak of the corruption of the will or suggest the impossibility of repentance, he does assume that if Israel is to be saved it must be by God's initiative, not Israel's, and he does borrow Jeremiah's image of the new heart. Like Jeremiah, therefore, he sees the necessity for God to remake his people's mind and will if the future is to be better than the past (*36*.26 f.).

The change of emphasis between Ezekiel and earlier prophecy is brought out by comparing three texts (Is. *1*.16, Jer. *2*.22 and Ezek. *36*.25). Isaiah puts the responsibility on the people: 'Wash yourselves, make yourselves clean.' Jeremiah sees that this is ineffective: 'Though you wash yourselves with lye, and use much soap, the stain of your guilt is still before me.' Ezekiel's answer is to shift the responsibility and initiative to God: '*I* will sprinkle clean water upon you, and you shall be clean.'

And note that for Ezekiel it is not a matter of *washing*, which is a word that belongs to the bathroom, but of *sprinkling*, which belongs to the sanctuary. More than any prophet who was before him, Ezekiel sees the point of cultic expiation, and of sacrifice. The earlier prophets are primarily moralists, which is to say that they see it as *man's* responsibility to behave himself, and to meet God's requirements. And what God does require is that he should 'do justly, love mercy, and walk humbly with his God' (Mic. *6*.8). Jeremiah sees the deficiencies of this approach, that man is not necessarily *able* to meet the divine demand in all its rigour, but he does not turn to the cult for the solution to the problem. Ezekiel, prophet and priest, does just that. He does not deny the need for moral seriousness, but he perceives that where men still fall short God has provided offering and sacrifice, whereby he may be satisfied.

## The place of encounter and atonement

For Ezekiel the presence of God is associated strongly with the temple. Yet as we have seen, God's presence is not *confined* to the temple. God's throne is wherever his people are. If they are in exile then in exile he can be encountered. When Ezekiel, in a vision, visits Jerusalem (Ezek. *8–11*) the throne chariot is there too. But it does not remain there. The temple is where the presence belongs, but it will not permanently return until the temple is renewed.

Chapters *40–48* of the book of Ezekiel describe a vision which the prophet had, in which he saw the restored temple. The first three of these chapters describe in some detail the temple itself. The writer then goes on to say something about the arrangements for worship and the rules governing priesthood. In chapter 47 he speaks of the river of life which will flow from the temple, and ends with detailed observations about the way the land of Palestine is to be divided up.

These chapters are problematical in many ways, and it is doubted by some scholars whether the prophet himself is responsible for them. Whether they really come from his pen or not, comparison of them with other parts of the book confirms that they do represent his outlook. Though parts of them make tedious reading, they are the quarry from which the author of the book of Revelation dug much of his imagery, and will repay study on that account alone. If they do represent Ezekiel's mind, then we can say without doubt that for him the temple is central. The new community which he foresees is a community centred on the temple and its ritual.

In Britain, when the Queen visits a military establishment, very elaborate preparations are made. Rooms and utensils, some of which the Queen will never see, are carefully cleaned, and, so popular legend has it, someone is even detailed to whitewash the coal. We may doubt whether the soldier who whitewashes the coal is spending his time well, and yet appreciate the feelings which prompt him to do so. Where *such* a guest is expected, can any trouble be too great? Ezekiel's elaborate specifications for the restored temple have something of the same feeling about them. His exact measurements of gateways, doorposts, thresholds, and his counting of steps, seem to us superfluous. But Ezekiel is preparing for a visitor, and everything must be *exactly* right. The climax comes in *43.1–5*, when the glory of the God of Israel comes from the east, the sound of his coming is like the sound of many waters, and the earth shines with his glory. The glory of the Lord enters the temple by the eastern gate; and the glory of the Lord fills the temple. The sovereign is again in residence.

Whatever may be said about Ezekiel's alleged individualism, his hope for the future is here expressed in terms of a restored and purified *community*, with God at its heart.

In his attention to details of the temple and its ritual Ezekiel is typical of post-exilic Judaism. Disregard of God's requirements had led to the punishment of exile. Hereafter nothing must be left to chance. Whether in moral matters or purely ritual ones, everything must be specified, and all specifications rigidly adhered to. Only so can Israel be certain that she does not offend.

### Hope in Ezekiel

Much of what needs to be said about Ezekiel's hope for the future has already been covered in other connexions. His hope for the community is bound up with the restoration and proper operation of the temple and its rites. His hope for his sinful people is expressed in images of renewal, of which we have already noted that of the new heart and the new spirit (36.26).

Chapter 37 offers us another striking vision, the vision of the valley of dry bones. Again, the object of this account is to encourage. The people were convinced that, now the temple had been destroyed and the best of the populace taken into exile, the nation was at an end. It was effectively dead. They saw no hope of recovery. Their hope was lost, they were clean cut off (37.11). The bones in Ezekiel's vision are a nation, or an army, and they are very dead indeed. 'Behold, they were *very* dry' (37.2). Can such bones live? The answer of the vision is that they can. They are called to life first of all by the word (which the prophet himself speaks—37.4 f.) and by the spirit. (The spirit of God is more prominent in Ezekiel's work than in that of any other prophet.)

It should be appreciated that this chapter has nothing at all to say about resurrection from the dead. The vision is not talking about the resurrection of individuals, but about the restoration of a nation. Within fifty years this hope of Ezekiel's for the restoration of the nation had, basically, been fulfilled.

### The watchman

John Wesley directed his helpers to 'preach as dying men to

dying men'. In doing so he reminded them that the preacher himself is a man under judgment. He shares the predicament of his hearers, and needs as much as they do the salvation which he announces to them. Now all the prophets display a strong sympathy with those to whom they speak, though some more than others. Even Amos, perhaps the least obviously sympathetic, claims to have prayed for Israel, to turn away disasters from them. Hosea and Jeremiah make no secret of the fact that their prophecies of disaster cut into their own souls. But even so, these prophets preach like righteous men preaching to sinners. The conviction that they are themselves men under judgment is never clearly articulated.

The only exception, before Ezekiel, to this general observation is Isaiah. Isaiah at his call recognizes himself as needing the purification to which he summons his nation. He is 'a man of unclean lips' dwelling 'in the midst of a people of unclean lips' (Is. 6.5). He knows that he cannot convert unless he is converted. Isaiah at his call also faces up to another problem. He faces the fact that he is being called to proclaim a message to which people will not listen. He solves it in 6.9 ff. (if solution it is) by accepting that his people's refusal to listen is all part of the plan. God *intends* them not to pay attention, until their punishment is complete. For us this answer raises more questions than it answers.

Ezekiel's parable of the watchman neatly brings together *both* the issues raised in Is. 6, the issue of the prophet's own salvation and that of the recalcitrance of his hearers. Though Ezekiel does not spell it out in so many words it is clear that he has thought of the commonsense answer to the problem of the audience that will not listen. If he knows at the start that they are not going to listen, why should he waste his time talking to them?

The commonsense answer is no answer, decides Ezekiel, because it ignores the matter of the prophet's own salvation. The prophet is a watchman (Ezek. 3.16–21, 33.1–9). The watchman's job is to warn of the enemy's approach. If he delivers his warning and no one pays attention and the city is destroyed, that is *their* fault. But if he says: 'No one is going to listen anyway, so why should I bother to deliver any warning?' the destruction will be the same, but this time it will be *his* fault.

The prophet's preaching, regardless of any effect it may have or fail to have on its hearers, is an expression of *his* obedience to God. To that extent, then, it is not even his business to *ask* whether anyone is listening. The prophet's business is to preach. The *response* to the preaching is for God to worry about. In a situation of that sort, where a whole people (apparently) is unresponsive to the divine will, it is something if only the prophet himself is responding. Their failure cannot excuse his. It does not improve the situation for the prophet himself to jump on the bandwagon of their disobedience.

There is, of course, a further answer to the problem, which Ezekiel does not mention, but which is at least hinted at in Elijah's experience in 1 Kings *19* (see especially v. 18) and is developed more fully in Jesus's parable of the sower. This further answer says that not only is the response God's business and not the preacher's, but that the response is always likely to be infinitely bigger than the preacher knows or hopes.

## DEUTERO-ISAIAH

'Deutero-Isaiah' or 'Second Isaiah' is the name we give to the prophet who was responsible for chapters 40–55 of the book of Isaiah. We know that these chapters were not the work of the eighth-century Isaiah, because the historical situation which they presuppose is quite different. They reflect the period around the end of the exile. By this time the Babylonian empire which had overthrown Judah was itself under threat. From the east was coming the conqueror Cyrus, who was busy founding the new Persian empire. He was known to have a very liberal policy towards conquered peoples and Deutero-Isaiah hails him as a great deliverer who will conquer Babylon and set God's people free and restore them to their land. He even greets Cyrus as God's messiah (anointed)—*45*.1.[1] Cyrus did in fact take over Babylon in 538 (though much more peacefully than 2-Isaiah seems to have expected), and very shortly afterwards he did allow the Jews to return to their homeland. (GBS, Chapter 10, i; Chapter 23, c.).

[1] Cf. also *41*.2, *42*.25, *44*.28.

It seems most probable that the first half of Deutero-Isaiah's work, up to chapter *48*, was produced in Babylon, when Cyrus was already active but before 538. It expresses high hopes. The second half, *49–55*, seems to reflect the years just after 538, when some of the Jews had already returned home. There is a note of disappointment in these later chapters. The more extravagant expectations had not been fulfilled. Cyrus is never even mentioned in this second half. The very first chapter of 2-Isaiah, chapter *40*, may have been written last of all, as an introduction to the entire work. It gathers up themes from both halves of 2-Isaiah.

It is generally assumed that 2-Isaiah really was a 'writing prophet' in the sense that he wrote down his words himself. These chapters do not consist of short oracles, as earlier prophetic books largely do, but of long poems in which the prophet's themes are intertwined in intricate patterns.

## The personality of the prophet

Of the prophet himself we know nothing. We do not even know his name. He gives us no account of his call, mentions no single incident in his life, and tells us nothing of how his message was received; i.e. no descriptions of visions or other communications. All we have is his message.

## The person of God in Deutero-Isaiah

Deutero-Isaiah produced his prophecy in Babylon, where he would be very familiar with the splendid worship of the Babylonian gods. The most striking aspects of Babylonian religion were its great festivals and pageants, when the images of the gods were carried in procession along ceremonial highways, and when priests indulged in elaborate rituals to determine whether the coming year would be prosperous or not. Indeed, the casting of oracles to discover the future was a very prominent feature of Babylonian religion throughout.

For the prophet, the worship of the true God involves a denial of nearly everything that the Babylonians understood by 'religion'. The Holy One of Israel is all that the Babylonian gods are not.

First, and most emphatically, there is only one of him. 'I am

God, and there is no other' (45.22). 2-Isaiah states the sole existence of God in an uncompromising way that goes far beyond what any earlier prophet or writer had said. Earlier prophets leave us in no doubt that Yahweh is the only God whom Israel *ought to worship*. They clearly imply that he is the only God who is *worth worshipping*. But they never give us an unmistakable statement that other gods *do not exist*. Typical of earlier prophets is Elijah's attitude on Mount Carmel (1 Kings *18*). In his contest with the prophets of Baal he does not say that there is no such person as Baal. He proves, rather, that Baal is powerless; that Baal can be insulted with impunity; that for practical purposes Baal can be ignored. He shows that Baal does not matter. This is what we might call '*practical* monotheism'. Elijah is prepared to *behave* as though Baal did not exist, though he might not have assented to that statement as a theoretical proposition. But for 2-Isaiah, both in practice and in theory, 'I am the first and I am the last; besides me there is no god' (*44*.6; cf. *43*.10).

He stresses God's *incomparability*. We cannot say what God is like, because he is unique, and therefore not like anything else whatever. He is therefore totally unlike these other so-called gods. 'I am God, and there is no other; I am God, and there is none like me' (*46*.9).

But the second consequence of God's incomparability is that it is futile to make images and idols. Much of 2-Isaiah's criticism of idolators is not of a very profound kind. No idolator ever identified his god with his image in the way which 2-Isaiah assumes. For real idol-worshippers the image *symbolizes* the god, helps to make god real to the worshipper. But 2-Isaiah conveniently ignores this and enjoys himself poking fun at gods made of wood or metal. A typical passage is *44*.9–20. He describes how idols are made, and suggests that the skill and creativity of the craftsmen who make them are far superior to any creative powers the idols themselves possess. He mocks the carpenter who cannot see the incongruity of lighting a fire to warm himself and cook his dinner, and out of the same piece of firewood salvaging a piece to make a god.

He mocks the idols further because they have to be carried in their processions, and end by being carried away by conquerors, ignominiously. Either way, they are simply a burden on the backs of weary beasts. They have no power to move about of their own accord, or even stand upright. Yet men appeal to them for help. The prophet contrasts them with Israel's God, who needs no carrying, but himself bears his people, has carried them and will carry them from birth to death (46.1–4).

The idol-gods therefore cannot carry anyone, and cannot *save* (45.20). This is what a god was really *for*. He was meant to be able to save those who served him. But there is only one saviour: 'I, I am the Lord, and besides me there is no saviour' (43.11; cf. 45.21).

Above all, the idols cannot say what will happen in the future. This was the most insulting thing which 2-Isaiah could say about the Babylonian gods, for prediction was supposed to be their strong point. In 41.21–29 the prophet challenges the gods. Let them declare what is to happen next, so that we can check and see whether their predictive powers are real! They have consistently failed in the past to predict important events. In particular, they failed to predict the rise of Cyrus. In 45.21 he repeats the challenge, and asserts that, by contrast with the idols, Israel's Lord did foresee and did predict through his prophets the events which are now taking place. (Cf. 44.7.)

Thus does 2-Isaiah, faced with the most impressive religion of the most powerful empire of his day, declare its splendour to be hollow and its gods a sham. Babylon looked as if she controlled the world, but the real control was exercised by the God of the tiny subject people, Israel.

## Images of creation and redemption

The imagery in which 2-Isaiah speaks of God's salvation is markedly different from that of the prophets before him. Once, at least, he refers to the old prophetic theme of the unfaithful wife, but only to deny that the relationship between God and his bride has ever been finally disrupted. 'Where is the certificate of your mother's divorce?' he asks the Israelites. It cannot be produced, is the implication. The relationship, in spite of appearances, has never been ended. Separation, perhaps; divorce, never! (50.1; cf. 54.5–7).

The images which 2-Isaiah does use, of creating, making,

forming, calling, redeeming, are not used separately. The themes are intertwined, overlying each other, appearing and reappearing in a complex pattern rather like the themes in polyphonic music (which is a sort of musical knitting).

A typical text is 43.7, which speaks of Israel as those who are 'called by my name; whom I created for my glory; whom I formed and made'. God is Israel's originator. He is responsible for her existence. He called Israel. But that does not mean simply that he summoned her. He actually called her into existence. 'To call', therefore, for 2-Isaiah, is to create. We are very close here to the thinking of the Priestly writer (who must in fact have been a near contemporary of the prophet). It is the Priestly writer's account of creation which speaks of God summoning things into being by his Word. (Cf. what 2-Isaiah says about the power of the divine word in 55.10–11.) The very word 'create' is a characteristic word of the Priestly writer. The words 'form' and 'make' are equally characteristic of the Yahwist's creation account. 2-Isaiah is thus picking up themes from several other writers in order to produce his own unique way of speaking.

44.1–2 introduces another idea in parallel with that of creation. Israel is not only the one whom God made and formed, but the one whom he *chose*. Now the verb 'to choose' is one of the Deuteronomist's favourites, and 2-Isaiah presses that into service too. But for 2-Isaiah, God's choosing of Israel is not a matter of looking at a row of existing nations and picking one out for himself. Israel did not actually exist as a people until she was chosen. She was *created* by being chosen. 'Choose', 'call', 'create' are all ways of speaking about the same activity.

The other great theme which in 2-Isaiah runs parallel to those of making, creating and calling is that of *redeeming*. In order to understand what the Old Testament means by redemption we must grasp a few facts about the way in which Israel's legal system operated. In those ancient times there was no police force. If a man suffered a wrong, it was up to him and his kinsmen to bring the wrongdoer to justice. If the man himself was charged with an offence, it was up to his kinsmen to support him in court. If a man was murdered, and thus no longer able to gain redress for himself, it was the kinsmen's job to secure vengeance. The nearest kinsman, on whom the burden principally fell, was called the *go'el*, which is generally translated, 'the redeemer'. This 'redeemer' had the duty to maintain the family's honour and integrity. If a man became poor, so that he was obliged to sell his land, the *go'el*, if he had at all the means to do so, was meant to step in and redeem it. If a man became so poor that he was obliged to sell himself into debt slavery, the *go'el* was meant to redeem the man himself; i.e. to buy him back. The 'redeemer', therefore, is the one who restores persons and property to where they rightly belong. He is the vindicator of his poorer kinsmen. We have already seen Jeremiah acting as a *go'el* (Jer. *32*), exercising the right of redemption by buying a field from his cousin Hanamel. In the book of Ruth, Boaz not only does the kinsman's duty by buying up Naomi's property but exercises another of the kinsman's ancient rights (more rarely appealed to in the Old Testament) of marrying the widow of his deceased and childless relative.

There was a second tier to this system. The king was meant to function as a sort of 'universal redeemer', who took up the cause of those of his subjects who were unfortunate enough to have no strong kinsman of their own to turn to. And if even the king failed, or if the king himself became the oppressor, then behind him and above him stood God, whose redeeming arm was strong enough for all eventualities. It is likely that those who wrote the book of Kings saw the death of Jezebel and the end of Ahab's house as such a 'redemptive' act, i.e. an act of God the Kinsman, avenging the blood of Naboth.

For 2-Isaiah God is Israel's redeemer. She belonged to him, for she had been created, formed, made, called and chosen by him. But now she is in slavery, captive in Babylon. But God can be relied on to do his kinsman's duty and restore her. Sometimes the prophet speaks as if God would buy his people back. In *43*.3 he offers Egypt and Ethiopia as a ransom for her, At others he sees God scorning to trade with the oppressor and threatening to deliver Israel by force. He will 'send to Babylon, and break down all the bars' (*43*.14, RSV). Cyrus, his anointed (*45*.1) will set them free 'not for price or reward' (*45*.13). They were 'sold for nothing', they 'shall be redeemed without money' (*52*.3).

All these creating, calling, choosing and redeeming activities of God are for 2-Isaiah merely different aspects of the one divine activity. He can speak of each of them in terms of the others. *51*.9–11 is a characteristic text. He speaks of God's creative work, using, astonishingly, a piece of pagan mythology. God is the one who 'cut Rahab (the old chaos-monster) in pieces', and built the world by dividing her watery body. But God's first great act of salvation, too, is one of dividing the waters, 'the waters of the great deep', for the redeemed to pass over. So the prophet makes the transition to speaking of the exodus for both creation and exodus are variations on the one theme of dividing the waters. And after God has brought his people through the sea, what do we expect him to do next? To lead them through the wilderness, of course. And this is exactly what God is about to do now, to lead his people back from exile, through the wilderness. Thus are God's great acts tied together, and thus are his ancient acts made the grounds for faith in his future salvation. Old exodus and new exodus are compared again in *48*.20–21. There was no thirsting in the desert last time, nor will there be this time. But the new deliverance will be even better than the old one, for this time they 'will not go out in haste' (*52*.12). It will not be an escape, but a triumphal procession.

## Hope in Deutero-Isaiah

After what has so far been said it will already be clear that hope is 2-Isaiah's main theme. Hope is based on the assurance of what God has done in the past, and on the reliability of his prophets. They accurately predicted the 'former things', and their predictions now of salvation can therefore be depended on.

For the most part, 2-Isaiah's hope is fixed on the near future. However much he dresses it up in poetic imagery its core is the expectation of political deliverance, the opportunity of the exiles to return home. But 2-Isaiah expressed his hopes for the return in such extravagant language (speaking of triumphal highways being raised across the desert, *40*.3: dry ground bursting into flower, e.g. *41*.18 f.; and so on) that it is not surprising that some found the reality of the return to be disappointing compared with the expectations he had raised. In later years, therefore, some readers re-interpreted his words, and took them to be referring to the far future, when the world would be re-created. There is enough in 2-Isaiah's imagery to make such re-interpretation plausible, for he can speak of the heavens vanishing, and the earth wearing out like a garment (*51*.6).

Though they are not prominent in his work, 2-Isaiah has not altogether forgotten the more traditional ways of expressing hope for the future. The restoration of the covenant with the royal house of David does get a mention (*55*.3), and the prophet also speaks of the glory of the restored Jerusalem (*54*.11 f.).

## Forgiveness

But for 2-Isaiah hope flows from forgiveness, and forgiveness flows from grace. The prophet has little to say of repentance, though there are some fine words on the subject in *55*.6 f. More characteristic is his appeal in *44*.22: 'Turn to me *for I have redeemed you.*' Repentance is asked for, but on the grounds that the redemption has already taken place or is already assured. God has already 'swept away like a cloud their transgressions, and like a mist their sins'.

The chapters of 2-Isaiah open with a similar statement. The time of punishment is over. Israel's hard service is ended, her iniquity pardoned; she has received the full measure of the penalty for her sins (*40*.2). But like Ezekiel, 2-Isaiah does not think of God waiting for Israel's response. Divine grace takes the initiative. 2-Isaiah uses language very like Ezekiel's when he says that he created Israel 'for my glory' (*43*.7) and that he will blot out her trangressions 'for my own sake' (*43*.25). What God does he does for 'his own sake', 'his name's sake', so that his name and glory might not be profaned (*48*.9, 11).

Unlike Ezekiel, 2-Isaiah seems to see little need for sacrifice or cult, and no need for a priesthood or any institution to stand between man and God and mediate God's forgiveness. He has some dismissive words to say about mediators in *43*.27. This is not necessarily to say that he would have abolished priesthood and sacrifice, but simply that they appear to play no part in his thinking.

Perhaps the suffering servant could be regarded as a mediatorial figure. And the prophet certainly uses sacrificial language when he speaks of the servant's self offering in

53.10. But with this exception all mediators pale into insignificance and for 2-Isaiah the stage is filled by the Redeemer, the Holy One of Israel, the Lord himself, in his person and in his name.

## The suffering servant

There are four passages in 2-Isaiah which are called the 'Servant Songs'. They were first picked out and given this title at the end of the nineteenth century. The passages are: 42.1–4; 49.1–6; 50.4–9; 52.13–53.12. They speak of someone called 'the servant of the Lord'. He is God's chosen, who does God's work, and yet he suffers and dies. Now 2-Isaiah several times speaks of the servant in passages quite apart from the 'servant songs', but, it was argued, the servant spoken of in the songs is a different figure from the servant mentioned elsewhere in 2-Isaiah. Hence the servant songs were treated as a separate problem, and some critics argued that they could not have been written by the same author as the rest of 2-Isaiah.

There are still scholars who treat them thus separately, but we shall not do so in this book. We shall look at what 2-Isaiah has to say about the servant, but without assuming that the servant in the songs is a distinct figure. 2-Isaiah does not use the servant idea with complete consistency, either within the so-called 'servant songs' or outside them. Sometimes the servant is explicitly said to be Israel (41.8; 49.3). At other times he is described in terms that seem to envisage an individual. (This is the case throughout the fourth 'song'.) And in 49.5 he is said to have a mission *to* Israel. In 44.26 the servant is explicitly said to be the prophet himself. Generally it is the servant's dedication to God's cause that is stressed, yet in 42.18–20 the servant's inadequacy and unfitness for his task are emphasized. The servant, in 2-Isaiah's mind, therefore, is not a single, particular figure, but an idea, and an idea which he exploits in different ways. He is not describing an individual but exploring a role. He is asking what *servanthood* means; what does it mean, what *might* it mean, to be the servant of the Lord?

What then are the characteristics of the servant as they emerge from 2-Isaiah's descriptions? He is chosen and appointed by God ('my chosen, in whom my soul delights' —42.1; cf. 44.1–2). He has, as it were, a destiny to fulfil. His inadequacy has been mentioned (42.18–20), but usually the prophet stresses his constancy. 'He will not fail, or be discouraged, till he has established justice in the earth' (42.4). He has a mission both to Israel and to the world at large (49.5–6). He is to be a 'light to the nations'. He has no apparent success, and has to say 'I have laboured in vain, I have spent my strength for nothing and vanity' (49.4). His meekness is emphasized. 'He will not cry or lift up his voice in the street', will not break the bruised reed or snuff out the smouldering lamp (42.2–3). In his own sufferings, 'he opens not his mouth', 'like a lamb that is led to the slaughter' (53.7). The suffering is a necessary consequence of his work (50.5–6) and he accepts it as such. In the last 'song', the well-known fifty-third chapter, the suffering is not so much a *consequence* of the task; it *is* the task, which God himself has laid on his servant, for 'it was the will of the Lord to bruise him; he has put him to grief' (53.10). The suffering leads even to death. 'He poured out his soul to death' (53.12). And yet somehow the servant is vindicated. He is vindicated partly in that his sufferings and death accomplish something. They make some kind of atonement for the sins of others. This is brought out strongly in the last 'song'. 'He has borne our griefs, and carried our sorrows' (53.4). He was 'stricken for the transgression of my people' (53.8). He 'makes himself an offering for sin' (53.10). He 'bears the sin of many' (53.12). But his vindication does not only lie in this kind of success, but in some honour which God bestows on him, 'dividing him a portion with the great' (53.12, and cf. 50.7 f.).

Who, then, is this servant? Of whom is the prophet speaking? The question was asked a long time ago (see Acts 8.32–34) and in our own generation many books and articles have been written in an attempt to answer it. The question can be understood in two quite different ways, and some of the confusion surrounding it is caused by failure to observe this.

Modern discussions of the question have often taken it to mean: *Where did the prophet get the idea* of the servant? There are a number of possible sources, and a number of possible models for the servant figure. Clearly we do not need to insist on selecting just one single model or source. The prophet's thinking may well have been influenced by several figures of the past, as well as by his own experience. We can make intelligent guesses as to what some of these influences were.

The suggestion made by the Ethiopian Eunuch in Acts 8 is that the prophet is thinking of himself. Now of course, we know nothing about the prophet and his life history, but it is more than likely that some of the experiences of suffering which he describes are his own. He himself doubtless shared with other prophets the strong feeling of divine vocation which he attributes to the servant, and like other prophets, he may have discovered that his divine vocation led him to face opposition and persecution.

In so far as he regards the servant as Israel herself the prophet must also have in mind the sufferings of his people. They were 'a people robbed and plundered' (42.22). They had passed through the experience of exile and the destruction of much that they had held dear. The prophet seems to be suggesting that if only they would face these sufferings not with resentment, and not merely as a punishment, but as something necessary to the task for which God had raised them up, then they might truly be 'a light to the nations'. But they would not.

There is equal likelihood that he has in mind also the experience of Jeremiah. The picture of the servant in the fourth song fits Jeremiah so well that it might almost be taken as a commentary on his career. He has the same divine vocation, the same intensity of purpose, the same gentleness, the same flintlike determination. He, too, is despised and rejected, but eventually vindicated by events. This is not to say that 'the servant *is* Jeremiah', but simply that the experience of this prophet is one of the sources on which 2-Isaiah drew.

Going further back into history, he may have been influenced by others who suffered to bring salvation to their people; by Moses, who offered himself in his people's stead (Ex. 32.32), or by Joseph, who also 'by oppression and judgment was taken away', so that his generation assumed that 'he was cut off out of the land of the living', and who yet prospered, and was exalted and lifted up, and made very high (Is. 53.8 and 52.13).

He may have had in mind, too, the sufferings of the kings.

We know that in countries around Israel, if not in Israel herself (and certainly in Babylon, where 2-Isaiah was writing) the abasement of the king was part of his coronation ritual, and annually repeated. The king was brought down from his throne, and stripped of his royal robes, sceptre and crown, and struck in the face by the priest. Only after he had been brought to tears was he given back his royal insignia and his dignity, and restored to his throne. None who have not suffered can rightly rule. In Israel we find the same theme repeated, not in ritual but in real life, in the story of David, the archetypal king. For David too has to undergo the experience of being cast down from his throne before being restored to true kingship. This was evidently felt to be an important story, for it takes up a very large part of the account of David's reign (2 Sam. *15–20*). 2 Sam. *15*.30 shows us a picture of the dispossessed David, going up the mount of Olives, weeping as he goes, and all the people with him, so that 'all the country wept aloud' (*15*.23). So goes the Lord's anointed. Only a messiah so rejected is entitled to return, down the mount of Olives, with his people rejoicing and the very stones crying out, 'Blessed is he who comes in the name of the Lord'.

All this 2-Isaiah must have known. The servant, as 2-Isaiah presents him, is repeating not only the experience of prophets but the experience of kings.

There is possibly yet another influence on 2-Isaiah's thought. We have seen that the ancient near east was familiar with stories of a dying god. The Canaanite Baal was such a one. The god died to bring life and salvation to his people, and then rose again. There is nothing in the servant passages to suggest that the servant rises again (though some interpreters have read such a notion into them). The fourth 'song' speaks of his vindication, not his resurrection. Nevertheless, it may have been in the back of the prophet's mind that even the pagans recognized that accomplishment could be found only through suffering, and life through death.

The other way of understanding the question: Who is the servant? is to take it in the sense: Who does the prophet think *will fulfil the servant's role?* Is it for the whole nation, or for some faithful remnant within the nation; is it for the restored king or for some messianic figure of the further future; is it for the prophet himself, or some other?

It is likely that the prophet himself could not have given any certain answer to this question. If the interpretation offered here is correct, then he is not describing a person at all, but an office. He is providing us, we might say, with a job specification. Whatever the servant's identity, this is what he will have to do and to be: he must not fail or be discouraged, but steadfastly set his face, giving his back to the smiters, and not hiding his face from shame and spitting; he must do no violence, and be silent like a lamb when led to slaughter, obedient even to death; he must be exalted and lifted up, and make his life an offering for sin, a ransom for many, making intercession, meanwhile, for the transgressors. Whoever will do this, in whatever age or place, takes upon himself the office and form of the servant.

# Section 5

## The Wisdom Traditions

### The Wisdom Books

WHAT *are* 'the Wisdom Books'? The principal ones are, in the Old Testament, Proverbs, Job and Ecclesiastes. In the Apocrypha we have Ecclesiasticus and the Wisdom of Solomon. But many other books contain passages of what we call 'wisdom materials', or develop 'wisdom themes'. One of the most characteristic elements of wisdom writing is the proverb, and proverbs crop up in practically every book of the Bible. There are also several psalms which are usually classified as 'wisdom psalms' because in their interests and their language they closely resemble the wisdom literature. (e.g. Ps. *37, 49, 73, 112.*)

Most of the wisdom books are, in their present form, quite late works, belonging to the post-exilic period, though some of them, especially Proverbs, contain collections which are very much older. But the roots of wisdom itself go back to the very earliest period of Israel's history, and beyond. One of these roots is in folk-wisdom, preserved and handed down in the tribal or family settting. It was in this setting that proverbs were coined, repeated, passed on, and possibly even put together into collections.

But the stream of folk-wisdom was eventually joined by another, the more sophisticated wisdom of the intelligentsia and of the court. These two were not necessarily all that far apart. Many of the materials which the professional 'wise men', the educated classes, were happy to collect and put into order no doubt originated in the popular folk-wisdom.

The typical professional 'wise man' was a government official. In countries where education is rare, the government has always been the chief employer of such educated talent as is available. This was as true in ancient times as today. The great courts of Egypt and of the Mesopotamian empires had trained and employed such professional wise men from centuries before Israel even existed as a nation. They were the administrators, the civil service, whose job was both to advise the government and to see that its decisions were carried out.

And like any other trade or profession part of their job was to train and educate the young men who would eventually be their successors. Some of our biblical wisdom literature, like the wisdom literature of Egypt and Babylon, was probably produced originally for the instruction of such 'apprentice wise men'. Much of it certainly envisages an audience of young men, and much of the advice given would be particularly appropriate to people whose careers would be spent at court.[1] How to behave in the presence of the king is a theme which appears quite often.

Joseph is in many ways a typical 'wise man'. He is a courtier, and specifically an administrator. His skills, however, are not merely the skills of management, and his wisdom is not limited to the common sense variety (though he has this in abundance). There is a supernatural dimension to it; for he receives some of his intelligence through dreams and visions (and has skill in interpreting other people's), and such a man as he 'can indeed divine' (i.e., practise divination)—Gn. *44*.15. That such skills in a wise man were not unique, but on the contrary fairly typical, is shown by the fact that the pharaoh, when he dreams, *expects* his wise men to be able to interpret (Gn. *41*.8), as, later, king Nebuchadnezzar does (Dan. *2*).

However, in spite of this 'supernatural dimension' to Joseph's wisdom, he achieves his ends mainly by the use of a sanctified intelligence. He succeeds by applying his mind. But Joseph is at once both rational and religious man. He applies his mind *in faithfulness to the divine will*. Daniel, as we shall see later, can also be regarded as a 'wisdom figure', for he shares many of the same qualities.

If the Joseph story is to be counted among the wisdom

[1] See e.g. Prov. *14*.35, *16*.12–15, *23*.1–3, *24*.21 f., *25*.6 f.

traditions of Israel it is quite an early example, for it is found in the J and E strata of the pentateuch. It is notable that one of its themes is the problem of suffering, a question with which much later wisdom writers were greatly preoccupied.

Traditionally, however, the biblical character most closely associated with wisdom is not Joseph but Solomon. One of the reasons why he acquired this connexion with wisdom may be that he was the first king of Israel to build up a thorough-going administrative system (based largely on Egyptian models). He must therefore have introduced into the country considerable numbers of that administrative class known collectively as 'the wise'.

But quite apart from this, Solomon himself built up a personal reputation as a wise man. Just what did Solomon's vaunted 'wisdom' consist of? The answer to this question helps us to understand some aspects of what Israelites understood by 'wisdom'. Solomon's wisdom is, first of all, a kind of quick-wittedness. There is a good example of this in the famous story of his judgment in the case of the two prostitutes who both laid claim to the same baby (1 Kings 3.16–28). Though the Bible cites this as an illustration of 'wisdom' our own inclination would be to call it 'cleverness'. It is precisely the sort of cleverness that was much admired in the ancient east. It could still be admired even when devoted to rather dubious ends. The Bible, after all, abounds in stories of sharp practice, which clearly delighted those who told and retold them. Such stories run from the very early one of Jacob's theft of the blessing right down to New Testament times and the tale of the Unjust Steward, whom the Lord commended (it may be recalled) 'because *he had done wisely*' (Lk. 16.8—RV).

Solomon's wisdom further consists in an encyclopaedic knowledge. He knew all about plants 'from the cedar that is in Lebanon to the moss that grows out of the wall', and about animals, birds, reptiles and fish (1 Kings 3.33). But especially is his wisdom demonstrated in his proverbs. 'He uttered three thousand proverbs; and his songs were a thousand and five' (1 Kings 3.32).

Yet those who describe Solomon's wisdom show an awareness that alongside all this cleverness there is a spiritual and moral dimension to wisdom. The real historical Solomon seems actually to have shown very little of this spiritual and moral grasp, but those who elaborated the Solomon legend were at pains to credit him with it nevertheless. The story of Solomon's dream in 1 Kings 3.3–13 attributes to him a humility and selflessness which in truth he may not have possessed, but which the storyteller knows is inseparable from true wisdom.

The same story also bears witness to another conviction, which is echoed and re-echoed throughout the wisdom writings of the Old Testament and Apocrypha, that wisdom can only be found by those who seek nothing else. The first step towards wisdom is to make wisdom one's *first* priority. In the story in 1 Kings 3 Solomon is said to have grasped this point. He seeks wisdom first, and all other things are added to him.

## Proverbs

So far we have spoken mainly of wisdom themes in narrative literature, but most wisdom literature is not of this type. The typical wisdom book consists largely of proverbs. The proverb is a brief, and sometimes witty saying. It may consist of a single line or statement, but more often, in the biblical tradition at least, it consists of a pair of parallel lines or statements, or occasionally even three. (GBS, Chapter 20, m.)

The bulk of the book which we call the book of Proverbs consists of long lists of such sayings. They are not, for the most part, arranged in any very logical way, but are almost random collections. The book is ascribed to Solomon, though it certainly does not go back any earlier than post-exilic times. Some of the proverbs it contains, however, may be very much older. It is conceivable that some might go back to Solomon himself. Some, we know, were originally Egyptian proverbs, for we have the Egyptian collections from which they were taken.

The contents of the book of Proverbs are of very uneven worth. Many of the sayings are mere truisms. Many contain such general advice that we are bound to wonder why the collector bothered to set them down. He admonishes his readers over and over again, in different words, to pursue righteousness and to abstain from wickedness and evil.

But much of his advice is more specific than this, and it does enable us to build up some sort of picture of the interests of the wise, and what they understood by the good life. Avoidance of evil involves, we discover, careful choice of friends and companions (*13*.20; *21*.24 f; *24*.1 f.). In particular, it involves careful choice of female companions. The author is not insensitive to the virtues of a good woman. He describes such a one at length in *31*.10–31. He is in favour of marriage, and tells us in *18*.22 that 'he who finds a wife finds a good thing'. But not all marriages are happy, and even in the authoritarian society of Israel, where a man would claim to be master in his own house, a 'contentious woman' was quite capable of making him miserable (see, e.g., *21*.9, 19; *25*.24; *27*.15 f.). However, the real threat, as the author sees it, is not within marriage but outside it. He spends a great deal of time warning young men against the 'wicked woman', the 'strange woman', the harlot and the adulteress. Chapter *5* is devoted entirely to this subject, and there are fairly substantial passages dealing with it in *6*.24–35 and *7*.6–27. See also *23*.27 f.

Over-indulgence in wine is another error against which the reader is quite frequently warned (*20*.1; *23*.20; *31*.4–7). The description of drunkenness in *23*.29–35 must surely have been written from experience.

Even more frequent are the warnings against laziness (*6*.6 ff.; *13*.4; *15*.9; *19*.24; *20*.4, 13; *22*.13; *26*.13–16). Laziness brings its own punishment with it, for its inevitable consequence is poverty. This is spelled out rather nicely in the parable in *24*.30–34.

Alongside the contempt for laziness goes a strong respect for discipline. Both learning and good character are rooted in discipline. And discipline is expressed in corporal punishment. Servants need it (*29*.19) but more especially do children. A child left to himself, without discipline, will end in disgrace (*29*.15), but one who is given plenty of it will be a credit to his family (*29*.17). Children are naturally stupid and stupidity has to be beaten out of them (*22*.15). Parents need not be afraid of being too severe, for discipline never killed anyone (*23*.13), and to spare the child is to do him a disservice (*13*.24)

If there is one characteristic above all others which marks out a wise man it is the care with which he speaks. Proverbs abounds in advice about watching one's words. The wise man does not gossip, or belittle his neighbour (*11*.12 f; *20*.19). He does not tell lies (*13*.5); speaks with restraint (*15*.1), and takes care to express himself both judiciously and persuasively (*15*.23; *16*.23 f; *25*.15). The power of words can hardly be exaggerated; the man who can handle them will not only keep of trouble (*21*.23) but will be able to make himself master of any situation (*18*.21).

The author's attitude to poverty is somewhat less straightforward. He certainly sees no virtue in it. Its disadvantages are only too apparent. The poor man has a hard time. He does not have very many friends. He does not always get the justice which he deserves. And yet, integrity is more important than wealth. It is better to be poor and wise than rich and foolish; it is better to be poor and upright than rich and wicked; it is better to be poor and content than rich and miserable.

Much of this, as will be seen, is sound practical advice rather than high-toned moral instruction. The author is very down-to-earth in his interests and very realistic in the advice he offers. He has little to say about religion, in the sense that he makes practically no reference to worship, sacrifice, festivals or the temple. Yet he mentions God a good deal. He assumes that God is there, undergirding everything. God is the guarantor of the moral order to which he so frequently appeals. He does not set out to offer us any religious truths, and yet the way in which he takes for granted a religious view of life is in its own fashion very impressive.

The book of Proverbs is the nearest thing we have in scripture to a 'secular' wisdom writing. It is at least secular in its interests, though as we have seen, the author in fact seems to take a basically religious view of the world. But later wisdom writings tend to be religious in far more obvious ways. We shall look next at the book of Ecclesiasticus (otherwise known as the Wisdom of Jesus ben Sira). We deal with it next, not because it was the next to be written, but because in some ways it is nearer in type to the book of Proverbs than any other scriptural book.

### Ecclesiasticus or The Wisdom of Jesus ben Sira

Like Proverbs, Ecclesiasticus is basically a collection of sayings. But it is not quite such a hotch-potch as Proverbs is. It does explore particular themes in an orderly way by building up *collections* of sayings on the same or related subjects. For example, Ben Sira deals with respect for parents in *3*.1–16; one's duty to the poor and underprivileged (*4*.1–10); relationships with women (*9*.1–9); friends and enemies (chapter *12*); relationships with people richer and more powerful than oneself (chapter *13*). Many of these collections are extremely revealing, not only about Ben Sira himself and his attitudes and prejudices, but about the times in which he lived.

One of the main differences between Ecclesiasticus and Proverbs is that Ben Sira's book displays a far more obvious interest in religion. And prominent in Ben Sira's understanding of religion is *the law*. This reminds us that Ben Sira wrote his book somewhere around 180 BC. We are beginning to get quite close to rabbinic Judaism, the Judaism we see at work in the gospels, and in which law has become all-important. Already for Ben Sira law and religion are so closely connected as to be almost the same thing. In *15*.1 'fear of the Lord' and 'holding to the law' are placed together in parallel as though they were identical. In *19*.20 a third element enters the equation. Both fear of the Lord and fulfilment of the law are in turn identified with wisdom. Thus, for Ben Sira, to be a wise man is to be a religious man, which is the same as being a law-keeping man. *32*.14–*33*.3 is a little dissertation about keeping the law, but *39*.1 ff. tells us that the wise man not only *keeps* the law, he *studies* it.

The law, thinks Ben Sira, has always been the basis of man's relationship with God. In the well-known list of 'famous men' in Ecclus. *44–50* the author emphasizes how all the great heroes of the nation were guided by law.

Since Ben Sira regards observance of the law as fundamental to religion he must necessarily accept the centrality of the cult which the law provides for. He clearly approves of the sacrificial system (*7*.31; *34*.18–20; *35*.1–11). He enjoins reverence for the priesthood and urges the duty of supporting it (*7*.29–31; cf. the 'praise of Aaron' in *45*.6–22). His positive attitude to the temple ritual also comes out strongly in his poem in praise of Simon the high priest (*50*.1–24).

Nevertheless, there is no suggestion that Ben Sira approves of the cult for the cult's sake, or sees any merit in worship that is not informed by moral obedience. He insists strongly that sacrifice and other forms of worship are useless unless they are genuine expressions of piety. *34*.18–26 is a collection of sayings that makes this point very emphatically (cf. *7*.9). In chapter *35* he expands his views on right religion. 'He who keeps the law makes many offerings' (*35*.1). 'Do not appear before the Lord empty-handed', he advises in *35*.4. But in *35*.7 he leaves us in no doubt that it is 'the sacrifice of a *righteous* man' that is acceptable. 'Do not trust an unrighteous sacrifice' (*35*.12). Prayer alone, quite unaccompanied by sacrifice, gets results just the same (*35*.13–17). 'He whose service is pleasing to the Lord will be accepted, and his prayer will reach to the clouds' (*35*.16).

Moreover, there are a few texts which speak of good deeds as an alternative means of atonement. Here again Ben Sira is being typically rabbinic. In *3*.30 we are told that 'almsgiving atones for sin'. In *3*.3 and *3*.14 honouring one's parents does likewise (cf. *29*.8–13). In *35*.2 the giving of alms is equivalent to a thank-offering. In *28*.2 the forgiveness of one's neighbour is said to procure the forgiveness of God, and *28*.5 reinforces this saying. *34*.26 implies that *fasting* is normally a means of procuring God's forgiveness, and asserts that it is unavailing if the one who fasts goes and commits the same sin again.

All this attention to religious topics certainly marks a development from the kind of wisdom writing which we have in Proverbs. There is one other respect in which Ben Sira marks a departure. Earlier wisdom writings display little or no interest in the way in which God has revealed himself in his historic acts of salvation, his redemption of his people. Ben Sira's 'praise of famous men' already referred to (*44–50*) does display such an interest. His list does not so much stress the revelation of God's character and will as the virtue of his human heroes, but nevertheless he does see Israel's history as significant.

## The Wisdom of Solomon

The Wisdom of Solomon is a much more important book, and a much more useful book for the Christian preacher, than its position in the Apocrypha might suggest. It is called 'The Wisdom of Solomon' because the writer is pretending (not very seriously) to be Solomon. The book was not really written by Solomon, but by a Jew of the inter-testamental period, probably around 100 BC. It was written in Alexandria, where a large Jewish colony was settled in a thriving gentile city. It was written in Greek.

The book was therefore written against quite a different background from any other Jewish wisdom writing, and for quite a different audience. The author stands firmly in the wisdom traditions of Israel, and yet he is addressing himself to problems which other wisdom writers do not face. He writes for people who are a religious minority in a pagan and occasionally hostile environment. They were people who were under constant pressure to assimilate and conform, either to give up their faith or to water it down. Nearly all of them had already abandoned the old Jewish languages of Hebrew and Aramaic. They spoke Greek, like all their pagan neighbours. If they went to school they learnt Greek philosophy and Greek science. They took for granted, in most respects, a Greek way of life. In their culture and their aspirations they were much like their fellow Alexandrians. How far could this process of assimilation go before they had lost all that was distinctive of them as Jews?

The pressure to conform was not just external pressure. They were surrounded by so much that they positively admired about Greek and pagan culture. When they read the poems of Homer, full as they were of the doings of pagan gods, they could not but respond to them as fine literature. When they passed in the street the objects of pagan worship, however much their own tradition might condemn the making of 'images', they could not help recognizing the statues as beautiful. When they read the pagan philosophers, they found them not only raising interesting questions but suggesting answers which were meaningful. Not only did the demands of practical living make it impossible to shut themselves off entirely from all that was pagan, these Jews were themselves too intelligent and sensitive and appreciative of beauty and reason to *wish* to do any such thing.

The situation of the second-century Alexandrian Jew and that of the present-day European Christian are not altogether remote from each other. For that reason the present-day Christian, especially if he is a well-educated and cultured Christian, is likely to find the book of Wisdom speaking to his condition in a way that no other biblical book does. For the author of Wisdom is taking a very positive attitude to the culture in which he lives. He is sensitive to what is good in it. And yet he is unwilling to abandon his own heritage of faith. He is indeed the inheritor of both cultures, and is trying to produce a way of thinking and a way of living that is not untrue to either of them.

We shall consider one or two topics which illustrate the writer's method of working, and the flavour of the synthesis which he works out.

### Wisdom and righteousness

The author is seeking wisdom, and he is trying to lead his readers to seek wisdom too. His aim is therefore not very different from that of many of the Greek philosophers whose works he had undoubtedly read. Plato, too, had sought wisdom, and tried to show others the way to it. And in so doing, Plato had spent a good deal of time trying to define the relationship of wisdom to righteousness. But Plato, like most of his fellow countrymen, had no doubt as to which of these two came first. If you wish to make people righteous you must *first* make them wise. That was the Greek philosopher's view. Righteousness is, in the long term, in a man's own best interests. If people act unrighteously, therefore, it must be because they are too stupid to recognize this. To get them to act righteously one must therefore convince them that it is the sensible thing to do. To make them righteous, one must first make them wise. Immorality, on this view, is simply a species of foolishness.

The author of Wisdom will have none of this. In the first five verses of his book he stands the philosophers' principle on its head. Those who crave wisdom, he says, must first of all be righteous. Wisdom is God's gift, and she will not enter a mind which is defiled by sin. 'Wisdom will not enter a deceitful soul' (*1*.4). Here he is being true to his Jewish tradition, which everywhere asserts that faithfulness to God is the way to wisdom ('The fear of the Lord is the beginning of wisdom').

The New Testament writers had the same battle to fight. They had to show that cleverness confers no special advantages in the sight of God (Mt. *11*.25; 1 Cor. *1*.17–*2*.8), and that there is no such thing as a special and better gospel to which only the 'wise' have access. There is indeed a wisdom which God gives to men (1 Cor. *2*.6–7), but it is offered only to the humble who ask for it (1 Kings *3*.7–9), and the way to it is through repentance and faith.

### The worship of idols

The author's Jewishness also shows itself in his treatment of idolatry. This is one of the points at which a Jew cannot compromise *at all* with the heathenism around him. The author of Wisdom repeats the same rather superficial criticisms of idolatry that we have noted in Deutero-Isaiah,[2] but he also makes some attempt to understand how such intelligent men as the pagan philosophers should be misled into polytheism and tolerate idol worship. The principle chapters in which he deals with this topic are chapters *13–14*.

He mocks the sailor about to put to sea, who prays for safety to his idol, 'a piece of wood more fragile than the ship which carries him' (*14*.1). Not that one ought to despise even a mere piece of timber; God has, before now, saved the world just with a piece of wood. (He is, of course, talking about Noah and the ark when he says this—*14*.6). 'Blessed be the wood by which righteousness comes' (*14*.7).

[2] Compare Wisd. *13*.11–19 with Is. *44*.13–20.

Many of the pagan gods were simply the forces of nature deified: Apollo was the sun, Artemis the moon, Poseidon the power of the sea, Demeter the power of the growing vegetation bursting into life, and so on. The author of Wisdom sees that the pagans' worship of these elements is a genuine religious response of awe and wonder; men worshipped them because they 'were amazed at their power and working' (*13*.4). There is nothing unworthy about the pagans' *feelings*. It was 'through delight in the beauty of these things that men assumed them to be gods' (*13*.3). They are perhaps 'little to be blamed' (*13*.6) for though they are distracted by the beauty of God's works into confusing them with 'the author of beauty' (*13*.3), they *are* engaged in a genuine search for God (*13*.6).

Other gods, he thinks, are simply deified human beings. People made images and statues of their kings, or to commemorate dead loved ones, and so skilful were the artists who created these images that men were seduced by the beauty of their work and came to regard as an object of worship the one whom shortly before they had honoured as a man (*14*.15–21). In spite of his Jewish horror of idolatry, therefore, the author is enough of a Greek to understand the appeal of artistic beauty, and to know how readily the response to such beauty passes into worship. This appreciation of artistic beauty is all the more welcome in that it finds expression nowhere else in scripture.

But the really pernicious thing about idolatry is not that men mistook the creature for the creator, it is idolatry's *moral effects*. Worship not directed towards the one proper object of worship becomes debased worship. So the pagans 'hold frenzied revels with strange customs'. They 'celebrate secret mysteries', some-times 'killing children in their initiations' (*14*.23). This corrup-tion spills over into the worshippers' private lives, so that 'they no longer keep either their lives or their marriages pure . . . and grieve one another by adultery' (*14*.24). Where the true God is not worshipped, all kinds of social disorder ensue, 'and all is a raging riot of blood and murder, theft and deceit, corruption, faithlessness, tumult, perjury, confusion over what is good . . . sex perversion, disorder in marriage, adultery, and debauchery. For the worship of idols not to be named is the beginning and cause and end of every evil' (*14*.25–27).


**The life to come**

If the author of Wisdom demonstrates his Jewishness in his condemnations of idolatry and in his insistence on the primacy of righteousness, he shows when he speaks of the life to come that he owes a good deal to the heathen philosophers too.

The Old Testament has virtually nothing to say about life after death. The ancient Israelites did believe in a place they called sheol, the abode of the dead, but they attached no positive value to it. The 'existence' which the dead enjoyed there (if 'enjoyed' is the right word) was of a very unsatisfactory sort. The dead survived as shadows of themselves.

Very late indeed in the Old Testament period did an idea of the resurrection of the dead begin to emerge. It is attested unambiguously in only one text, Dan. *12.2*, which speaks of a resurrection of 'many' (not of all). Dan *12.2* seems to suggest that the especially righteous (like the martyrs) who had not received their reward in this life, are to be raised to life; likewise the especially wicked (like the persecutors) who had not received due punishment.

But the author of Wisdom has quite another idea about the future of the righteous. Of the righteous who have suffered he says that their hope is 'full of immortality' (*3.4*). This immortality which they will inherit is the destiny for which God originally intended all mankind. They were meant for 'incorruption' (*2.23*), i.e. they were intended by God to live for ever, if the devil's envy had not spoiled his original plan. In chapter *8* he tells us that immortality is also one of the gifts of wisdom (*8.13, 17*). But this immortality is nothing to do with the resurrection of the body. What is immortal is the *soul*. It is 'the *souls* of the righteous' which 'are in the hand of God' (*3.1*).

This idea of the soul, the essential part of human personality, which survives death, is so well established in Christian tradition, and so much taken for granted by so many believers, that we may easily miss the fact that it is not at all well grounded in scripture. It appears neither in the Old Testament nor in the New, but only here, in this single book of the Apocrypha. It has been taken over by our author from the Greek philosophers. In *8.19* he even seems to be taking it for granted that the soul is pre-existent, i.e. that souls exist, independently, before they take on particular bodies and are born into the world.

Yet even here the author of Wisdom has not simply adopted the Greek notion of immortality uncritically. Most of the Greeks would have said that the soul was *by nature* immortal. It was that part of man which had such an affinity with the divine that it could not perish. Our author does not appear to believe this. Through wisdom one might *gain* immortality. The righteous man will be *awarded* immortality. No one possesses immortality as a natural right. He seems to think that the punishment of the wicked is that there is no immortality for them. He speaks of the fate of the wicked in entirely negative terms. Their punishment is not that there is a nasty future in store for them, but that they will have no future at all.

Moreover, alongside the talk of immortality there does run another idea, which is not perhaps altogether reconcilable with it. The author does appear to believe in some sort of last judgment. The righteous are not only immortal, but there is a 'time of their visitation', when they will 'shine forth' (3.7). 'They will govern nations and rule over peoples, and the Lord will reign over them for ever' (3.8). In 5.15 f. we learn not only that 'the righteous live for ever more, and their reward is with the Lord', but that 'they will receive a glorious crown, and a beautiful diadem from the Lord's hand'.

### The righteous sufferer

Several times it is made clear that the righteous who are to be so rewarded are the *suffering* righteous. Who *are* these righteous sufferers of whom the book of Wisdom speaks? Although the book was written in Alexandria and not Palestine, it is possible that the author was thinking, at least in part, of the Maccabean martyrs. He was probably writing barely a generation after the martyrs' time. But whether this be so or not, there can be little doubt that his own Jewish community in Alexandria had experienced suffering too. From as early as the fifth century BC there had been sporadic anti-Jewish riots in Egypt, and as the Jewish community in Alexandria became more numerous, antipathy to it became more marked, and sometimes that antipathy broke out in violence. Some commentators have suggested that the 'wicked' who, according to Wisdom, persecute the righteous, are not gentile opponents of the Jews, but rather hellenizing Jews themselves, who persecuted those who wished to remain faithful to their ancestral faith. However that may be, there is every reason to suppose that the problem of the suffering righteous man was one which the author had met at first hand. In dealing with it he takes up the themes and the language that we have already seen used in other parts of scripture.

The righteous man is persecuted because his every existence is an offence to the wicked (2.14). He reproaches them for sins against their own law (2.12). He 'calls himself a servant of the Lord' (3.13) and 'claims that God is his Father' (3.16).

The sufferings of the righteous man are therefore a sort of trial of strength, a testing, not so much of the righteous man himself as of God. The wicked are putting him to the proof. (This is partly the theme of Job. Job's constancy, though he does not know it, is a justification of God as against Satan.) Thus the wicked say: 'Let us see if his words are true, and let us test what will happen at the end of his life; for if the righteous man is God's son, he will help him, and will deliver him from the hand of his adversaries' (cf. Ps. 22.8). 'With insult and torture let us put him to the test, that we may find out how gentle he is, and make trial of his forbearance.' (The theme of the servant's willingness and acceptance of suffering is prominent in 2-Isaiah. Cf. Is. 50.6; 53.7.) 'Let us condemn him to a shameful death, for, according to what he says, he will be protected' (Wisd. 2.17–20).

For the righteous man himself the sufferings are a kind of refining process, like the testing of Abraham, and Job (see Job 23.10). God tries the righteous 'like gold in the furnace' (Wisd. 3.6). But for others the sufferings of the righteous have an atoning value, for God accepts those sufferings 'like a sacrificial burnt offering' (3.6; cf. Is. 53.10).

But most important of all, in spite of his sufferings, and even death, the righteous man is somehow vindicated. 'The righteous man who has died will condemn the ungodly who are living' (4.16). Just what the nature of this vindication is is not entirely clear, but it results in the total discomfiture of the wicked. 'Then the righteous man will stand with great boldness before the face of those who have afflicted him . . . When they see him, they will be shaken with dreadful fear, and they will be amazed at his unexpected salvation . . . In anguish of spirit they will groan, and say, "This is the man whom once we held in derision . . . Why has he been numbered among the sons of God? And why is his lot among the saints?" ' (Wisd. 5.1–5).

### Wisdom and the History of Salvation

We remarked earlier that the older wisdom writings, as exemplified in Proverbs, take little interest in God's great saving acts, by which he revealed himself to his people. They do not mention such events as the exodus or the conquest of Canaan as revelations of God's power or love. Jesus ben Sira, as we saw, does find some usefulness in an appeal to history, which he presents as a catalogue of faithful men (Ecclus. 44–50). The author of Wisdom, too, in the second half of his book does something rather similar, but he tries to demonstrate how the great events and the saints of old were all guided by *wisdom*.

He begins at 10.1 with the creation and traces the action of wisdom through the successive events of biblical history. He never mentions any of the ancient heroes by name, but refers to them all rather obliquely. Wisdom 'saved a righteous man by a paltry piece of wood' (Noah). She 'rescued a righteous man when the ungodly were perishing' (Lot). 'When a righteous man fled from his brother's wrath, she guided him on straight paths' (Jacob).

Our author breaks off his account of wisdom's guidance of Israel's history to give us a long excursus (chapters *12–15*) on the sins of Israel's enemies, both the sins of the Canaanites whom Israel dispossessed and those of the Egyptians from whom she fled. The chief of these sins, of course, is idolatry. The Egyptians, particularly, made images of their gods in animal form, and so it was especially appropriate that in the ten plagues they were punished largely through the agency of animals, frogs, flies, lice (*15*.18–*16*.4).

This leads the author back to his history, and he spends the rest of the book on an elaborate description of the plagues. This description has a number of signficant features. First, we must recall the author's own position, and that of his first readers. They were Jews, living in Egypt, in the midst of an Egyptian community which had often shown itself hostile to them. They felt that they were the victims of discrimination. This helps to explain the evident delight with which the author describes the misery of the plague-ridden Egyptians, and the smugness with which he recounts how the Israelites living among them escaped all affliction. This again illustrates how important it is to know the background of a biblical book if we wish to understand why an author writes as he does.

These chapters about the plagues are important in another way. The author of wisdom is not simply re-telling the Bible story. He is clearly familiar with more fanciful accounts than the Bible provides. The Jewish traditions which we call *midrash* often elaborated the biblical stories by adding all kinds of miraculous details (usually with the purpose of bringing out the religious message of the story) and our author is evidently drawing on midrashic traditions of this sort. For example, the tenth plague, the death of the firstborn of Egypt, is not carried out, as in Exodus, by the Lord himself, or by 'the destroyer', but by the divine Word, a huge figure, standing astride the earth while his head touched the sky. 'Thine all-powerful Word leapt down from heaven, from the royal throne, into the midst of the doomed land; a stern warrior, carrying the sharp sword of thine authentic command' (Wisd. *18*.15). This reminds us that a typical Jew of this period (and that means the New Testament period too), whether he lived in Palestine or in the Dispersion, would be familiar with his biblical stories not simply in their biblical form, but in these elaborated forms. We shall understand some features of our New Testament better if we remember that its writers took such midrashic interpretation for granted.

The last significant point about Wisdom's interpretation of the plagues is that alongside the fancy, and intertwined with it, goes a good deal of rationalism. This appears most obviously in the author's description of the plague of darkness (chapter *17*). Not only, he tells us, were the Egyptians bound in darkness, but it was such a darkness that nothing could pierce it. There were no stars, and even if the Egyptians struck a light or lit a fire it gave no visible brightness (*17*.5). Moreover, in the darkness the Egyptians were terrorized by hideous, nightmarish shapes, and by fearful sounds. Yet in all this there was no darkness for the Israelites. Ex. *10*.23 states that while the Egyptians had darkness it was light for Israel, but implies that this was because Israel lived in a different part of the country. Wisdom makes it clear that Israelites and Egyptians were living and working *in the same places (18*.1–2). The Egyptians could hear the Israelites as they went unhindered about their work. There is more than a strong hint in *17*.21 that the Egyptians' darkness was a *subjective* darkness. It was a darkness in the mind. The sounds which so terrified them were the ordinary sounds of the wind blowing or the birds singing (*17*.18–19). The shapes and spectres which turned their lives into a continuing nightmare were the products of their own fear and their own evil consciences (*17*.9–15). Thus the author of Wisdom, while with one hand he seems to be exaggerating the miracle, with the other he offers us something like a rational explanation of what was going on. The wisdom writers manage to hold together a strong conviction of divine power and an equal conviction that the universe is a rational place, rationally governed.

### The figure of Wisdom

One striking feature of the book of Wisdom is the way in which Wisdom herself is personified. She is described as if she were an actual individual, a kind of divine or semi-divine being.

Now the author of Wisdom has not originated this way of speaking. It is found already, in a less developed form, in the book of Proverbs, especially in chapters *8* and *9*. It is significant that the description of lady Wisdom in Prov. *8–9* follows immediately after the descriptions of the adulteress and the 'strange woman' in chapters *6* and *7*. An explicit contrast is being suggested. The 'strange woman' seduces the fool to illicit delights and leads him on to death. She sits in her window, winking and soliciting. Now the lady leaning from the window is a well-known pagan *religious* motif. We have a number of pictures of her surviving from heathen sources. Among the Greeks she is Aphrodite, the goddess of love. Among the Canaanites she is Astarte. The writer of Proverbs, describing the 'strange woman', is implicitly equating immorality and religious infidelity. Here at least in the wisdom writings is one of the old prophetic themes taken up, for this is the prophets' idolatry/adultery identification in a new guise. But what is characteristic of the wisdom traditions is that an extra term is added to the equation; not only does adultery equal idolatry, but adultery also equals foolishness.

The wise, by contrast, have succumbed to the attractions of lady Wisdom. They are literally 'in love' with Wisdom. She does not wink from windows, but openly in public places she issues her invitations (Prov. *8*.1 ff.), summoning men to her blameless delights, and to life rather than death.

Some of the New Testament's most potent images are rooted here in the description of Wisdom. 'Wisdom has founded her house' (Prov. *9*.1) and the house of Wisdom is always well founded, for as the gospels tell us it is founded on rock (Mt. 7.24–27; cf. Lk. *6*.47–49).

And Wisdom also prepares a feast (Prov. *9*.2 ff.). And having prepared she sends out her servants to summon the guests and say that all things are now ready. And the invitation is an open one, to anyone who will hear (*9*.4). We shall see this theme of the great feast appearing again in the apocalyptic writings, where it is the feast of the messiah. And it figures prominently in the parables of Jesus, whose open invitation is to 'the poor and maimed and blind and lame' (Lk. *14*.16–24; cf. Matt. *22*.1–10), and from whose supper only the *foolish* shut themselves out (Mt. *25*.1–12).

Wisdom, therefore, is the secure builder; she is the evangelist, inviting men to life; she is the eternal host. But she is also much more. According to Prov. *8*.22–31 she is the firstborn of God, begotten before all worlds. The Lord got Wisdom first, and then by Wisdom created all things besides (cf, Prov. *3*.19). In this passage of Proverbs God expresses through Wisdom not only his *mastery* of the creation, but his *delight* in it (Prov. *8*.30–31).

The author of the Wisdom of Solomon builds on these ideas which we have found in Proverbs, accepting them and adding to them. He accepts the idea of Wisdom the evangelist, telling us that not only is Wisdom easily found, but she positively goes out of her way to make herself known to those who desire her (see Wisd. *6*.12–16). 'He who rises early to seek her will have no difficulty, for he will find her sitting at his gates.' 'She goes about seeking those who are worthy of her.'

Both authors stress the rewards which Wisdom offers. The profit from Wisdom is better than profits of money (Prov. 3.14). She is the pearl of great price, with which no other jewel can compare (Prov. 3.15). Wisdom offers riches and honour, as well as long life and happiness (Prov. 3.16–17). According to Wisd. 6.18 Wisdom shows the way not merely to long life but immortality; and not merely riches and honour but a kingdom (Wisd. 6.19–20). Those who seek Wisdom first will have all these things added to them (Wisd. 7.8–11). 'All good things came to me along with her.' (Note in this passage too the reappearance of the image of the 'priceless gem'—7.9.)

The author of Wisdom takes up the idea of 'falling in love' with Wisdom in a very explicit way. 'I loved her and sought her from my youth, and desired to take her for my bride, and I became enamoured of her beauty' (Wisd. 8.2). He describes the bliss of being married to lady Wisdom: 'When I enter my house, I shall find rest with her, for companionship with her has no bitterness, and life with her has no pain, but gladness and joy' (8.16).

But it is in his account of Wisdom's relation to God that the author of the Wisdom of Solomon most decisively goes beyond the author of Proverbs. He takes for granted her part in creating the world, describing her as 'the fashioner of all things' (7.22). Interestingly, he at one point identifies Wisdom with God's Word. Thou 'hast made all things by thy word, and by thy wisdom hast formed man' (9.1–2). Wisdom 'is an initiate in the knowledge of God, and an associate in his works' (8.4). Yet her relationship to him is more intimate even than that. 'She is a breath of the power of God, and a pure emanation of the glory of the Almighty . . . She is a reflection of eternal light, a spotless mirror of the working of God, and an image of his goodness' (7.25–26). She is thus the breath of God, and the divine light.

The importance of these descriptions of Wisdom, and the claims made for her, is that when the first Christian thinkers were trying to express their understanding of the relationship of Christ to God they found this language ready to hand. They could take over the kind of statements which had been made about Wisdom and apply them to Christ. In Wisdom they recognized already a figure who was in some respects clearly to be distinguished from God, and yet was in essence herself divine, partaking of the divine nature. They were able to point to her and say: Christ is like that. They felt able to make the same claims for Christ as had been made for Wisdom, that he was there 'in the beginning', and that 'all things were made through him'.

## Ecclesiastes and Job

With the books of Ecclesiastes and Job we step back a little in time. It is not altogether certain when either of them was written, but they are assuredly somewhat earlier than Wisdom and Ecclesiaticus. Together these two books, Ecclesiastes and Job, make up the literature of Israelite scepticism. The importance of Ecclesiastes lies not so much in what it says, as in the mere fact that it exists. There *is* such a thing as Israelite scepticism, that is what is significant. Most of the Old Testament books give us the impression that their writers had never even considered the possibility that God might not exist, and that the entire religious enterprise might be a waste of time. This possibility is one that every modern believer has to face. Perhaps the writer of Ecclesiastes never does go quite so far as to doubt God's existence, but he certainly queries the *usefulness* of belief in God and of the practice of religion. Things go on, says Ecclesiastes, much as they have always gone on. There is no progress. There is no grand design. There is no great purpose to whose fulfilment the creation moves (Eccles. *1*.4–11). At a blow, therefore, he devalues the whole prophetic tradition, and dismisses the notion that God reveals himself to men in his mighty acts.

In his wisdom he doubts the value even of wisdom. Wisdom *seems* to be preferable to folly, and the writer has set his mind to acquire it, and yet he acknowledges that in the end the wise man and the fool meet the same fate (*2*.12–16). Righteousness is preferable to wickedness, and yet there is no guarantee that righteousness will be rewarded. In practice, the righteous seem rather to be at a disadvantage. The moral he draws from this is: 'Be not righteous overmuch' (6.15–17; cf. *8*.14).

If all this sounds depressing, Ecclesiastes is determined not to be depressed about it. Things may seem futile, but we may as well get on as best we may with the business of living. 'Whatever your hand finds to do, do it with all your might; for there is no work or thought or knowledge or wisdom in the dead land to which you are going' (9.10). And we may as well enjoy what pleasures life provides, while they last. 'Go, eat your bread with enjoyment, and drink your wine with a merry heart . . . Let your garments be always white; let not oil be lacking on your head. Enjoy life with the woman you love, all the days of your vain life which he has given you under the sun' (9.7–9).

Ecclesiastes offers us no answers to these doubts which he expresses, though some later editor, shocked at his outspokenness, has added one or two more orthodox comments to his work. In the last resort, he does not even take his own doubts too seriously. He ends by reminding us that, though he has taken the trouble to write a book about them, writing books is a futile activity, and reading them is a great bore (12.12).

But the important thing, to repeat, is not that he answers these doubts, but that he voices them. The mood which Ecclesiastes expresses is one which all today's believers must experience from time to time, and his sceptical view of the world is one which we must all acknowledge as a possible and defensible one. There is a kind of comfort in the fact that in the pages of scripture such moods and such opinions are acknowledged.

The book of Job is an altogether more serious piece of work. Job, too, has his doubts, but he cares intensely about the answers to them. He will not leave them unresolved.

The question Job faces is: How can I go on believing in God? The immediate problem which raises this question for him is the problem of suffering. The book opens with a scene in heaven, in which God boasts about the virtue of his faithful servant Job. Satan replies that Job's virtue is dictated by mere self-interest. If God were to take away his prosperity his virtue would be exposed as a sham. God gives Satan permission to test Job, and as a result he suffers grievous loss, poverty, horrible sickness and distress.

His wife offers him no support, but advises him to curse God and die. His friends come to visit him, and offer him the kind of platitudes which only make his sufferings worse. His arguments with them occupy the bulk of the book. He insists throughout that he ought not to be suffering in this way. There is no justice in life. He demands to see God himself and argue his own case. In the end, God answers Job out of the whirlwind. He is satisfied. God's case against Satan is proved, and the book ends neatly with the restoration of Job's prosperity.

In all this, what answer to the problem of suffering is the

book offering us? A number of different answers are in fact proposed, most of them being unambiguously rejected. Eliphaz argues that Job cannot plead innocence, because all men sin. So suffering can never be undeserved. Bildad reasons that men do not suffer only for their own sins. Other members of a man's family, such as his children, may sin and bring suffering on him. Zophar simply asserts that exceptional suffering is proof of exceptional guilt, and that if an apparently virtuous man is suffering then he must really be a hypocrite. The speeches of Elihu (which most scholars say were not originally part of the book but have been added later) develop the theory that suffering is meant to be educative, it teaches us something, if we react to it rightly. Job argues vehemently against all of these, and seems to be vindicated by God for doing so. For in Job *42*.7 God says to the friends: 'You have not spoken of me what is right, as my servant Job has.'

The prologue and epilogue to the book, which speak of God's argument with Satan, are suggesting a better answer. At its lowest this answer says that God may have reasons for allowing suffering which men cannot know about. But a more profound version of it suggests that man, in accepting suffering and not allowing it to destroy his faith, is somehow fighting God's battle for him against the powers of evil.

But this can hardly be *the* answer which the author of the book is proposing. When God answers Job out of the whirlwind Job professes himself satisfied, and yet this is before we get to the epilogue. Job's answer must lie in the final speeches of Yahweh.

What, then, have the speeches of the Lord (chapters *38–41*) to say about the problem of suffering? To be brief, nothing. They do not raise the question of suffering at all. One might even say that they speak of everything *but* the problem of suffering, for they are nothing if not discursive. So Job, baffled by the problem of suffering, is satisfied by a speech which never addresses itself to the problem at all?

The answer to this anomaly is that the problem of suffering is not the *main* issue for Job. It is only the way into the main issue. His problem is: How can I go on believing in God? And the answer he gets is the answer he has contended for all along. He sees God himself, or at least speaks with him. His answer, that is to say, is the answer of religious experience. He can go on believing because he has met God for himself. This being so, the problem of suffering can be left on one side. It is still there, but it no longer matters in the way it did before. Job still cannot answer it, but he can live with it, because he has met God, and knows God and trusts God. 'I knew of thee only by report, but now I see thee with my own eyes' (42.5).

Although the wisdom writings in general are in some ways quite distinct from the other streams of Old Testament tradition, having little to say about God's covenant or his great revealing acts in history, and even less about the temple, the holy city, or the atoning sacrifices, we do find in the book of Job *some* themes echoed from the rest of the Old Testament.

The theme of the suffering servant of God is quite central to the book. We have seen this theme exemplified in the Pentateuchal traditions in the person of Joseph, and in the prophetic traditions in Jeremiah and in the servant of the Lord in Deutero-Isaiah. Here it is taken up by a wisdom writer, and in a slightly different and perhaps more realistic way. The prophetic sufferers, and perhaps Joseph too, know what they are suffering *for*. They have a mission, a work to accomplish, and suffering is part of it or a necessary condition of it. Suffering is inevitably easier to bear if one is suffering for a reason. But the tragedy of most of the suffering which men encounter in the world is that there is no reason for it, or none that can be discerned. The depressing thing about much suffering in real life is the apparent arbitrariness, pointlessness and sheer wastefulness of it. It is this kind of suffering which is in question in the book of Job. The author of the book is telling us that Job's suffering has indeed got a purpose, but by the nature of the case, Job himself cannot know that.

But in Job the theme of the suffering servant is combined with another, the theme of the man who contends with God. This is a less developed theme in the Old Testament, but it is detectable at a number of points. Abraham, in his great argument in Gn. *18*, is taking it on himself to call God to account. In a much less articulate way Jacob too is a God-fighter (Gn. *32.22–32*). Moses, also, has to argue with God to keep him true to his gracious purposes (Ex. *32*). Jeremiah argues in a manner strongly reminiscent of Job himself (see the 'confessions' of Jeremiah). But Job outdoes them all in his outspokenness, his force of argument, his determination not to let man's case go by default but to present it fully before the throne of grace.

## The wisdom writers' understanding of God

Most wisdom writers, as we have noted, show little interest in the *apparatus* of religion. They rarely refer to worship or festivals, and seldom mention prayer or sacrifice in any very positive way. They refer to them often enough to make it clear that they accept such things as a natural and proper part of civilized life, but there is not much indication that they attached great positive value to them.

Yet, as we have seen, all the wisdom writers refer frequently to God. They take his existence for granted, and they assume his control of human affairs. This is so even among the earlier and more 'secular' writings. The later writers are often preoccupied with questions which are deeply religious questions. Even though they do not concern themselves, therefore, with the structures and institutions of religion, they take a profoundly religious view of life.

In spite of this, we miss in the wisdom writings at large any strong feeling of God as a person. He is the upholder of the rational order rather than a warm, personal being who can actually be met. The exception is provided by the book of Job. Job is extremely dissatisfied with the upholder of the rational order. Job has grave doubts about the rational order itself. In his own case it does not feel as if it is working as rationally as it is supposed to do. Job reflects a wise man's dissatisfaction with the God of the wise. For Job has problems which can only be met by the God of the prophets, and by the God of Abraham, of Isaac and of Jacob; a God whom a man can grasp, and by whom he might be grasped. Job's comforters have offered him theology; but Job craves the meeting with the living God, without which the theology is only so much verbiage. Job illustrates the shortcomings of wisdom, for there are some questions which cannot be answered by reason alone, but only out of the whirlwind. It is only when he steps outside the boundaries of the wisdom tradition that Job gets his answer. Out of the travail of his soul he hears God speak to him, and is satisfied.

# The Psalms and the Apocalyptic Writings

## The Psalms

READING the psalms is like reading the whole of the Old Testament in miniature, for all the Old Testament's major themes, and most of its minor ones, are reproduced here. The reasons for this are apparent enough if we consider the *function* of the psalms. The book of Psalms is for all practical purposes the hymnbook of ancient Israel; i.e. it consists of songs and poems whose primary purpose was to be used in worship. Most of them were written initially for use in the worship of the temple. In later days they were taken over and used in the rather different context of the synagogue. Now in a hymnbook we *expect* to find hymns for all occasions and all festivals, and on all the important religious topics.

Moreover, the psalms are representative of the Old Testament in another way. The book of Psalms seems to contain material from a wide variety of different periods. Now in fact it is very difficult to date individual psalms with any degree of precision, but even so it is quite evident that we have many psalms from the pre-exilic period, some of which may go back to the very early days of the monarchy. It is equally evident that some reflect the ideas, and the literary style, of the post-exilic period.

The main reason why it is difficult to date psalms with exactitude is that liturgical songs and poems rarely have occasion to refer to particular historical events. Our own hymnbooks always indicate the author of each hymn, and give his dates of birth and death. If they did not, how easy would it be to deduce the date simply from the content of the hymn? This is the situation we find ourselves in with the psalms. There is a hymn in the Methodist Sunday School Hymnbook which refers to 'Gay trams and bright buses that roar up and down'. It could easily be calculated that the hymn must have been written during the few decades when trams were a common sight on our city streets. Similarly, the psalm which begins: 'By the waters of Babylon, there we sat down and wept', gives itself away as having been written very shortly after the exile (Ps. *137*). But both these pieces of literature are very rare in offering such readily datable references.

It is much easier, and perhaps more useful, to determine from the content of our hymns and psalms what was their specific function in the worship of the community. We may not reliably guess when they were written, but we can often deduce *how they were used.* If we again consider the analogy of our own hymnbooks, it is very easy to see that some hymns are meant to be sung in celebrating Christmas; some are obviously intended as funeral hymns; others are communion hymns, and so on. And even if our hymnbooks were not divided into sections with titles which indicate these uses, it would still be quite obvious from the content of the hymns concerned. We can make many of the same sort of deductions about the psalms. Even when we cannot say precisely how they were used in worship, we can classify them according to subject matter (again as our own hymnbooks tend to do). There are penitential psalms, appropriate for making public or private confession of sins. There are psalms which cata-logue the great saving acts of God, which would be suitable for singing on the great festivals when Israel celebrated these historic events. There are psalms which seem to be designed to accompany the offering of sacrifices, and some which appear especially suitable for singing in procession. There is a large class of 'pilgrim psalms' which pre-suppose that the worshipper is approaching the sanctuary, and in which he claims that he fulfils the conditions of 'clean hands and a pure heart' which the Lord demands from those who enter his courts. When we read or study a psalm it is nearly always helpful to ask ourselves: How did the man who wrote this psalm expect it to be used? What can I deduce from its content as to how it fitted in to the worship of the Israelites?

One very obvious distinction that can be drawn is between psalms which seem to be meant for individual use and those which are written throughout in the plural, suggesting that they were intended for use by a whole congregation. It used to be thought that the individual psalms, which speak throughout of 'I' and 'me', were perhaps not used in public worship, but were written as purely private prayers. This is still possible, but scholars are generally less sure now that the 'I' psalms *are* purely individual. Worshippers do not necessarily find it odd to speak of 'I' and 'me' even when worshipping together in a body. Ps. *51* is phrased in very individual terms, ('Have mercy upon me, O God, according to thy loving kindness . . .') yet in Christian worship it is not infrequently said together by whole congregations as a kind of 'general confession', without, it appears, any great sense of inappropriateness. If such personal language comes quite naturally to us in public worship, there is no reason why it should not have come equally naturally to an Israelite. And to use our own hymns once more for comparison, what could be more personal and individual in its expression than a hymn like Charles Wesley's 'Jesu, lover of my soul'? Yet congregations sing it quite happily together. And that is merely an example taken at random; there are plenty of others.

When considering the use made of the psalms we must always bear in mind that the psalms have had a long history. They have been not only used but re-used, and often re-interpreted in the process. A striking example of re-use and re-interpretation relates to the group of psalms known as the royal psalms. These are psalms which refer explicitly to the king. Most scholars are now agreed that these psalms go back to the period of the monarchy, and that when they were written they were meant to be taken at their face value. The king they referred to was the king of Israel, the reigning monarch. The reason why there are so many psalms which speak directly of the king is that the king was an important *religious* functionary. Kingship was a sacred office. The king very likely had a vital part to play in the celebration of the great festivals. He ruled as God's regent on earth. He had a priestly function: he represented God to the nation, and he represented his people before God. All this we may deduce from the royal psalms.

Some of them celebrate his coronation (which was probably repeated annually), when God adopted the king and
called him his son. Ps. *2.7*: 'I will tell of the decree of the
Lord: he said to me, "You are my son, today I have begotten
you".' The coronation psalms promise the king victory over
all his enemies. He will 'break them with a rod of iron, and
dash them in pieces like a potter's vessel' (Ps. *2.9*). Psalm *21*
is a good example of a psalm of this type. Some celebrate the
covenant which God made with the house of David (e.g. Ps.
*89* and *132*) reminding God of the promises which he made,
not only to perpetuate David's descendants upon the throne
but to safeguard the holy city, and the sanctuary which
David's son built. The most extraordinary of the royal
psalms is Ps. *45*. It was not only written, as its content bears
witness, for the specific occasion of a royal wedding, but it
refers to the king quite bluntly as 'God'. 'Your throne, O
God, is for ever and ever' (*45.6*) and 'Therefore, O God,
your God has anointed you . . .' (*45.7*). These statements
are so difficult to accept that translators have traditionally
obscured what the text really says, but they do point to the
very high position of dignity which Israelites attributed to
their king.

There were evidently occasions in the worshipping life of
the nation when it was felt appropriate to express such sentiments. But that was before the exile, when Israel had its own
kings. After the exile Israel had no king, except for the
succession of foreign emperors who ruled her. Why were
these psalms kept in the collection? Surely they were redundant! They were kept because they were re-interpreted. In
the later worship of the temple, and in the worship of the
synagogue, all the royal psalms were taken as referring to the
coming messiah, the king whom God would restore to the
throne of his people. A psalm such as Ps. *72*, which not only
promises the king victory over his enemies but extols his
justice, was very readily re-interpreted in that way, but the
others, too, were subjected to the same process.

Ps. *72* reminds us that the process of re-interpretation did
not stop with the synagogue. We still sing Ps. *72* in our
Christian worship, in the shape of a paraphrase which beings:
'Hail to the Lord's anointed, great David's greater son.' For
the royal psalms were taken by Christians to refer not to the

coming messiah, but to the messiah who has come already, Jesus Christ.

When we ask the question about the use of the psalms, therefore, we must remember that the question may have several answers, just as there may be several answers to the questions about what a particular psalm *means*. The meaning for the man who wrote it, and the use for which he intended it, may not be the meaning and use which were given to it in the later temple or the synagogue, and the meaning which the same psalm has for Christians may be different again. In re-interpreting scripture in this way we are not necessarily doing anything illegitimate, as long as we *know* what we are doing. There is a long Christian tradition of such re-interpretation of scripture. Jesus himself accepts the messianic interpretation of Ps. *110*, and applies it to his own person (or seems to be doing so) (Mk. *12*.35–37 and parallels). And we cannot in any case be forbidden to see a meaning in an ancient text which its author did not see. For a text may take on a significance in the light of later events which it could not have had at the time when it was written.

## The psalmists' understanding of God

All the psalms are prayers, of one sort or another. It goes without saying, therefore, that they are focused on God, and a very rich picture of the divine character emerges from them. Since the psalms were not, of course, all written by the same person, and indeed reflect the thinking of very different periods, the picture of God which emerges is not an entirely consistent one, but it is consistent in its main features.

(A striking example of inconsistency, if one is needed, is provided by Pss. *115*.17[1] and *139*.8. The one takes it for granted that God is a God of the living, and that his writ does not run in the kingdom of the dead. The other asserts confidently that even in the abode of the dead there is no escaping either his judgment or his care.)

The majority of the psalms are concerned with one aspect or another of praise and thanksgiving. This is a marked feature of Jewish worship to this very day. A glance through the Jewish prayer book will quickly convince the reader that

[1] Cf. Ps. *6*.5.

worship for the Jew is centred on God and his greatness.
In much Christian worship, by contrast, especially in the
non-conformist tradition, we spend a great deal of time talking about ourselves. The psalms suggest that this God-
centredness has been characteristic of the worship of Israel
since biblical times.

## God as Creator

God is, first of all, creator. Most of us, if asked what the Old
Testament has to say about God as creator, would automati-
cally think of the opening chapters of Genesis. The opening
chapters of Genesis are of course important, but the understanding of creation which they express is by no means typical
of the Old Testament as a whole, and it is significant that no
other Old Testament writer refers back to the Genesis
account of creation in any extensive way. The psalms reveal
that Israel had several distinct ways of speaking of the creation; several different pictures of it, as it were.

Pss. *74*.13 and *89*.8–10 refer to the old creation myth,
widespread in the near east, that God created the world by
killing the chaos-dragon and splitting open her body. The
same myth is mentioned by Deutero-Isaiah in *51*.9. The
Priestly writer clearly knows the myth, but he has rationalized
it by depersonalizing chaos and speaking of it simply as 'the
abyss', or 'the great deep'. In this picture of creation God is a
warrior and the process of creation a battle. The ordered
world is the fruit of God's victory. He creates, as he saves,
with strong hand and outstretched arm.

There is an alternative picture in the psalms which is very
common. God is thought of as *building* the world, 'setting the
earth on its foundations' (Ps. *104*.5), 'founding it upon the
seas' (Ps. *24*.2; cf. *102*.25). Associated with this same picture
is the idea of God spreading out the heavens 'like a tent' (Ps.
*104*.2). Again 2-Isaiah shows himself familiar with the picture
(Is. *40*.22). It may seem at first sight as if these two features of
laying the world's foundations, as if in stone, and yet making
its roof like a vast curtain, are incompatible, as if the writers
could not make their minds up whether they were thinking of
a tent or a building. Recent archaeological finds in the Sinai
peninsula suggest that the Midianites, who might be called
Israel's spiritual ancestors, constructed their semi-permanent

desert shrines in exactly this way, with a stone base but a
tent-like top. The Old Testament writers may well have
known that the primitive tabernacle was of this sort. If this is a
correct interpretation, then what God was constructing when
he built the world was *a sanctuary*, a holy place.

Occasionally we have reference to the idea of God *fabricat-
ing* his creation. The Yahwist in Gn. *2*.7 speaks of God
shaping man out of the dust, and Ps. *139*.13–16, rather more
intricately, thinks of God shaping the bodies, with their
organs, of individual men. Ps. *8*.3 extends this notion to larger
scale phemonema and talks of the heavens as 'the work of thy
fingers'.

And to add to all these, we have also in the psalms the idea
familiar to us from both the Priestly writer and Deutero-
Isaiah, that God creates simply by uttering his powerful word.
'By the word of the Lord the heavens were made' (Ps. *33*.6).
In Ps. *147*.4 God *names* the stars, asserting his control over
them (cf Is. *40*.26) (as in Gn. *2*.18 ff. he gave Adam the
privilege of sharing his creative work and divine authority by
inviting him to name the animals.) Ps. *147*.15 ff. shows how
God's word is not only powerful in creation, but in the continuing maintenance of the created order. 'He sends forth his
command to the earth; his word runs swiftly. He gives snow
like wool; he scatters hoarfrost like ashes . . . He sends forth
his word and melts them . . .'

These different pictures of the creation are not to be seen as
contradicting each other. The same biblical writer is capable
of using more than one picture simultaneously, proving that
for Israelites themselves there was no felt inconsistency. The
tale of the smiting of the chaos-dragon was certainly not taken
literally by writers such as 2-Isaiah, and it is more than possible
that none of the other pictures were either. They are simply
alternative ways of speaking, all of them useful in some measure. Ancient men in general were probably much more able
to see through the shortcomings of their own imagery than we
give them credit for. How we picture the universe and envisage the processes of its formation is not therefore of primary
importance. It does not much matter whether we think of the
earth as flat, and roofed over by a solid sky, or whether we
think in terms of galaxies, millions of light years apart. The
eye of faith sees either the flat earth or the galaxies as the

handiwork of God, and sees them, too, as witnesses to their creator's power and constancy.

## God as saviour

The power that created the world and upholds the world is demonstrated also in God's mighty acts, his 'wonders' as the psalmists often call them. Ps. *78* is a good example of one which celebrates God's classic saving acts. It recounts the history of the exodus and the wanderings, but it does not merely extol God's greatness. It reminds us of some of the prophetic interpretations of history in that it emphasizes over and over again the faithlessness of Israel and her lack of proper response to what God was doing for her. It recalls the repeated punishments which God was obliged to inflict, and his eventual rejection of the Northern Kingdom. It ends by affirming the Lord's choice of Zion as the place of his sanctuary, and of David's dynasty to be his kings.

Ps. *68* gives a less comprehensive account of God's saving acts, but it is interesting in that it seems to be drawing on very ancient traditions about Yahweh the warrior God, the 'One of Sinai'. It rejoices that this warlike strength is still active and still available to save God's people. But the festal procession which celebrates this strength and salvation is directed not to Sinai but to Jerusalem and its sanctuary. The psalmist seems to be trying to relate the old meeting place with the new, Sinai with Jerusalem. Or perhaps we could say that he is trying to relate the unrepeatable events of history with the repeatable celebration of them in the cult. The relation between the events of the exodus and the covenant-making on Sinai, on the one hand, and their repeated celebration at the great festivals, is rather like the relationship in Christianity between the events of Christ's life and death and their celebration in the church. The crucifixion and resurrection of Jesus are unrepeatable. Christ died 'once, for all'. And the witnesses of those events are unique. No other generation can share their experience in quite the same way. Yet Christians can appropriate for themselves these unique events and their significance, first, by receiving the Holy Spirit (for Pentecost is in principle a repeatable event which must happen again and again in every generation, and indeed to every individual

Christian) and secondly by sharing in the sacraments. Both the Israelites' celebration of their festivals and the Christian celebration of the Lord's supper are referred to in the Bible as acts of 'remembrance'. In biblical language 'to remember' is a strong word. It does not just mean 'to reminisce', or 'to call idly to mind'. Ritually to *remember* God's mighty acts means to re-enact them in worship, to relive them, to enter into them and make them one's own. It was to accompany such acts of remembrance that many of the psalms were written.

Not surprisingly, since the psalms seem mostly to have been written for use in the temple at Jerusalem, Jerusalem figures quite largely in them, and the sanctuary which was its chief glory. Love for Jerusalem itself comes out especially strongly in the pilgrim psalms. Glorious things are spoken of her (Ps. *87*). As the mountains stand round about her, so the Lord is round about his people (Ps. *125*). The pilgrim goes lovingly around her, counting her towers and marvelling at her walls (Ps. *48*). He longs for the courts of the Lord, and the lovely dwelling place of God (Ps. *84*) and is glad when they say to him: 'Let us go up into the house of the Lord' (Ps. *122*).

The reason why Zion's sanctuary is so important is that it is God's own dwelling, his house, the place where his glory dwells (Ps. *26*.8; cf. *46*.4–5). It is also the place where he can be met. 'The God of gods is to be seen in Zion' (Ps. *84*.7—older translations usually translate this verse quite differently). It is the place where his face shines forth, bringing salvation (Ps. *80*).

The same love for Jerusalem which appears in the pilgrim psalms is expressed in the very different psalms which lament her destruction. Ps. *79* mourns the defilement of the temple. Ps. *137*, written for singing in exile, swears never to forget Jerusalem. Ps. *129*, perhaps even more movingly, portrays Zion as the servant of God, whose fate has always been to suffer. 'The ploughers ploughed upon my back, making long their furrows.' 'Sorely have they afflicted me from my youth, yet they have not prevailed against me.' In this little psalm all the main elements of the suffering servant tradition are taken up, and applied not to an individual, but to the holy city. Jesus was not the first to weep over Jerusalem.

When the psalmists speak of God as saviour they are not

always thinking of him as a *national* saviour. God is also the personal saviour of individual Israelites. Thus, many psalms are appeals to God to save the worshipper from what are very evidently quite personal troubles. Ps. *71* is an example of this kind, where the psalmist seems to be afflicted by many enemies. In other cases the psalmist's language suggests that his trouble is sickness. Ps. *38* is typical of such psalms. It would be impossible from this psalmist's list of symptoms to diagnose his trouble, for he seems to have everything possible wrong with him. But the reason for the comprehensive list of symptoms is that we are dealing with liturgical poetry, and liturgical poetry is rarely specific. It has to meet the needs of a variety of worshippers. Just as a 'General Confession' cannot be very specific about sins, so a general prayer for healing, which is what Ps. *38* seems to be, cannot be very specific about symptoms.

Ps. *77* demonstrates that Israelites did not keep the ideas of personal salvation and national salvation entirely separate in their minds. The psalm starts off as a quite personal appeal for help. The psalmist seems to have fallen on hard times. God does not help him any more. He cannot sleep for worrying about his problems. But in verse 11 he remembers to his comfort the great deeds of God, and especially the passage of the Red Sea. The implication is that the God whom the sea obeys is surely competent to deal with the individual troubles of the worshipper.

Not all the psalmists are in trouble. Even those who are not express the same confidence in God's care, and their words convey a deep sense of personal trust. Ps. *91* is one of the loveliest examples of this kind. It does, perhaps, lay itself open to misinterpretation. 'A thousand may fall at your side, and ten thousand at your right hand; but it will not come near you' (*91*.7). Such words, taken at their face value, might encourage the wrong kind of confidence in God, which is why the devil could quote this very psalm in the temptations of Jesus. But there is a right way to understand such confidence.

The twin ideas of God's power and his concern for his people are brought out in a series of images which we find used elsewhere in the Old Testament but which are perhaps specially characteristic of the psalms. First there are the images of king and shepherd. We deal with these together because they belong together. It may seem strange to associate what seem to us to be very different ways of describing God, but for the men of the ancient east they were not very different at all. A king was seen as the shepherd of his people, owing them the same duty of care as a shepherd owed his flock. It was not only Israelites who thought like this, for in Mesopotamia, too, men used shepherd language when speaking of their kings, and the Pharaoh of Egypt from time immemorial had carried a crook and flail. It must not be forgotten that Israel's first really great king, king David, began life as a shepherd. David was looked back on as the ideal king, who cared for his people as he had learnt to do for his flock. And the messiah, David's son, is seen as one who will follow in his father's footsteps, a king/shepherd.

The content of this idea of the shepherd-ruler is spelled out in detail by Ezekiel in chapter *34*, where he criticizes the 'shepherds of Israel', i.e. her rulers. Ezekiel makes it clear that it is the lord himself who is the chief-shepherd. Those whom he is criticizing are the hirelings, who have allowed the sheep to be scattered and to become a prey (*34*.6, 8), and have not searched for those that were lost (*34*.5 8). Therefore the Lord himself, the good shepherd, will seek them (*34*.11 f.).

Having said all this about the way in which the two images of king and shepherd are related, it has to be admitted that in the psalms themselves they tend to occur separately. 'The Lord is king.' A number of psalms open with that statement, see, e.g. Pss. *93*, *97* and *99*. (In RSV the words are translated 'The Lord reigns'.) In Ps. *93* God's kingship is thought of in terms of his creative power and ability to control the universe. In Ps. *97* the same themes occur but his kingship is also expressed as his authority over the other so-called gods, the idols. In Ps. *99* his kingship is expounded in terms of his rule of justice and salvation over his people Israel.

But also, 'The Lord is my shepherd'. The famous Ps. *23* sets out the meaning of shepherding for the individual believer. The shepherd *leads* his sheep and looks after them. It is a well-known fact that eastern shepherds lead their flocks and do not drive them. They do not use sheep dogs, nor do they need any. The significance of this is that the eastern sheep is a much more responsive and intelligent animal than the European sheep. For the British motorist, to meet a flock of sheep on a country road is a frustrating experience. If one meets a flock of sheep on a country road in Israel one does not even bother to slow down. The shepherd, when he hears the car approach, simply tells the sheep to step on to the verge, and they do. (This may sound incredible, but the writer has actually observed it.) This is a good example of the way in which a biblical image may make a very different impression on ourselves from the one which it was designed to make. To compare God to a shepherd is acceptable. The corollary, that we are the sheep, seems too unflattering. But it would not have appeared so to an Israelite.

Ps. *80* begins by considering God not as the shepherd of the individual worshipper, but of the whole flock of Israel. (It also goes on immediately to recall God's kingship by speaking of him as 'enthroned upon the cherubim'.) But it quickly makes a transition to a quite different image, that of God the husbandman, the vinegrower. In vv. 8 ff. it speaks of God's planting of his choice vine, in terms that recall Is. *5*. But whereas Isaiah uses the parable of God's vineyard as a parable of judgement, to prophesy what God will do to the vineyard that fails to produce good fruit, the psalmist laments the vineyard's destruction and appeals for God to restore it.

The New Testament draws on this image of Israel the vine or the vineyard, developing it in its own ways. Jesus, in Matt. *21*.33–41 (and parallels) makes use of it to condemn the tenant husbandmen, rather as Ezekiel had condemned the hireling shepherds. He develops it quite differently in the parable of the true vine (Jn. *15*). And even Paul, who is not much given to parables, uses something rather like it in Rom. *11*.17 ff, though here the vine has become an olive tree.

The other great image of caring which the psalmists use, that of God the father, is not very prominent, but it does appear. Ps. *103*.13 says: 'As a father pities his children, so the Lord pities those who fear him.' 'Pities' is an unfortunate translation here, and it is regrettable that even some modern translations (such as RSV) retain it. Even the NEB's 'has compassion on' is not quite right. The Hebrew word conveys not pity or compassion but the spontaneous natural affection that exists between parent and child.

In all these images, king, shepherd, father, husbandman, we see the psalms taking up and echoing ideas from elsewhere in the Old Testament. And since the psalms were used regularly in worship these images were being constantly presented and re-presented to the worshippers, being engraved on their consciousness, ready to be appealed to when they were taken up by Jesus and his apostles.

## The psalmists' understanding of man

The best introduction to the psalmists' understanding of man, or indeed to the Old Testament's understanding of man, is Ps. 8. Some regard Ps. 8 as a royal psalm, though it does not explicitly mention the king. But whether it is describing the king as representative man, or whether it is describing mankind as such, is not of crucial importance for our present purposes.

Though Ps. 8 *is* setting out the psalmist's understanding of man, it is significant that it begins with God. It begins with the hallowing of his name, and with the praise of his work in salvation and creation. To understand man rightly he must *first* be understood in relation to his creator. He must also be understood in relation to the rest of created things. In relation to the vastness of God's created universe (and it must be remembered that the psalmist's idea of its vastness was infinitely more restricted than ours) man appears insignificant. 'When I look at thy heavens, the work of thy fingers, the moon and the stars which thou hast established; what is man that thou art mindful of him, and the son of man that thou dost care for him?' (8.3–4). Man is therefore 'put in his place' very firmly.

Yet in spite of his insignificance man is given great dignity. He has been made 'little less than God' (8.5). Older translations read, 'a little lower than *the angels*'. There is absolutely no justification for this. The Hebrew text does not mention angels. The rendering merely reflects the translators' uncomfortable feelings about the outspoken statement. Man is God's regent on earth, 'crowned with glory and honour' (8.5) and given dominion over all God's works (8.6). All things have been put under his feet, 'all sheep and oxen, and also the wild animals, the birds of the air, and the fish of the sea . . .' (8.6–8). This is simply making explicit what is there in the creation narratives of Genesis. P expresses the same thought by saying that man is made in God's image and by saying that he has dominion over creation (Gn. *1*.29). J does it by speaking of his naming of the animals (Gn. *2*.18 ff.).

But since man is so insignificant in himself, this position of honour and authority in the world can only be attributed to him by grace. He holds his position from God, and apart from God he cannot sustain it.

The psalmists are equally clear that man needs grace for another reason, that he continually falls short of the glory which God intends for him; in brief, that he is a sinner. Ps. *8* speaks of his insignificance, it does not speak of his sin. Ps. *103* steps from one topic to the other by focusing on man's *weakness*. Man's weakness does not excuse his sin, but it explains his proneness to sin, and makes God readier to forgive, because he understands man's situation: 'He knows our frame; he remembers that we are dust' (Ps. *103*.14). The psalm goes on to contrast this weakness of man's with the everlasting power of God (*103*.15–18; cf. Is. *40*.6–8).

Not all the psalmists seem to be conscious of sin. Some psalms, on the contrary, are protestations of innocence. We, brought up on the doctrine of universal sin, react rather unsympathetically to such protestations, but they need to be seen in their social context. In an Israelite law court there seems to have been little in the way of examination of witnesses or bringing in of evidence. If someone was suspected of a crime his accuser would bring him to court and he would be asked to swear an oath. If he felt able to swear then that was taken as sufficient evidence of innocence. The only alternative to such an 'oath of exculpation' was a confession of guilt. In Jos. 7, after Achan's grievous wrongdoing, lots are drawn to indicate the likely culprit. Once Achan is indicated he is not immediately condemned. He is simply invited to swear an oath, for that is what the words 'Give glory to the Lord God of Israel' (7.19) mean. Achan cannot swear, and can only say '*Hatathi*', which we translate as 'I have sinned', as if it was a religious word . But in a judicial context it is better translated as a plea of guilty. (It is the same word as David uses when challenged by Nathan, 2 Sam. *12*.13.)

Now when the Israelite suffered misfortune he felt it as an accusation. It was God's punishment for sin. And if he felt that he had done nothing to justify it he reacted as he did to any other accusation, by resorting to the oath of exculpation. Ps. *26* is a good example of such an oath. It was probably associated with a special ritual, for *26*.6 speaks of the psalmist washing his hands in token of his innocence, and then circling the altar. The same ritual of hand-washing is found in Dt. *21*.6–9, where the elders of a city disclaim responsibility on their city's behalf for an unsolved murder (and it is found also of course in Matt. *27*.24). The worshipper is behaving before God as he would in a court of law. One might say that the whole of the book of Job or at least of Job's own speeches is a kind of oath of exculpation, a protestation of innocence.

The people who used these exculpatory psalms were probably much less self-righteous than they make themselves sound. The writer of Ps. *32* has evidently tried the exculpatory technique and has found that in his case it did not work. 'When I declared not my sin, my body wasted away . . . for day and night thy hand was heavy upon me' (*32*.3–4). He has therefore resorted to the alternative of penitence and confession (*32*.5), with more success.

The situation implied by the famous Ps. *130* is probably similar. 'Out of the depths have I cried to thee, O Lord.' The 'depths' are probably not depths of guilt, but of distress. The psalmist does not seem to know what in particular he has done wrong. He observes that everyone has sinned, so that in a sense everyone deserves punishment. 'If thou, O Lord, shouldst mark iniquities, Lord, who could stand?' (*130*.3). 'But there is forgiveness with thee, that thou mayest be feared' (v. 4). He is asking for the forgiveness without which no man could survive.

The writer of the best known penitential psalm of all, Ps. *51*, does seem to know what he has done wrong. He appears to have quite definite offences in mind, though he never says what they are. In *51*.4 he acknowledges the justice of the punishment which God has inflicted on him: 'So that thou art justified in thy sentence and blameless in thy judgment.'

But he goes further than this, telling us that he was 'brought forth in iniquity' and 'conceived in sin' (v. 5). This sounds very like the Christian doctrine of original sin, but it is probably not meant to be so understood. It is not even certain that the psalmist is intending to make a statement about mankind in general. He is rather pointing to the intensity of his own feelings of guilt. He sees that nothing will answer his condition short of a remaking of his personality. He needs a clean heart, a newly created heart, and a new and right spirit (v. 10). This is very similar to the language Jeremiah uses when he speaks of the new covenant (Jer. *31*.31 ff.) and which Ezekiel echoes (Ezek. *11*.19; *18*.31; *36*.26).

This psalmist's attitude to sacrifice is also very interesting. He does not see sacrifice as a way of obtaining the forgiveness he desires. He declares bluntly: 'Thou hast no delight in sacrifice; were I to give a burnt offering, thou wouldst not be pleased' (v. 16). This seems to follow the tradition of Amos *5*.25 and Jer. *7*.22, which deny that sacrificial worship is any proper part of Israel's religion. Other psalms support the same viewpoint. 'Sacrifice and offering thou dost not desire' (*40*.6). And Ps. *50*.13 mocks the whole idea of sacrifice. 'Every beast of the forest is mine, the cattle on a thousand hills . . . If I were hungry, I would not tell you.' 'Do I eat the flesh of bulls, or drink the blood of goats?'

Yet in spite of these denials, which are very remarkable in liturgical poems, intended for use in the temple, the great place of sacrifice, sacrifices do figure prominently in the psalms elsewhere. Even Ps. *51* itself has had a little contradictory appendage added to it (*51*.18–19) to bring it into line with majority opinion.

However, it is noteworthy that even the psalms which mention sacrifices with approval never explicitly connect them with expiation or forgiveness. When the purpose of the sacrifices is spoken of they are always being used to express thanksgiving, or in fulfilment of vows. Forgiveness is obtained by penitence and prayer, not by sacrifice.

Under the heading of sin and forgiveness we have already raised one aspect of the question of innocent suffering. The psalmists, like the wisdom writers, were very conscious of the problem. It was not just the sufferings of the righteous which gave rise to concern, but the prosperity of those who were known to be anything but righteous.

Ps. *37* suggests that the problem is really illusory, or at least temporary. The wicked may flourish for a while, but not for ever. 'Yet a little while, and the wicked will be no more; though you look well at his place, he will not be there. But the meek shall possess the land' (*37*.10–11; cf. *37*.35–36). The psalmist simply asserts that righteousness does get its reward. 'I have been young, and now am old; yet I have not seen the righteous forsaken or his children begging bread' (37.25). There are many of us who would not confirm his observations. This psalmist is really offering us the same answer as the friends of Job, that in the last resort the universe *is* organized on moral lines.

The author of Ps. *73* looks a little further into the problem. He too is very impressed by the rewards of wickedness. He is moved to envy the wicked (73.3). 'For they have no pangs; their bodies are sound and sleek. They are not in trouble as other men are' (73.4–5). Because they prosper they have social approval also (73.10). So he complains: 'All in vain have I kept my heart clean and washed my hands in innocence' (73.13). In spite of his virtue the psalmist has not escaped affliction, 'for all day long I have been stricken, and chastened every morning' (73.14).

His first answer to the problem is the same as that of Ps. *37*. God sets the wicked in slippery places. They look safe, but suddenly they are down and ruined. They disappear as a dream disappears on waking (73.18–20). Yet the last section of the psalm suggests a better answer to the problem. 'Nevertheless I am continually with thee; thou dost hold my right hand. Thou dost guide me with thy counsel.' 'Whom have I in heaven but thee? And there is nothing upon earth that I desire besides thee. My flesh and my heart may fail, but God is the strength of my heart and my portion for ever' (73.23–26). This suggests, though it does not say so explicitly, that the writer sees his fellowship with God as something better than the rewards of wickedness. The wicked only have wordly success. The righteous man has God's own friendship.

### Sickness and death

Ps. *73* introduces us to another topic. The quotation above from 73.18–20 carefully omitted half a verse. The whole text (in RSV translation) reads: 'Thou dost guide me with thy counsel, and afterwards thou wilt receive me to glory.' We omitted the words because they are misleading. The Hebrew text of the second half of verse 24 does not make grammatical sense, and cannot be what the psalmist originally wrote. The

RSV translation represents the traditional attempt to make sense of the verse, and it does so by reading into it what looks like a reference to life after death.

There are several verses in the Psalms which look as if they might be references to life after death. One or two, like Ps. 73.24, are produced by translators trying to cope with a corrupt text, but most are simply metaphorical references to deliverance from sickness or serious trouble. It is most unlikely that any psalmist had arrived at the notion of resurrection or immortality, and no text in the psalms clearly attests either of these ideas.

The men who wrote the Bible did not see the sharp distinction between death and life that we tend to see. Life and death were simply different parts of a continuous spectrum. Some people are much more alive than others. All of us are more alive at some times than at others. (We sometimes say, 'I feel half dead this morning'.) They saw a sick man as having moved towards the death end of the spectrum. Sickness is a mild attack of death. In severe cases the sick person moves well towards the end of the spectrum. He may move so far that he does not recover. But just as some of the living are more alive than others, some of the dead are more dead than others. This is why the raising of Lazarus was so striking (Jn. 11), because Lazarus was very dead indeed (11.39). To people who think in these terms there is no sharp distinction between healing a very sick person and raising to life a dead person. We are inclined to see these two activities as different in kind. An ancient Israelite would have seen them as different only in degree.

Thus, when such an Israelite did recover from serious illness, it came very naturally to him to speak of coming back from the pit, and having been rescued from sheol (the abode of the dead). In our terms, this language is metaphorical.

### The uncongenial elements in the psalms

In all parts of the Old Testament we are likely to encounter sentiments which to a Christian are unacceptable or objectionable, but nowhere are we so conscious of them as in the psalms. We are perhaps more conscious of these objectionable elements in the psalms because traditionally the psalms have been used a great deal in public worship and we have expected congregations actually to sing them rather than just hear them read. We may notice them more because the unacceptable features often appear side by side with expressions of the loftiest and noblest sort, and they stand out by contrast. And we may find the same features more objectionable because they appear in a context of devotion, of prayers actually addressed to God. If a man has murderous feelings about his enemies we may sympathize. When we find him trying to enlist God in support of such feelings we react with shock.

Be that as it may, there are two chief kinds of material in the psalms which Christians find difficult. About the expressions of self-righteousness in many of the psalms we have already said something. The other unpleasant kind of material is the prayers for vengeance on enemies. Perhaps the best known of these is at the end of Ps. *137*, which says of Babylon: 'Happy shall he be who takes your little ones and dashes them against the rock.' This is speaking of public enemies, but more frequently it is the psalmist's private enemies who are cursed.

It is no use trying to pretend that such statements are not there. We must not try to explain them away by suggesting that they do not really mean what they say. Neither may we justify them by suggesting that since they occur in Holy Scripture there must really be good reasons for them. We simply have to accept the fact that those who wrote the Old Testament disagreed with our estimate of what is morally acceptable, and disagreed at some quite important points. It is passages such as these which remind us that the Old Testament is a pre-Christian book.

But neither is it reasonable to write off the entire Old Testament simply because it contains some expressions which are sub-Christian. Because there are some points at which their moral perceptions disagree with our own we do not need to discount everything which the Old Testament writers say. They still have a very great deal to teach us.

### The Apocalyptic writings – the book of Daniel
(See also GBS, Chapter 20, 1, Chapter 24, k.)

The book of Daniel was written during the persecutions

which led to the Maccabaean revolt. At this period Palestine was ruled by the Greeks and was part of the Seleucid Empire, centred on Antioch in Syria. Under the king Antiochus IV, known as 'Epiphanes', an attempt was made to stamp out Jewish religion. All copies of the scriptures were seized and burnt; it was forbidden to circumcise children; and all Jews were to be compelled to offer sacrifice to heathen gods and to eat pieces of pork (forbidden by the Jewish law). The temple at Jerusalem was taken over as a pagan sanctuary and a statue of Zeus set up in it (this statue is referred to in scripture as 'the abomination of desolation').

Many Jews complied with the new demands, but many resisted. Some fled to the wilderness, and lived in 'dens and caves of the earth', and eventually mounted a quite successful guerrilla war. Others were captured and were hideously 'tortured, refusing to accept release'. (2 Macc. 6–7 gives us gruelling accounts of the kind of thing that went on.)

The Jews who lived at this period had two great questions facing them. First, before the outright persecutions began, they had to decide how far they could accept the habits and customs of the Greek rulers who were their masters, and of the Greek soldiers and settlers who lived among them in considerable numbers. This was a specially acute problem for the Jewish upper classes who had to have daily dealings with the Greek rulers. Secondly, when persecutions began in real earnest, the problem was how to survive and yet keep faith with their own religious traditions. The book of Daniel is designed partly to encourage the faithful Jews who were faced with this unprecedented attack on their religion, and partly to answer some very practical and mundane questions.

The book begins by telling some instructive stories about a man called Daniel and about three friends of his. Daniel and his friends are said to have lived at the time of the exile, and to have been carried away as captives to the Babylonian court. There they were selected because of their special abilities to become officials and palace servants. They were given the training which such officials were normally given. Daniel and his friends are faithful Jews, and the stories illustrate some of the problems which they met and how they surmounted them.

All kinds of practical questions are answered by these

stories; questions which may seem trivial to ourselves, but which were of great moment to Jews living in a hostile pagan world. The book of Daniel demonstrates that even in the most difficult environment of all, that of the pagan court itself, a proper Jewish way of life can be sustained.

If a Jew in the imperial service is embarrassed by his Jewish name and is given a foreign name by his master, can he accept it? This was not an idle question, for foreign names were sometimes theophoric names, i.e. they contained embedded in them the name of a pagan god. Daniel is offered the name Belteshazzar; his friend Azariah is called Abednego. These contain the names Bel and Nego (otherwise Nebo) well known Babylonian gods. They are accepted without demur. The author seems to be saying: What's in a name?

But what about the Jewish food laws? Can a good Jew eat the food offered to him by his pagan masters? The answer suggested in Dan. *1* is that the Jew in such a position should ask for vegetarian meals. The pagans will think him rather odd but it won't be too embarrassing, and it will be good for his figure (*1*.15). Modern Jews still resort to the same device. It sidesteps the most important Jewish food laws, which all relate to meat.

If, however, the pagans make a direct assault on the Jew's religion there is no scope for compromise. If they try to prevent him saying his prayers (Dan. *6*) and worshipping as Jewish custom demands, he must resist even at the risk of his life (this is the occasion on which Daniel goes into the lions' den). And if the pagans insist that the Jew worship an image, especially the image of a divinized heathen king (Antiochus made himself out to be god incarnate) then he must resist *at all costs*, and God will be with him in the fire. This is the point of the famous story of Shadrach, Meshach and Abednego in the burning fiery furnace (Dan. *3*). For Daniel's first readers, as 2 Macc. *6–7* shows us, the burning fiery furnace was not merely something in a fairy tale, but a real life threat. Shadrach, Meshach and Abednego, faced with this threat, display a fine confidence. 'Our God whom we serve is able to deliver us from the burning fiery furnace, and from your hand, O king' (Dan. *3*.17). But Daniel's first readers can hardly have been so easily satisfied. They knew that miraculous deliverances were not to be counted on. For the aged Eleazar (2

Macc. 6.18 ff.) and the widow and her seven sons (2 Macc. 7) there had been no fourth man in the fire. The author of Daniel is making no pretences. He knows that miracles are not guaranteed, and for that reason the confident statement by the three young men is not their last word. 'Our God whom we serve is able to deliver us . . . *but if not*, be it known to you, O king, that we will not serve your gods or worship the golden image which you have set up' (Dan. 3.18). Miracle or no miracle, deliverance or no deliverance, nothing releases the Jew from his absolute obligation to obey the first and second commandments, to worship no other god and to acknowledge no image.

In all this, it is to be noted, the book's attitude towards gentile civilization is by no means entirely negative, and the picture presented of the pagan kings is not in every case unsympathetic. The king Darius in chapter 6 is basically well-intentioned, and well-disposed towards Daniel himself. His mistake is simply that he allows himself to be manipulated by his courtiers. And king Nebuchadnezzar, though in chapter 3 he appears in a very bad light as the king who sets up his golden image for all to worship, is much more sympathetically treated in chapter 4. In chapter 4 Nebuchadnezzar's great sin is pride. He is warned against it by his own dream, interpreted by Daniel. This is the dream of the great tree, which fills the earth, and the birds of the air nest in its branches. But it is cut down, and its stump bound with a band of iron and brass, amid the tender grass of the field. The tree is Nebuchadnezzar himself, says Daniel, and unless he breaks off his sins by practising righteousness he will be cut down in like manner, until he knows that heaven rules.

All this came upon Nebuchadnezzar. He succumbs to the sin of pride. Walking on the roof of his palace one day he looks over the city and says: 'Is not this great Babylon, which I have built by my mighty power?' Now the point of this pride is that, humanly speaking, it is justifiable pride, and Daniel knows this. Babylon was one of the wonders of the ancient world. The empire centred on it was the most civilized that the world had so far produced. For Nebuchadnezzar pride was hard to avoid, because he genuinely had so much to be proud of. Nevertheless, his pride is sinful. In chapter 4 the author of Daniel is telling us that the Nebuchadnezzars of this world, whatever their achievements, stand under condemnation; and that the kingdoms of this world are to be judged—judged, but not written off. In chapter 4 the author still seems to think that there is hope even for Babylon and its ruler. The stump of the great tree remains, and is preserved, 'bound with a band of iron and brass'. The idea of the remnant, the saved remnant, which the prophets had applied to Israel, is here applied to the gentile world (cf. Is. 6.13). And moreover, there is hope of repentance for the gentiles too. In Daniel's story Nebuchadnezzar does repent, and is restored to his kingdom (cf. Jonah 3).

In chapter 5, however, a very different picture is drawn. In the person of Belshazzar the negative side of the pagan empire is presented. There is nothing civilized about Belshazzar. Nebuchadnezzar could be saved because he was, in the end, prepared to acknowledge his position before God. Belshazzar only treats the things of God with contempt. Belshazzar's sin is not pride (for he no longer has anything to be proud of) but only arrogance. He personifies a civilization become corrupt, and wholly unresponsive to God; a civilization which has been found wanting and whose days are numbered, but whose best minds cannot read the writing on the wall.

It is thought likely by many scholars that these stories in the first part of the book of Daniel originally circulated quite separately. They do seem to reflect different situations. Chapter 1 seems to reflect a time when Jews had their problems in relation to the gentile world, but when they were not actively persecuted. Chapter 4 still sees hope for the pagan world. Chapter 6 reflects a background of presecution but is suggesting that it is not being encouraged by the highest imperial authorities themselves, but by their subordinates. In chapter 3 it is the king himself who takes the initiative in persecution.

At some stage, probably when the persecution of Antiochus was at its height, these stories have been collected and published together with some quite different material, the visions of the second half of the book. The visions are very strange and complex. The only thing at all like them in the first half of the book is the description of Nebuchadnezzar's dream in chapter 2, his dream of the great image.

The visions of Daniel have something in common with

prophetic visions, especially the sort of visions which are described in the later prophetic books. (Those recounted in the early chapters of Zechariah are good examples of late prophetic visions, and their similarity in style to the visions of Daniel is unmistakable.) They are lengthier and more elaborate than most of the visions described in earlier prophecy, and their imagery tends to be bizarre. After the book of Daniel was published a whole new category of literature sprang up, probably in direct imitation of Daniel's work. Elaborate descriptions of visions, full of strange imagery, became this literature's stock in trade. This new category of literature is now known by the name of 'apocalyptic'. Apart from the second half of the book of Daniel and the book of Revelation in the New Testament, none of it was accepted into the canon of scripture, but it was nevertheless very important for a while, as we shall later see.

Daniel chapter 7 makes a good introduction to apocalyptic visions and imagery. It is less difficult to understand than many others and it illustrates some of the main characteristics of such passages. It is about a series of four beasts, which appear one after the other. After the beasts appears a fifth figure, in human form (or to use Daniel's own words, 'one like a son of man'). The last and most terrible of the four beasts is judged and destroyed. The second half of the chapter gives the interpretation of the vision.

The beasts are composite animals. The first is like a lion but has eagles' wings, but it loses its wings and goes on two legs. Another is like a leopard, but has four wings and four heads. Compound animals, with quadruped bodies but with wings, and occasionally human heads, are commonplace among the sculptures of the Mesopotamian lands. This illustrates one aspect of apocalyptic imagery. It is often drawn from pagan mythology. It would have seemed much less unfamiliar to Daniel's first readers than it appears to us.

Secondly, the imagery of the apocalyptists is to a large extent *conventional*. There were accepted ideas about what image stood for what reality. A beast, as in Dan. 7, is normally an empire. A beast with several heads is an empire with several successive dynasties of kings. Daniel's fourth beast has only one head but ten horns. For those familiar with the code being used, 'horn' equals 'ruler'. After the ten horns an extra horn sprouts and uproots three of the others. This little horn has eyes, and 'a mouth speaking great things'. In fact this little horn stands for Antiochus Epiphanes, the persecuting emperor. The 'great things' are Antiochus's claim to be god incarnate.

When Daniel goes on to tell of the judgment of the great beast by 'the Ancient of Days' he is predicting the immediate overthrow of the Seleucid Empire by the intervention of God. And as the beasts symbolized the pagan empires, so the 'one in human form' who is to receive the kingdom personifies the 'saints of the Most High'.

This shows a third feature of apocalyptic imagery. It is often *topical*. It refers to events and persons who were 'in the news' in the writer's time. In the case of Dan. 7, we are fortunate in knowing enough of the history of the period (which 1 and 2 Maccabees, in the Apocrypha, give us in some detail) to recognize who 'the little horn' is meant to represent; but things are not always so easy. Many of the details in apocalyptic visions which are obscure to us were probably crystal clear to their first readers.

Perhaps the nearest thing in our own culture to the apocalyptic vision is the political cartoon. They may seem very different phenomena. The cartoon is a visual medium, the apocalyptic vision a literary one. But they have some features in common. Again, the imagery is conventional. Political cartoons of the old-fashioned sort used to use the figures of John Bull, or Britannia or Uncle Sam. Everyone knew what these figures meant. Sometimes they pictured a large bear. It did not need to be labelled. Everybody knew it stood for Russia. Some cartoonists, like some apocalyptists, develop their own private conventions. There used to be one whose political satires often displayed a carthorse. At first he used to indicate its significance by writing the initials TUC on some part of its anatomy, but after a while he stopped doing so, because his regular readers knew what the carthorse stood for.

But the political cartoon, like apocalyptic, is above all *topical*. It speaks to the moment, and when the moment is past it may have little meaning. To look through a collection of cartoons even twelve months old may set the reader quite a problem in recollecting to what events some of them refer.

How much greater is our problem with apocalyptic, which was topical two thousand years ago!

Our consideration of Daniel's imagery has brought out its connexions with *prophecy*. Perhaps Daniel's connexions with prophecy hardly need to be stressed. Daniel is so like a prophet that those who translated the Old Testament into Greek, and at the same time reorganized the canon on what seemed to them logical lines, placed Daniel after Ezekiel but before the 'minor' prophets. They thus made it clear that they saw the book quite definitely as a prophetic book, and they have been followed by most translators and editors since. Our English Bibles customarily place Daniel where the Greek translators placed him.

To position Daniel thus among the prophets can certainly be defended. He takes up both many ideas and some literary techniques from the prophetic literature. But Jewish tradition never did classify Daniel among the prophets, and does not do so to this day. The Hebrew Bible places the book outside the section where the prophets are, in the third section of the canon, the 'other Writings'. We shall look shortly at why this is so. For the moment, let us examine one respect in which apocalyptic writing is both like and unlike prophecy. Let us look at the *view of history* which we find in the two sorts of literature.

The vision in Dan. *2* is fairly typical of apocalyptic treatments of history. The 'great image' of which king Nebuchadnezzar dreams is presented as a model of world history. This history is divided into successive ages: there is the age of gold, the age of silver, the age of bronze (in descending order of excellence—it is part of the apocalyptists' philosophy of life that everything gets worse) and these are followed by the age of iron, which is ruled by strength but with horrible ferocity. Finally we get to the feet of the image, the lowest point; and the feet are feet of clay. When these fragile feet are shattered (by a stone, cast by no human hand) the image falls, world history is at an end.

The important characteristic of this scheme (which is typical of apocalyptic writings generally) is its rigidity. World history passes through fixed stages. Nothing that men do can make much difference to them. When world history has run its course, then the kingdom of God takes over.

The prophets never speak as if the future was fixed. They confidently predict what the future will be, but their predictions are always *conditional*. They tell people what will happen *if* they continue to behave in certain ways. If people change their ways the way is open to a different future. How the system operates depends on how people choose. For the apocalyptists the future is fixed. There is no choice about how the system operates. There is only a choice *within* the system. For history ends with the judgment of the powers of this world, and with the victory of the saints, and *individuals* have a choice as to which side they will be on when the day comes.

To understand this we have to remember that throughout most of the period when apocalyptic writing was being done (from the second century BC to the second century AD) the Jews were politically powerless. They were ruled for most of the time by foreign kings. They were always the victims of decisions taken elsewhere, which they had no power to influence. Caught up in a godless system over which they had no control the believers simply did their best to keep faith, and hoped for the day when the godless system would be swept away and replaced by the new divine order.

There are of course Christians in the world today who feel themselves to be living under just such conditions, and to them the apocalyptic books speak with a powerful voice. And if 'secularization' proceeds apace, and the political structures of the western world became progressively less responsive to Christian values than they are now, they are conditions under which we might all eventually live.

There is a further point of comparison between prophets and apocalyptists with regard to their views of history. Both prophets and apocalyptists have their eyes set on the future—though as we have pointed out, it is in both cases the *near* future that interests them most. For the prophets the future holds both judgment and salvation, though the balance between the two differs from prophet to prophet. Amos is virtually all judgment. At the other end of the scale is Deutero-Isaiah, for whom the time of judgment is past and only salvation is left to look forward to. Most prophets however envisage a future in which both elements have a place. The apocalyptists again see trouble and salvation as falling into a rigid scheme. They foresee a time of suffering for the people of God, which will progressively become more intense. The worse things become, the more hopeful God's people can be, because at the point at which things cannot possibly get any worse God will intervene.

The word 'intervene' is the clue to a major difference between the prophetic and apocalyptic outlooks. For the prophets, God does not 'intervene'. He does not need to. Everything in the world is under his control all the time. When the time of salvation comes, therefore, it will be brought in by the normal processes which we all know and understand. For the prophets the time of salvation will be brought in by the reign of a righteous king, who will govern wisely, lead the nation to economic recovery, and by military victories establish her as a centre of empire. Salvation, that is to say, will come about through the ordinary operations of politics and economics.

For the apocalyptists it is far otherwise. They have lost faith in the ordinary processes of politics and economics. By the ordinary processes of politics things only ever get worse. Salvation will come, therefore, when God calls a halt to the operation of ordinary political processes and creates a new heaven and a new earth, working according to new and more satisfactory rules. On this view, God does 'intervene', because for the time being the world is under the domination of forces opposed to God, and is not running in the way he intended.

Examination of their views of history and the future has shown us that apocalyptic is not merely prophecy in another guise. It has a good deal in common with prophecy, but it has developed along independent lines. The Jews have always refused to class Daniel among the prophets for the simple reason that he falls outside the prophetic age. Among some sections of Judaism prophecy was thought to have come to an end in the time of Ezra, and nothing written since that time shared prophetic inspiration. By the time the book of Daniel was written, therefore, the prophetic section of the canon was closed. We may not wish to operate by such arbitrary criteria, but we can see how apocalyptic shares some features of other kinds of literature as well.

Among the Jews, religious writing could take a number of different forms. It could be prophecy, it could be history

writing, it could be wisdom, or it could be law. We have seen
what Daniel and the other apocalyptists owe to prophecy. We
have seen how they handled the writing of history. But
perhaps we ought to look a little more closely at that subject
before passing on, because it may seem at first sight strange to
call history a kind of religious writing. Not all history is
religious, of course, but among the Jews all history was religious, because if God is in control of all events we cannot
speak of events without, at least by implication, saying something about God.

Among the Jews, if one had a case to argue, one of the
approved ways of doing so was to retell the story of God's
people in such a way as to demonstrate one's point of view.
The Pentateuch itself, though it contains a good deal of law,
sets all the law in a context of history; a history which starts off
as the history of the human race and narrows down to a
history of the people of Israel up to the entry into the Promised Land. The Deuteronomic School set out *their* understanding of life in the form of a history too, which may be seen
as beginning with Deuteronomy itself and which traces the
ups and downs of the Israelites until the exile of Judah. The
Chronicler, who wrote the books of Chronicles, Ezra and
Nehemiah, has a rather different case to present, and he too
does it by re-writing history. Ezekiel, more briefly, represents the history of Israel as a history of failure, in accordance with the needs of his own preaching.

In the New Testament we find the same thing still going on.
Stephen, before his accusers, simply tells again the history of
his people. But he tells it in such a way as to make two points.
He finishes his history at the foundation of the temple, which
he presents as the great act of apostasy; and he brings out as
he tells his story the fact that Israel have always resisted new
truths (as they are now resisting the gospel). Paul, in the
speech recorded in Acts *13*.16 ff., also begins with a retelling
of history, but unlike Stephen's, his intention is to show how
the history of Israel leads up to Christ, so he stops with the
anointing of David, Jesus's ancestor.

Thus the author of Daniel is not doing anything strange
when he reorganizes history around his own convictions. He
organizes the history of the world around a culminating point
just ahead of his own time, which he believes is the end time.

This last point, that for Daniel (and the other apocalyptists) the end is imminent, needs some emphasis. It is easy when reading apocalyptic writings, such as Daniel and Revelation, to get the impression that they are looking towards some far off future. There are two reasons for this. First, Daniel is set in the exile. Its words are therefore being put into the mouth of a seer of several centuries before the writer's own time. The character, Daniel, is presented as looking centuries into the future. But for the author and his first readers that 'future' is actually the present. Later apocalyptic authors followed the same convention. They ascribed their work to figures of the remote past. They claimed that they were prophecies and visions by men such as Moses, Ezra or Noah, or most popular of all, Enoch. They thus very easily *give the impression of* gazing into the distant future. Their real interest, however, is always the present, or the very immediate future of the author and his first readers. In this respect they are once more very like the prophets.

Secondly, since Daniel and his apocalyptic successors are often speaking of the last times and the final judgment it is again very easy to imagine that it is the remote future they are thinking of. But for the apocalyptists the last times are *now*.

So then, Daniel and the apocalyptists have drawn on prophecy, and on history writing. They have also drawn on Wisdom writing. Daniel himself is very much the typical 'wise man'. He is many ways similar to Joseph. He is a courtier. He is skilled in giving counsel, especially in the interpretation of dreams. But even in a pagan environment he is faithful to his God and serves the purposes for which God sent him, even though it involves suffering. Daniel, though in the end he succeeds, has to face death by being thrown into the lions' den. His wise friends have to pass through the fiery furnace. The theme of the suffering wise man which we have seen emerging at so many points in scripture (the Joseph stories, Job, the book of Wisdom) emerges strongly here.

Fourthly, as we noted at the beginning of our treatment of Daniel, the book turns out to have something in common with *Law*. It does not enunciate laws in the manner of the pentateuch, but it does contain *case law*. It attempts to show how the keeping of the law might work out for Jews who find themselves in a pagan world.

What the author of Daniel has done, therefore, is to take elements from all the main kinds of Jewish religious writing, and from them produce something which is essentially new. This new thing, which we call apocalyptic writing, is not, for many modern readers, the most congenial kind of writing in the Bible, and yet it has some valuable features, which it is as well to be aware of.

First, it places before men a number of clear choices. It presents the world as a place where decisions have to be made. All these decisions flow from one basic decision; are we for or against the rule of God?

Secondly, there is an urgency about the decision. The time for decision is *now*. In a while it will be God's turn to decide, and then it will be too late for men to change their minds.

Thirdly, the decision is a momentous one, for on it hangs our eternal destiny. The idea of a life after death, in which men will be rewarded according to their works, emerges clearly only with the book of Daniel (Dan. *12*.2). Other apocalyptists took up the idea and it eventually became very influential.

Fourthly, Daniel, and the apocalyptists generally, emphasize the *cosmic scale* of God's activities. The world is not controlled by politicians, or by generals, or by economic forces, but 'the Most High rules over the kingdom of men' (Dan. *4*.32).

And though Daniel himself does not make this clear, it is very clear in other apocalypses that when God acts in salvation his salvation too is cosmic in scale, for after the judgment, and the dissolution of all things, God will create a new heaven and a new earth.

Apocalyptic writing eventually fell out of favour, first among the Jews and then among the Christians. This is why there is so little of it in the canon of scripture. But during its hey-day it was very influential indeed. The reason why it is so important for us to understand something about it is that it was during that hey-day that Christianity appeared on the scene. Much of the language of the first Christians, and of Jesus himself, is apocalyptic language. They took for granted many of the apocalyptists' ideas. They assumed that Satan and demonic forces were at large in the world, but that God was intervening to reassert his control over it. The urgency of

Jesus's message, his conviction that the last times have begun, and that now is the time when men must decide for or against the rule of God—all these are features which are drawn from apocalyptic thinking.

This is the final reason for paying attention to apocalyptic writing. Whether we feel it has a message directly for ourselves or not, we shall understand Jesus and his apostles better when we have done so.

# Local Preachers' Studies:
# Old Testament Study Scheme

**Text-books:** W. David Stacey, *Groundwork of Biblical Studies*; Henry McKeating, *Studying the Old Testament*.

A six-monthly course is envisaged, taking a fortnight over each study, save that Studies 6 and 7 will probably need a month each. Students working by correspondence course should send the answers to two questions for studies 3–9 and one question for Study 10 to the appointed tutor at the appropriate time. There will be no further notification after receiving the tutor's name and address. Other students may wish to use the questions for discussion in groups or for examination practice.

## Studies 1 and 2

The aim of the first two studies is to give the student a first reading of introductory and background material to prepare him/her for study of the Bible. The student will need to refer back to this material as he/she works through Studies 3-10. No questions are set directly on the prescribed chapters in Studies 1 and 2 neither in the Study Scheme nor in the examination and the student should omit at a first reading passages which he/she finds too difficult.

## Study 1

Read *Groundwork of Biblical Studies*
*Section    1    The Student and his Approach*
Chapter    1    Introduction
Chapter    2    The Basic Disciplines of Biblical Studies
Chapter    3    The English Versions of the Bible
Chapter    4    Aids to Bible Study
*Section 2        Background Material*
Chapter    5    Transculturization
Chapter    6    The Geography of the Bible

## Study 2

Read *Groundwork of Biblical Studies*
*Section    2    Background Material*
Chapter    7    Climate, Seasons and Calendar
Chapter    8    Biblical Cosmology
Chapter    9    Social Structure
Chapter  11    Archaeology and the Bible
Chapter  12    The Languages of the Bible, Paragraph a
Chapter  13    The Canon, Paragraphs a–c
Chapter  14    The Ancient Manuscripts, Paragraphs a–f
Chapter  16    The Political Map in OT Times
Chapter  17    Cities, Settlements and Shrines of OT Times
Chapter  26    The Growth of the Old Testament

## Study 3

The Study material now becomes essential reading. Be sure to look up the biblical references:

*Groundwork of Biblical Studies*
Chapter  10    The History of the Biblical Period, Paragraphs a–k
Chapter  18    Yahweh and the Gods of Canaan
Chapter  20    Literary Types in the Old Testament

QUESTIONS:

Chapter  10   Discuss with reference to the relevant passages in the Bible, the difficulty of giving a full and accurate account of the Exodus, the Wilderness Wanderings and the Entry into Canaan.

Chapter  18   What were the main points of contrast between the religion of Yahweh and the religion of Baal?

Chapter  20   Discuss the uses of the word 'myth' in relation to the Old Testament material.

## Study 4

*Groundwork of Biblical Studies*
Chapter  21   The Pentateuch

*Studying the Old Testament*
Section   1   The Pentateuchal Traditions

*Bible passages for study:*
Gn. *1–4, 6–9, 11.1–9, 12, 15, 18, 19, 22, 28, 32, 37–47, 50.*
Ex. *3, 11–12, 14, 19–20, 21–23, 32.*
Lv. *5.1–6.7, 16, 19.9–18.*

QUESTIONS:

1. In what respects might the Pentateuch's ideas of sin be called 'sub-Christian'? What insights of permanent value into the nature of sin do we find there?
2. What do the pentateuchal writers (apart from Deuteronomy) tell us about covenants?
3. In what ways, according to the J, E and P traditions, does God reveal himself and his will?

## Study 5

*Groundwork of Biblical Studies*
Chapter  22   The Former Prophets

*Studying the Old Testament*
Section   2    The Deuteronomic Traditions

*Bible passages for study:*
Dt. *5–8, 12, 13, 15, 16, 18, 20, 21, 24.5–25*.4, *26*.
Jos. *24*.
1 Kings *8*.
2 Kings *22–23*.

QUESTIONS:

1. How far is it accurate to describe the Deuteronomic laws
   as 'humanitarian'?
2. What do the Deuteronomists think it means to 'love the
   Lord your God with all your heart . . . soul . . . and
   might'?
3. 'The Deuteronomic historians, in propounding the theory
   that faithfulness to God is always rewarded and unfaithfulness punished, did a grave disservice to Israelite religious thinking.' Do you agree with this statement?

**Study 6**

*Groundwork of Biblical Studies*
Chapter  19    Prophets, Priests and Kings
Chapter  23    The Latter Prophets

*Studying the Old Testament*
Section   3    The Prophetic Traditions (1)

*Bible passages for study:*
Num. *11*.1–30, *16*.
1 Sam. *8–10, 13*.1–15.
2 Sam. *7, 11–12*.
1 Kings *11*.26–*14*.20, *17–22*.
2 Kings *2*.1–*3*.20.
Hos. *1–3, 5*.13–*6*.6, *11–14*.
Amos *1–9*.
Is. *1, 5–6, 7*.1–*9*.7, *11, 28*.

QUESTIONS:

1. What does the Old Testament understand by the word 'prophet'? What were the prophet's functions?
2. Is it accurate to say that the prophets before the time of Amos were more interested in politics than religion?
3. Give an account of the leading ideas of *either* Amos, *or* Hosea *or* Isaiah of Jerusalem.

## Study 7

*Studying the Old Testament*
Section   4   The Prophetic Traditions (2)

*Bible passages for study:*
Jer. *1.1–3.5, 7, 8.18–9.1, 11–12, 15, 17–21, 24, 26–29, 31–32, 36–38, 40–43.*
Ezek. *1–5, 16, 18, 23, 33.1–20, 34, 36.22–32, 37.*
Is. *40–46, 49.1–6, 50, 52–55.*

QUESTIONS:

1. 'Jeremiah was fundamentally an optimist.' Do you agree?
2. Give an account of Ezekiel's understanding of sin and grace.
3. 'Deutero-Isaiah has more to say about God as creator than any other prophet.' Suggest reasons why this is so.

## Study 8

*Groundwork of Biblical Studies*
Chapters  24  The Writings

*Studying the Old Testament*
Section   5   The Wisdom Traditions

*Bible passages for study:*
1 Kings *3.*
Job *1–3, 29–30, 38–42.*

Prov. *1–9, 24, 31.*
Eccles. *1, 9, 12.*


QUESTIONS:

1. How far is the wisdom writers' view of life a genuinely religious one?
2. What do the wisdom writers contribute to Israel's understanding of God?


**Study 9**

*Groundwork of Biblical Studies*
Chapter 27   Temple and Synagogue

*Studying the Old Testament*
Section  6   The Psalms and the Apocalyptic Writings

*The Psalms*

*Bible passages for study:*
Pss. *2, 8, 22, 23, 24, 26, 32, 45, 48, 51, 72, 73, 78, 91, 103, 104, 129, 132, 137, 147.*


QUESTIONS:

1. What do the psalmists understand by 'salvation'?
2. What have the psalms to say about sin and forgiveness?


**Study 10**

*Studying the Old Testament*
Section  6   The Psalms and the Apocalyptic Writings

*The Apocalyptic Writings*

*Bible passage for study:*
Dan. *1–6, 7.*

QUESTIONS:

1. What ideas of permanent value can be found in the apocalyptic writings?

# Index